Artificial Intelligence and International HRM

This book offers an in-depth and recent account of the research in Artificial Intelligence (AI) technologies and how it is impacting and shaping the field of international human resource management (IHRM).

Grounded in contemporary developments in the field of technological change and the Future of Work and the fourth industrial revolution (4IR), the book lays down a solid foundation by offering a comprehensive review of the field of AI and IHRM. It includes empirical research, including case studies of global MNEs and conceptual chapters focusing on the impact of AI on IHRM practices and therefore business-level outcomes of productivity, efficiency, and effectiveness through the adoption of AI-assisted HR applications. The chapters in this volume evaluate individual IHRM practices and study how they impact employee-level outcomes of job satisfaction, personalization, employee commitment and so on. Finally, the book concludes by identifying current gaps in the literature and offers directions for future research for scholars to develop and advance future research agendas in the field.

This volume will be of great use to researchers, academics and students in the fields of business and management, especially those with a particular interest in new age technologies of operating business. The chapters in this book, except for Conclusion, were originally published as a special issue of *The International Journal of Human Resource Management*.

Ashish Malik is Associate Professor and Head of Management Department at Newcastle Business School, University of Newcastle, Australia. Ashish is also the Workforce Resilience Cluster Lead and is an Associate Editor of *Journal of Business Research* (Methods Section) and *Asian Business & Management* journal. He serves on the Editorial Review Board of *Human Resource Management Review* and *Journal of Knowledge Management*. Ashish has published over 100 research outputs, including 10 books and his research features in top-tier academic journals such as the *Harvard Business Review, MIT Sloan Management Review, Human Resource Management (US), British*

Journal of Management and *Industrial Marketing Management*, among others. He has won several awards and has secured research income of more than AU$ 5 million over a range of HRM and multidisciplinary projects.

Pawan Budhwar is the 50th Anniversary Professor of International HRM, Head of Aston Business School, and an Associate Pro-Vice Chancellor International (India) at Aston University, UK. He is also the Joint Director of Aston India Centre for Applied Research and the Co-Editor-in-Chief of Human Resource Management Journal. He received his doctorate from Manchester Business School and is globally known for his research in the fields of strategic and international HRM and emerging markets with a specific focus on India. He has published over 150 articles in leading journals and has also written and/or co-edited over 25 books. Pawan is the co-founder and first President of Indian Academy of Management, an affiliate of Academy of Management. He has served as an advisor to the Commonwealth Commission for six years, as Co-Editor-in-Chief of the *British Journal of Management* for 7 years (2014–2020) and is a Fellow of the Higher Education Academy, British Academy of Management, the Academy of Social Sciences, and the Indian Academy of Management. He has won numerous awards for his research.

Artificial Intelligence and International HRM

Challenges, Opportunities and a Research Agenda

Edited by
Ashish Malik and Pawan Budhwar

LONDON AND NEW YORK

First published 2023
by Routledge
4 Park Square, Milton Park, Abingdon, Oxon OX14 4RN

and by Routledge
605 Third Avenue, New York, NY 10158

Routledge is an imprint of the Taylor & Francis Group, an informa business

Introduction, Chapters 1–3, 5, 6 © 2023 Taylor & Francis
Conclusion © 2023 Ashish Malik and Pawan Budhwar
Chapter 4 © 2021 Akanksha Jaiswal, C. Joe Arun and Arup Varma. Originally published as
Open Access.

With the exception of Chapter 4, no part of this book may be reprinted or reproduced or
utilised in any form or by any electronic, mechanical, or other means, now known or hereafter
invented, including photocopying and recording, or in any information storage or retrieval
system, without permission in writing from the publishers. For details on the rights for
Chapter 4, please see the chapter's Open Access footnote.

Trademark notice: Product or corporate names may be trademarks or registered trademarks,
and are used only for identification and explanation without intent to infringe.

British Library Cataloguing in Publication Data
A catalogue record for this book is available from the British Library

ISBN13: 978-1-032-45452-8 (hbk)
ISBN13: 978-1-032-45454-2 (pbk)
ISBN13: 978-1-003-37708-5 (ebk)

DOI: 10.4324/9781003377085

Typeset in Minion Pro
by Newgen Publishing UK

Publisher's Note
The publisher accepts responsibility for any inconsistencies that may have arisen during the
conversion of this book from journal articles to book chapters, namely the inclusion of journal
terminology.

Disclaimer
Every effort has been made to contact copyright holders for their permission to reprint
material in this book. The publishers would be grateful to hear from any copyright holder
who is not here acknowledged and will undertake to rectify any errors or omissions in future
editions of this book.

Contents

Citation Information   vii
Notes on Contributors   ix

Introduction: Artificial intelligence – challenges and
opportunities for international HRM: a review and research agenda   1
Pawan Budhwar, Ashish Malik, M. T. Thedushika De Silva
and Praveena Thevisuthan

1   Humanoid robot adoption and labour productivity: a
perspective on ambidextrous product innovation routines   33
Manlio Del Giudice, Veronica Scuotto, Luca Vincenzo Ballestra
and Marco Pironti

2   The adoption of artificial intelligence in employee recruitment:
The influence of contextual factors   60
Yuan Pan, Fabian Froese, Ni Liu, Yunyang Hu and Maolin Ye

3   May the bots be with you! Delivering HR cost-effectiveness
and individualised employee experiences in an MNE   83
Ashish Malik, Pawan Budhwar, Charmi Patel and N. R. Srikanth

4   Rebooting employees: upskilling for artificial intelligence
in multinational corporations   114
Akanksha Jaiswal, C. Joe Arun and Arup Varma

5   Beliefs, anxiety and change readiness for artificial intelligence
adoption among human resource managers: the moderating
role of high-performance work systems   144
Yuliani Suseno, Chiachi Chang, Marek Hudik and Eddy S. Fang

6 Artificial intelligence, robotics, advanced technologies and
human resource management: a systematic review 172
Demetris Vrontis, Michael Christofi, Vijay Pereira, Shlomo Tarba,
Anna Makrides and Eleni Trichina

Conclusion: AI and HRM - Future Research Agendas 202
Ashish Malik and Pawan Budhwar

Index 208

Citation Information

The chapters in this book were originally published in *The International Journal of Human Resource Management*, volume 33, issue 6 (2022). When citing this material, please use the original page numbering for each article, as follows:

Chapter 1

Humanoid robot adoption and labour productivity: a perspective on ambidextrous product innovation routines
Manlio Del Giudice, Veronica Scuotto, Luca Vincenzo Ballestra and Marco Pironti
The International Journal of Human Resource Management, volume 33, issue 6 (2022), pp. 1098–1124

Chapter 2

The adoption of artificial intelligence in employee recruitment: The influence of contextual factors
Yuan Pan, Fabian Froese, Ni Liu, Yunyang Hu and Maolin Ye
The International Journal of Human Resource Management, volume 33, issue 6 (2022), pp. 1125–1147

Chapter 3

May the bots be with you! Delivering HR cost-effectiveness and individualised employee experiences in an MNE
Ashish Malik, Pawan Budhwar, Charmi Patel and N. R. Srikanth
The International Journal of Human Resource Management, volume 33, issue 6 (2022), pp. 1148–1178

Chapter 4

Rebooting employees: upskilling for artificial intelligence in multinational corporations
Akanksha Jaiswal, C. Joe Arun and Arup Varma
The International Journal of Human Resource Management, volume 33, issue 6 (2022), pp. 1179–1208

Chapter 5

Beliefs, anxiety and change readiness for artificial intelligence adoption among human resource managers: the moderating role of high-performance work systems
Yuliani Suseno, Chiachi Chang, Marek Hudik and Eddy S. Fang
The International Journal of Human Resource Management, volume 33, issue 6 (2022), pp. 1209–1236

Chapter 6

Artificial intelligence, robotics, advanced technologies and human resource management: a systematic review
Demetris Vrontis, Michael Christofi, Vijay Pereira, Shlomo Tarba, Anna Makrides and Eleni Trichina
The International Journal of Human Resource Management, volume 33, issue 6 (2022), pp. 1237–1266

For any permission-related enquiries please visit:
www.tandfonline.com/page/help/permissions

Notes on Contributors

C. Joe Arun, Loyola Institute of Business Administration, Chennai, India.

Luca Vincenzo Ballestra, Department of Statistical Sciences "Paolo Fortunati", Alma Mater Studiorum University of Bologna, Bologna, Italy.

Pawan Budhwar, Aston Business School, Aston University, Birmingham, UK.

Chiachi Chang, International Business School Suzhou, Xi'an Jiaotong-Liverpool University, Suzhou, China.

Michael Christofi, University of Nicosia, Nicosia, Cyprus.

M. T. Thedushika De Silva, Newcastle Business School, University of Newcastle, NSW, Australia.

Manlio Del Giudice, University of Rome "Link Campus University", Rome, Italy; Paris School of Business, National Research University Higher School of Economics, Paris, France; National Research University Higher School of Economics (HSE), Moscow, Russian Federation.

Eddy S. Fang, International Business School Suzhou, Xi'an Jiaotong-Liverpool University, Suzhou, China.

Fabian Froese, Faculty of Business and Economics, University of Goettingen, Goettingen, Germany.

Yunyang Hu, School of Management, Jinan University, Guangzhou, Guangdong, China.

Marek Hudik, Faculty of Business Administration, Prague University of Economics and Business, Prague, Czech Republic.

Akanksha Jaiswal, Loyola Institute of Business Administration, Chennai, India.

Ni Liu, Faculty of Business and Economics, University of Goettingen, Goettingen, Germany.

Anna Makrides, University of Nicosia, Nicosia, Cyprus.

Ashish Malik, Newcastle Business School, University of Newcastle, Australia.

Yuan Pan, Faculty of Business and Economics, University of Goettingen, Goettingen, Germany.

Charmi Patel, Henley Business School, University of Reading, Reading, UK.

Vijay Pereira, NEOMA Business School, Reims Campus, France.

Marco Pironti, ICxT Innovation Interdepartmental Center, University of Turin, Turin, Italy.

Veronica Scuotto, Research Center, Pôle Universitaire Léonard de Vinci, Paris La Défense, France; Department of Management, University of Turin, Torino, Italy.

N. R. Srikanth, Technology Services, Bengaluru, India.

Yuliani Suseno, Newcastle Business School, The University of Newcastle, Newcastle, Australia.

Shlomo Tarba, Birmingham Business School, University of Birmingham, University House, Birmingham, UK.

Praveena Thevisuthan, Newcastle Business School, University of Newcastle, NSW, Australia.

Eleni Trichina, University of Nicosia, Nicosia, Cyprus.

Arup Varma, Quinlan School of Business, Loyola University Chicago, Chicago, IL, USA.

Demetris Vrontis, University of Nicosia, Nicosia, Cyprus.

Maolin Ye, School of Management, Jinan University, Guangzhou, Guangdong, China.

Introduction: Artificial intelligence – challenges and opportunities for international HRM: a review and research agenda

Pawan Budhwar, Ashish Malik, M. T. Thedushika De Silva and Praveena Thevisuthan

ABSTRACT

Artificial intelligence (AI) and other AI-based applications are being integrated into firms' human resource management (HRM) approaches for managing people in domestic and international organisations. The last decade has seen a growth in AI-based applications proliferating the HRM function, triggering an exciting new stream of research on topics such as the social presence of AI and robotics, effects of AI adoption on individual and business level outcomes, and evaluating AI-enabled HRM practices. Adopting these technologies has resulted in how work is organised in local and international firms, noting opportunities for employees and firms' resource utilisation, decision-making, and problem-solving. However, despite a growing interest in scholarship, research on AI-based technologies for HRM is limited and fragmented. Further research is needed that analyses the role of AI-assisted applications in HRM functions and human–AI interactions in large multinational enterprises diffusing such innovations. In response to these combined issues—the fragmented nature of research and limited extant literature, we present a systematic review on the theme of this special issue and offer a nuanced understating of what is known, yet to be known, and future research directions to frame a future research agenda for international HRM. We develop a conceptual framework that integrates research on AI applications in HRM and offers a cohesive base for future research endeavours. We also develop a set of testable propositions that serve as directions for future research.

Introduction

The Fourth Industrial Revolution (4IR) marks an increased use of emerging technologies, such as artificial intelligence (AI), big data, machine learning, mobile technology, the Internet of Things, geo-tagging, virtual reality, speech recognition, and biometrics (Azadeh et al., 2018; Shank et al., 2019). The application of these advanced technologies transforms the way business is conducted locally or globally and has had a considerable impact on the way work is designed, workers are engaged, and workplace processes changed (Abraham et al., 2019; Agrawal et al., 2017; Duggan et al., 2020; Malik et al.,

2020a; 2022; McColl & Michelotti, 2019). Indeed, serious concerns and reservations have been voiced regarding the role of AI in causing job destruction and humanity's very basis and essence (Agar, 2019, 2020; Charlwood & Guenole, 2022; Malik et al., 2020b). Nevertheless, AI and other related intelligence-based applications bring opportunities for organisations to achieve optimal strategic business outcomes, such as enhancing service quality, productivity, cost-effective service excellence (CESE) (Wirtz, 2019), return on investment (Torres & Mejia, 2017), operational efficiency, customer engagement and loyalty (Prentice & Nguyen, 2020), employees' service quality (Nguyen & Malik, 2022) and reducing considerable operational and capital cost (Wirtz, 2019). Moreover, such research also delivers positive individual-level outcomes, such as positive levels of employee and talent experiences, intention to quit and job satisfaction through the use of AI-assisted human resource (HR) applications (Malik et al., 2020c, 2021; Nguyen & Malik, 2022). More recently, Malik, Budhwar and Kazmi (2023, in press) have developed an extended strategic framework for understanding how AI-assisted human resource management (HRM) can impact a range of business and employee outcomes through the lenses of human and machine learning, strategic HRM literature and AI-mediated social exchanges.

AI refers to a broad class of technologies that allows a computer to perform tasks that generally require human cognition, including adaptive decision-making (Tambe et al., 2019, p. 16). A growing debate in academic research examines different types of AI digital tools and techniques and whether firms can benefit from such business solutions (Aouadni & Rebai, 2017; Castellacci & Viñas-Bardolet, 2019). In this regard, the recent calls for academic scholarship on AI in HRM have received considerable attention in premier HRM journals, including other related disciplinary areas such as international management, information technology, and general management (see Budhwar & Malik, 2020; Buxmann et al., 2019; Jain et al., 2018; Kaplan & Haenlein, 2020; Meijerink et al., 2018). Thus, research at the interface of AI and HRM assumes an increasingly multidisciplinary character (Connelly et al., 2020). However, there is still limited understanding in the AI-HRM literature about how AI and related technologies can offer solutions for effective HRM and sub-functional areas and how AI-enabled HRM functions link to other operational tasks to deliver better results outcomes for their organisations (Agrawal et al., 2017).

Despite the limited knowledge on AI-HRM scholarship, a growing body of knowledge asserts that contemporary developments in automation technologies offer remarkable benefits for HRM (Bersin & Chamorro-Premuzic, 2019; Maedche et al., 2019; Prikshat et al., 2021). Further, organisations from local and multinational enterprises (MNEs) have understood the benefits of AI-based tools and techniques to enhanced employee satisfaction, commitment and job engagement (Castellacci & Viñas-Bardolet, 2019), productivity (Wirtz, 2019), job performance, HR cost-effectiveness (Azadeh & Zarrin, 2016), employee retention (Malik et al., 2020c, 2021; Nura & Osman, 2013), effective decision-making (Azadeh et al., 2018), while reducing HR-related and other operational costs (Torres & Mejia, 2017). The growing interest in examining AI and its impact on sub-functional areas of HRM is rising. For example, scholars argue that emerging AI-based HRM technologies can support talent acquisition, development, assessment, and retention in large technology MNEs (Bersin & Chamorro-Premuzic, 2019; de Kervenoael et al., 2020; Malik et al., 2021). It can also assist from recruitment to selection, assessing, and interviewing the most suitable candidates (Torres & Mejia, 2017; van Esch et al., 2019), including Industry 4.0 advertisements to take out new job profiles (Pejic-Bach et al., 2020) and assess employees' training effectiveness (Sitzmann & Weinhardt, 2019). The above has implications for International Human Resource Management (IHRM) as contextual influences, such as linguistic, cultural, institutional differences across borders will need sufficiently diverse databases for AI applications to minimise any inherent biases in narrow databases and single country contexts.

Although the extant literature on AI-enabled HRM reports optimistic outcomes, others argue for examining the negative consequences of these advanced technologies for both organisations and employees (Huang et al., 2019). Not attending to adverse aspects may lead to unintended consequences, such as high employee turnover, decreasing job satisfaction, loss of customer satisfaction, incurring high costs, and eventually affecting organisations' overall business performance and goodwill (Li et al., 2019). Furthermore, scholars point out that limitations usually happen when adapting AI in HRM due to the complex nature of HR phenomena, constraints of the small data sets, accountability questions associated with fairness and other ethical and legal issues, and possible adverse employee reactions to management decisions via data-based algorithms (Tambe et al., 2019).

Analysing the use of automation technologies in HRM suggests there is still limited knowledge of how AI-enabled HRM functions affect workers, their work outcomes, and overall organisational outcomes (Castellacci & Viñas-Bardolet, 2019). Furthermore, there is a need to show how these HR-focused AI applications improve positive outcomes while reducing negative consequences. Thus, we argue that the influence of the socio-technological context, such as flexible organisational structure, proper training, dealing with fear and change management, and upskilling employees, can further strengthen to achieve favourable outcomes. We also argue that it is also vital to consider personal employee factors, such as personality and emotional intelligence, as they can influence business outcomes (Huang et al., 2019).

There is also an ongoing argument in the AI-HRM literature about identifying the attributes of employees when adapting AI and intelligence-based technologies in organisations to deploy these technologies effectively. However, despite the considerable opportunities provided by advanced technologies in HRM, employees are better able to perform several tasks that machines cannot do (Agrawal et al., 2017; Maedche et al., 2019). Thus, scholars argue that augmenting humans with AI applications rather than replacing them leads to optimised organisational benefits, as both AI and humans can collectively excel and perform well (Wilson et al., 2017). We argue that AI-enabled HRM produces favourable outcomes through human–AI configuration mechanisms. The research base on AI applications from an IHRM perspective is relatively small, though there are some emerging signs of empirical evidence from single-country contexts (Nguyen & Malik, 2021, 2022; Pan et al., 2021; Suseno et al., 2021) or subsidiaries of large technology multinationals (Del Giudice et al., 2021; Jaiswal et al., 2021; Malik et al., 2020c, 2021).

Considering the above calls and limitations, a systematic review of the literature can provide some pathways for researchers. Taking a global view of the use of AI and advanced technologies in the field of HRM, we believe this systematic review provides a rigorous assessment of the extant literature for answering the following research questions:

1. What is the current knowledge of AI and intelligence-based technologies in the global business context in the field of HRM?
2. How do AI-enabled intelligence technologies affect employee and organisational outcomes in the global business context?
3. What are the main directions for consideration for future research?

This review aims to answer the above questions focusing on adopting AI applications in HRM functions in a global context. Second, this review contributes to AI literature on how automation and AI-based technologies affect HRM functions by studying outcomes at both employee and organisational levels, and considering the positive and negative consequences evident in the extant literature, thus proposing future research directions. Third, this review presents how key social-technical and personal factors influence positive outcomes at the workplace. Fourth, we highlight how human–AI configurations play a vital role in strengthening positive individual and business unit outcomes. Fifth, by focusing on the themes of AI and its impact on HRM, we propose future research propositions to guide theory-building efforts. By focusing on the how and why of AI adoption, business and HR leaders must learn to effectively manage the opportunities and challenges posed by AI applications through appropriate social-technical and personal interventions and configurations. Sixth, we build a framework that shows the linkages between AI and intelligence technologies, HRM functions and their consequences on employee and organisational outcomes, and how some of these outcomes could be achieved through social-technical and personal factors by augmenting social-technical and personal factors.

Methodology

Employing a systematic literature review approach as our guiding research methodology (Snyder, 2019), this review aims to provide a thorough assessment of the extant literature on AI and advanced technologies in the field of HRM, which has implications for the management of HRs globally. Systematic reviews involve a process of collecting and critically analysing the literature and the themes emanating from the chosen studies that are within the scope of the research questions posed and to constitute a concrete foundation for advancing the knowledge and theory development on a given topic (Paul & Criado, 2020; Snyder, 2019). Furthermore, such an approach allows a repeatable and transparent process for synthesising findings that ensure overall reliability (Tranfield, Denyer & Smart, 2003). Therefore, guided by the suggestions of Tranfield et al. (2003) and Snyder (2019) for undertaking a systematic literature review in business and management research, we decided on a systematic approach as the appropriate method for this review to provide comprehensive coverage of the literature and to locate emerging themes while ensuring its repeatability.

Selection of articles and qualitative assessment

Driven by our above-mentioned research questions for this review, we included studies that have focused on the use of AI or advanced technologies in the field of HRM across the international boundaries and a temporal boundary of the last decade as this is a relatively new phenomenon that has gained prominence since 2010 (2010–2020). A 10-year time frame was also decided to capture the recent development of studies that explored AI-advanced technologies and HRM as the field of AI, and intelligence-based technologies have significantly developed in recent years. Based on the focus, a range of specific keywords relating to AI, robotics and other intelligence-based technologies and the HRM discipline were included and combined in the search string using the Boolean operators, 'OR' and 'AND'. The keyword search algorithm applied for this review is as follows:

("Artificial Intelligence" OR "AI" OR "robotics" OR "bots") AND ("human resource management" OR "HRM" OR Human resource management functions" OR "HRM functions" OR "HRM cost efficiency" OR employee-level outcomes OR "individual outcomes" OR "organisational outcomes" OR "firm level outcomes" OR "human-collaboration" OR "employee-experience").

The next critical decision was to decide which relevant electronic databases to use as search engines. Given that the scope of the review is in the context of management discipline and technology-related fields, we selected three well-known search engines that are widely used by management and business scholars, such as ABI/ProQuest, SCOPUS and Web of Science. Having decided on the three databases, we applied the search algorithm on each search engine and filtered the initial research results for full-text, peer-reviewed articles in the English language and keeping the time frame of 2010–2020. Then, an initial screening based on the relevance was performed for the titles, keywords or abstracts to identify the papers and subsequently screened using inclusion and exclusion criteria decided for the review. Following other comprehensive systematic reviews conducted in management (e.g., Christofi et al., 2021), we excluded non-peer-reviewed journal articles, papers not in English (due to language limitations), books, book chapters, editorials, commentaries, executive summaries, and (peer reviewed) conference papers. In addition, we only included papers from the top journals listed in the Australian Business Deans Council (ABDC – A* and A) rankings as a proxy and signalling frame for selecting high-quality peer-reviewed articles we included papers published in journals which are ranked high in a combination of leading journal ranking lists, such as the Australia's ABDC and the UK's CABS list.

Like with any research design, researchers have managed the trade-offs of time, effort and quality in terms of the number of data points (out-puts) to include in the analysis. We believe the rigour of reviewing in top-tier journals is much more robust and demanding than other categories of outputs. This is particularly true for an emerging field which faces challenges in being accepted in the mainstream premier outlets. Thus, in our bid to focus more on high-quality outputs, we may have lost some excellent papers published in the lesser ranked journals and other outputs identified above as well as some additional themes.

Nevertheless, we performed a manual cross-check to screen the papers for the inclusion criteria further. Moreover, due to different approaches and perspectives contributed to this emerging field of AI and advanced technologies and limited papers in the literature, we decided to include all three types—empirical, conceptual and review papers for the review. Having 110 papers based on the inclusion and exclusion criteria, and after removing the duplicate papers, a qualitative approach was undertaken to further refine the articles by reading the full text of these papers. Following a preferred guideline for using two reviewers to select the final sample of articles (Snyder, 2019), two authors of the research team were deployed to mutually decide on the final sample of articles for this review, ensuring the quality and the reliability of the search protocol. During the qualitative assessment, two authors from the authorship team rated the 110 papers for relevance on an individual basis after full-text reading and then compared the relevance with each other. Any deviations in ratings was resolved at discussion meetings with the rest of the team for including the papers in the final sample. Out of 110 papers, 40 papers were eliminated during the qualitative assessment, as these papers did not focus on the central questions posed by this literature review. The process applied for the review is depicted in Figure 1. A final search yielded a total of 70 papers that were published in 38 journals. A list of journals and the frequencies of articles published has been presented in Table 1.

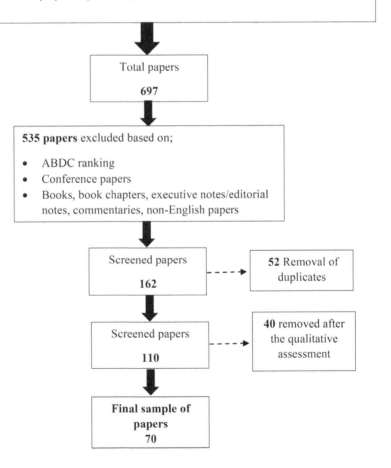

Figure 1. Screening flow chart.

Table 1. List of journals and the frequencies of articles published.

No	Journal name	Journal rating Abdc/caBs	No. of articles
1	Academy of Management Annals	A*/4*	1
2	Annals of Operations Research	A/3	1
3	Annual review of organizational Psychology and organizational Behavior	A*/3	1
4	Australasian marketing Journal	A/1	1
5	Business & Information systems engineering	A/2	1
6	California management review	A/3	3
7	Comparative labor law and Policy Journal	A	1
8	Computers & Industrial engineering	A/2	2
9	computers and operations research	A/3	1
10	computers in human Behavior	A/2	7
11	Decision support systems	A*/3	2
12	European Journal of Work and organizational Psychology	A/3	1
13	Harvard Business review	A/3	2
14	human resource management review	A/3	4
15	human–computer Interaction	A/1	1
16	Industrial marketing management	A*/3	1
17	International Journal of accounting Information systems	A/2	1
18	International Journal of hospitality management	A*/3	1
19	International Journal of human resource management	A/3	1
20	International Journal of Information management	A*/2	5
21	International Journal of Production research	A/3	1
22	Journal of Business research	A/3	3
23	Journal of computer Information systems	A/2	1
24	Journal of hospitality marketing and management	A/1	2
25	Journal of Information Technology	A*/4	1
26	Journal of retailing and consumer services	A/2	1
27	Journal of service management	A/2	2
28	Journal of service research	A*/4	3
29	Journal of service Theory and Practice	A/1	1
30	Journal of strategic Information systems	A*/4	1
31	mIT sloan management review	A/3	7
32	Organizational Dynamics	A/3	1
33	Public management review	A/3	1
34	Public relations review	A	1
35	Safety science	A	1
36	Technological forecasting and social change	A/3	2
37	The leadership Quarterly	A*/4	1
38	Tourism management	A*/4	2
	Total		**70**

Data coding and analysis

Relevant data from the selected articles were extracted into (Tranfield et al., 2003) an Excel spreadsheet containing simple categorical data, such as the article details, year of publication, author details, type of paper, methodology, research context (industry), key findings and future research directions that aided easy reading and forming the descriptive analysis (Tranfield et al., 2003). Following Ererdi et al. (2021), the coding was conducted using two authors from the authorship team independently to ensure the inter-coder reliability and any coding discrepancies were discussed at research meetings for this review. The agreement between the two authors was 96% and the discrepancies were resolved by mutual consensus. Once extraction and coding were completed, in-depth thematic analysis was conducted to locate themes emerging. As a result, we identified a few common categories of articles on *micro-foundation of AI/robotic collaboration, AI/advanced technology influence on HRM functions* leading to the *individual, team and organisational level outcomes*, a range of *intervention factors that influence the use of AI/robotics in the field of HRM* and *organisational settings*. In addition, several articles had an international focus and included research on the adoption of AI for HR and related activities by multinational firms (e.g., Dwivedi et al., 2021; Li et al., 2016; Oesterreich et al., 2019; Pejic-Bach et al., 2020; Suen et al., 2019).

Key themes

To visualise the comprehensive picture of how AI and AI-based technologies affect HRM and human–machine configurations at work and their influences on employee and organisational level outcomes, we develop an overarching conceptual framework through this review. This is presented in Figure 2 and aligns with the above-identified themes in this review.

Theme 1: AI and intelligent technologies in HRM functions

A key emphasis has been on how AI and other related intelligence-based tools and techniques could impact the HRM function as a whole and its sub-functional domains. Analysing the literature enabled us to focus on AI-enabled HRM functions by concentrating on sub-functional domains, such as HR planning, recruitment and selection, training and development, compensation and benefit and performance management, and analyse how these AI-enabled digitalised functions provided novel opportunities for firms and employees.

HR planning and recruitment and selection. Assigning the right person for the right job is the major challenge for HR planning. However, AI and other automation technologies make this task even easier in organisations. Mainly, AI assists in HR planning by determining future employee needs and making effective recruitment decisions (Karatop et al., 2015). It is also evident that AI-enabled recruitment and selection play a crucial role in attracting and selecting the most talented work pool to the organisations, as these advanced technologies can access data and make decisions at a speedy pace and can handle large volumes of information in a time that far exceeds human capacity (Torres & Mejia, 2017). As a result, AI algorithms can improve job candidate identification, that is, who

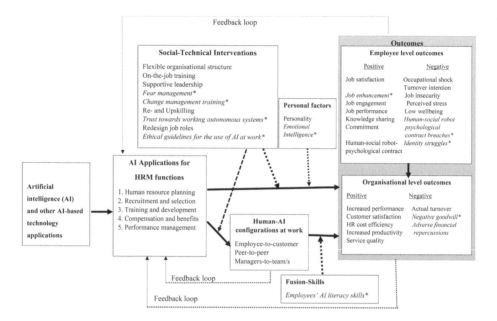

Figure 2. An integrated conceptual framework of the influence of AI-based applications technologies on employee and organisational level outcomes. *Note.* Items in italics and asterisks are indicative of areas which need to be tested in future research.

is most interested and suited for the job and provide better communication of the job opening. Influencing job seekers' technology increases their participation in AI- enabled recruiting (van Esch et al., 2020). AI also assists in making the job interview process more effective, so that the interview process is now changed from face-to-face to internet-based interviews, such as asynchronous video interviews (AVIs) (Torres & Mejia, 2017). Moreover, Pessach et al. (2020) found in their studies that using a hybrid decision-support tool helped HR professionals in the recruitment and placement processes and increased the impact of recruiters and maximised organisational return on investment. AI Algorithms allowed HR professionals to identify suitable profiles for job vacancies, eliminating cognitive biases of race, gender and sexual orientation that mars human judgement in recruiting activities.

Training and development. The literature highlights that AI supports the training and development of employees more effectively. Most importantly, systems could save each current employee's electronic resumes that provide the organisation with an electronic inventory of its employees. This can help to track shortages in skills or to develop suitable training programmes. It can also help organisations to search for an appropriate candidate within the organisation. Moreover, employees could use these systems in order to manage their prospective careers. If employees lack any skills, these AI systems help them identify their training needs and complete the required courses. Further, online or virtual training provides a couple of benefits for both the organisation and employees. AI assists HR managers to assess training effectiveness and making decisions on employee competency, including emotional and intellectual capabilities and experiences level, in order to assign the right employee with the corresponding talents to the correct positions (Karatop et al., 2015; Sitzmann & Weinhardt, 2019).

Compensation and benefits. Our analysis presents that automation in payroll systems supports HR professionals in efficiently handling all HR payroll and related value-added activities. This is because AI technologies can track all types of employee data, including employee personal details, changes in personal information such as dependants, or marriage and beneficiary changes (Bussler & Davis, 2002). Moreover, the skill supply and demand gap obtained from the databases helps determine an organisation's compensation and benefits plans (Pessach et al., 2020). AI systems also assist managers and experts in collecting the most pertinent information about required employees' compensation and benefits systems. Specifically, these systems help to calculate and determine the salary parameters of employees concerning their jobs (Mehrabad & Brojeny, 2007).

Performance management. AI-enabled performance management tools and techniques also provide multiple opportunities for both employees and organisations. For instance, a fuzzy multi-attribute decision-making tool leads to a fair evaluation of employees. Notably, this tool helps identify employees who need further improvements in some factors and the magnitude of improvements needed (Manoharan et al., 2011). Moreover, digital performance tools assist managers to assess employee performance or to recommend any required improvements and take corrective actions for an employee based on expert opinion such as providing training, talent enhancement and further qualification wherever required (Azadeh et al., 2018; Manoharan et al., 2011).

Implementation challenges. Although many studies highlight the need to adopt AI and automation intelligence technologies in HRM to obtain optimised benefits, how these systems are running is still a bottleneck in AI research. Most importantly, how organisations make decisions on employees based on the outputs provided by AI-based systems is not primarily transparent to employees (Connelly et al., 2020). There is an argument how employees like gig workers and workers, who work distantly from customers and organisations, monitor through AI-based technologies (Connelly et al., 2020). Scholars further claim that when employees do not understand how decisions have been made using AI-based systems or cannot accept these decisions, it leads them to adversarial behaviours in organisations (Tambe et al., 2019). However, only limited research is noted on examining how to diminish negative consequences due to the technology adaptions in HRM functions.

Ethical and legal issues. Employees need to know what data is collected about them and determine whether they are provided with the opportunity to verify their collected information produced by the relevant systems. Employees also need to know how these AI-based decisions affect their outcomes, including their attitudes and behaviours (Connelly et al., 2020). In this regard, employees need open and transparent communication to ensure the AI systems are working promptly, securely and reliably (Wilson et al., 2017). On the other hand, the literature points out that organisations communicate to employees what technologies are being used and how expert systems make employee-related decisions (Connelly et al., 2020). Furthermore, ethical issues from China and Global South-East Asian countries point to intensifying surveillance and 'getting in workers' heads' (Houser, 2018; Kshetri, 2021; Wong & Liu, 2019), and there are several racist and sexist biases prevalent in some AI applications (Moosajee, 2019).

Way forward. Some studies emphasise that AI-enabled HRM functions, particularly e-based performance management and training and development, become more effective when improving communication (Bharadwaj & Shipley, 2020; Bititci et al., 2016). For instance, IBM uses clear dialogues between managers and employees on all valuable insights that have been obtained from analytics and AI capabilities, and they are readily available to both the HR division and employees (Kiron & Spindel, 2019). It is also argued that a feedback loop is needed for learning and innovation in organisations (Grønsund & Aanestad, 2020). Furthermore, Castellacci and Viñas-Bardolet (2019) argue there is a need for developing automation-based communication technologies in organisations as these advanced algorithms facilitate communications and informal networks, enrich the information flow between employees and organisational managers and create new bonds with external agents. Thus, future research needs to focus on the how, why, and questions concerning the nature of feedback flow between organisations and employees related to AI-enabled HRM applications to minimise the impact of any unfavourable consequences at the workplace. Accordingly, we propose several propositions. For this theme we propose that:

Proposition 1. *A two-way, open and timely feedback incorporating inter- cultural and contextual knowledge in local and global organisations in the design and implementation of AI-enabled HRM applications can minimise the negative consequences of AI applications.*

Theme 2: impact of AI-enabled HRM applications on business and employee outcomes

Positive individual outcomes. We found from the extant literature that AI-enabled HRM affects both employees and organisations. Most importantly, these AI-focused HRM create favourable employee outcomes such as job satisfaction, commitment, employee engagement, and participation, thereby increasing their performance (Aouadni & Rebai, 2017; Azadeh et al., 2018; Castellacci & Viñas-Bardolet, 2019). Employees can also use the internet to create realistic expectations and perceptions of their working conditions and to foster their competencies and training (Castellacci & Viñas-Bardolet, 2019). Moreover, AI applications can free up humans and their time for several predictable and routine tasks (Maedche et al., 2019). On the other hand, the literature also points out how these automated technologies can negatively affect employees. For instance, job insecurity, high employee turnover intentions, increased stress and negative attitudes and behaviours towards new technologies implemented are negative employee consequences that an organisation must confront. Moreover, employees' interaction with internet use raises issues of employees' well-being at the workplace (Castellacci & Viñas-Bardolet, 2019).

Positive business-level outcomes. Automation technologies in HRM impact not only employee-level outcomes but also influences business-level outcomes. The literature on AI-enabled HRM adoption suggests that it leads to productivity gains, cost reduction and operational efficiencies (e.g. flexibility, scalability, safety and reliability), customer engagement and loyalty (Botha, 2019; Lu et al., 2020; Prentice & Nguyen, 2020; Ransbotham et al., 2017; Tarafdar et al., 2019). AI can also yield greater returns on investment by providing cost-effectiveness to the organisation (Torres & Mejia, 2017). The other business-productivity outcome of the AI technology is cost-effective service excellence (CESE), which refers to organisations simultaneously among the best performers in their competitive market regarding customer satisfaction and productivity. For example, *Amazon*, a world-leading online retailer, and *Singapore Airlines* have achieved the CESE milestones. Emerging technologies such as AI, big data, machine learning, mobile technology, the Internet of Things, geo-tagging, virtual reality, speech recognition, and biometrics bring enormous opportunities for extensive service innovations that have the potential to enhance the customer experience, service quality and productivity richly, all simultaneously (Wirtz, 2019). Service robots and AI are the other examples that are also likely to provide exceptional economics of scale and scope, as they only incur bulk costs at their development stages. However, robots used at information counters incur a low cost, whereas entirely virtual robots (such as voice-based chatbots in an app or on a website) incur close to zero incremental costs. Robots can collect data from various sources: the internet, cameras, microphones, sensors, and organisational knowledgebase and CRM systems. The robot can identify a customer using biometrics (facial and voice recognition systems) and can provide highly customised and personalised service on a scale at a small marginal cost (Wirtz, 2019).

Negative individual outcomes. Although the positive consequences of advanced technologies are emphasised in the literature, several negative issues have also been identified. For instance, improper use of such technologies in HRM may lead to high employee turnover. Although service robots significantly contribute at the market level, employees are considered the most critical assets in people-intensive services. Moreover, service robots can only perform cognitive and analytical tasks that require low levels of emotional or social complexity.

On the other hand, services connected with high emotional or social complexity require emotional authenticity, which typically humans are more adept at displaying. Moreover, tasks that are highly complex and need high emotional-social skills need to be performed by humans. However, such tasks may be augmented by robots and AI. Therefore, service robots may not be a key source of competitive advantage beyond the short-to-medium term (Wirtz, 2019).

Adverse business-level outcomes. While the 4IR transforms the way of doing significant activities in organisations, it is still a debatable topic how effectively it impacts the organisation's people, process, system, and structure it is still a debatable topic. More studies discuss the severe effects of adapting automation-based technologies in the workplace. For instance, Dwivedi et al. (2021) claim that, by 2030, 70 per cent of business operations will have adopted some form of AI technology within their business or manufacturing processes. Scholars further predict that Smart Technology could replace 57% of existing jobs within the OECD, by AI, Robotics, and Algorithms, and most organisations are under pressure to make any progress on building AI data analytics capabilities (Brougham & Haar, 2020).

System-level challenges. Brougham and Haar (2020) also found in their study that threat of technological disruptions leads to employee job insecurity and thereby increased turnover intentions. They also argue that employees feel fewer technological disruptions when they have fewer job mobility options. This study further asserts that, although employees leave organisations, turnover leads to adverse effects, including low employee job satisfaction. Thus, many studies assert that technological advancements in organisations increase fear among employees for their tasks and jobs, which may be adversely affected due to these advanced technologies. Moreover, employees' negative attitudes towards technological evolutions are another significant barrier to successfully adopting and implementing advanced technologies in the workplace (Brougham & Haar,

2020). Thus, there is a need to answer how to alleviate fear among employees for the implementation of new technologies in HRM functions.

In this regard, researchers argue that proper and meaningful training is highly valued for reducing employees' negative feelings towards new technological adaptions (Brougham & Haar, 2020). Furthermore, Tambe et al. (2019) argue that organisational change practitioners need to accommodate change perspectives required to carry out technology innovation in organisations. Training also enables employees of organisations to learn routines, memorise relevant information and understand how to use IT systems (Wirtz, 2019). Thus, creating a new culture and organisational redesign helps overcome the technological obstacles at the workplace.

Also, scholars claim that appropriate organisational culture is required for the successful long-term implementation of automation technologies (Bititci et al., 2016). However, reducing fear among employees is not studied well in the literature. This needs further investigation. Therefore, we formulate the following proposition:

Proposition 2. *Lack of effective fear and change management training can rouse employees' fear of AI-enabled HRM functions, thus increasing their intentions to leave their organisations or negatively impact their performance.*

Theme 3: configurations of human-AI-enabled technologies interplay at the workplace

Use of digitalized co-workers. It is not uncommon to see different forms of AI-driven technologies deployed in organisational contexts, for example, involving logical decision-making and enhanced cognition, previously performed by humans (Grønsund & Aanestad, 2020). The extant literature provides limited evidence of such applications as the field is still evolving. However, there has been a noticeable surge in studies concerning human--AI collaboration in the last 5 years (2015–2020). Nevertheless, this is not steady and consistent, leaving more room for conceptual and empirical studies within AI/BOT applications and human interactions. Recent research on service employees, in particular studies on customer service frontline employees, offers evidence of utilisation of intelligent bots and automation (e.g. voice recognition assistants, chatbots and other service automation systems) to streamline processes and improve task efficiency (e.g. Henkel et al., 2020; Li et al., 2019; Prentice et al., 2020b).

Gradual job-replacement thesis. Firstly, in our observations of extant literature, scholars have acknowledged the role of AI and intelligent technologies in accelerating specific tasks and processes while noting that AI deployment resonates a risk of 'human replacement' (Li et al., 2019). In their theory of job replacement through AI, Huang and Rust (2018) significantly contributed to the literature concerning this double-edged effect of AI in services as to conceptualise how AI reshapes service and how AI may replace service workers entirely, thus suggesting employees to develop specific skills—intuitive and empathetic skills that AI is not yet capable of holding to it. Furthermore, their theory asserts that while service employees focus on developing their intuitive and empathetic skills, AI may help take care of analytical tasks that save human time and resources.

Apart from this theory, only a handful of studies have theoretically or empirically investigated the effects of human–AI configurations, what tasks can be best performed by AI and intelligent technologies, and what skills and competencies employees need to develop in AI-driven organisational settings. A significant number of scholars have recently acknowledged more ethical and justice to consider the human worker in the loop where most of the studies encouraged augmenting employees, rather than a replacement as the technology itself in organisational contexts (e.g. Dwivedi et al., 2021; Glikson & Woolley, 2020; Grønsund & Aanestad, 2020; Maedche et al., 2019; Metcalf et al., 2019). These studies have alluded to different roles or acts or skills that employees should play and develop at work to remain in the loop and cope with their roles being augmented from AI/intelligent technologies for better organisational results. Several scholars agree that employees must acquire new skills—to work with AI or expand their existing skills focused on emotions, judgement, innovation, personal relationships and soft skills (e.g. Agrawal et al., 2017; Huang et al., 2019; Huang & Rust, 2020; Larivière et al., 2017; Rampersad, 2020; Ransbotham et al., 2017; Wilson & Daugherty, 2018). Doing so will help utilise their knowledge and skills in heterogeneous tasks organisational value addition activities. The role of AI and AI-enabled technologies can play a complementary rather than competing a competing role with humans, as it helps interact with customers or co-workers/team members and amplifies human capability by dealing with high volume analytical and routine tasks or offering efficient, personalised services on a scale (e.g. Agrawal et al., 2017; Huang & Rust, 2020; Wirtz et al., 2018). Building on different capabilities that human workers and AI/intelligent technologies can offer, we can develop a better human–AI configuration, and thus, the following propositions are offered:

Proposition 3a. AI/intelligent technologies can augment human capacity by delivering routine (homogeneous) high volume analytical tasks while leaving the non-routine (heterogeneous), judgment-based low volume and non- analytical tasks to be performed by humans.

Proposition 3b. With the increased augmentation of humans, HR managers can leverage AI/intelligent technologies to deliver transformative and innovative solutions for acquiring, developing and retaining talent, thus enhancing employee experience and engagement propositions.

Re-inventing and re-imaging self for better alignment. In further reaction to the above proposition, we assert our argument on employees' particular skills to better fit human–AI configurations? The extant literature notes the importance of re-skilling, job redesign and training workers to use intelligent agents or AI technologies (e.g. Aleksander, 2017; Grønsund & Aanestad, 2020; Larivière et al., 2017; Ransbotham et al., 2017). Nevertheless, this stream of research tends to be less conclusive on which specific skills a worker should adopt or develop to work together with AI depending on the nature of AI technology(ies) being used at work. Wilson and Daugherty (2018) introduced the term 'fusion skills'—to define the skills that employees need to develop that enable them to work effectively in the human–AI interplays at work. They assert that organisations and the management teams should use the full potential machine and human intelligence through effective collaboration to transform their operations into the next level of business competition to capitalise on market opportunities. Malik et al. (2021) found the presence of talent supply chain bots for acquiring, developing and retaining talent and enhancing their employee experience (EX) through hyper-personalisation of the talents' EX. To this end, literacy on using algorithm-based systems and intelligent agents, we would call 'AI literacy', help human workers better collaborate with the systems and ensure the work is getting through AI/ intelligent technologies. The underline notion that the positive effect of AI/intelligent technologies can be enhanced when employees have better fusion skills and literacy to work with AI/intelligent technologies, we propose the following:

Proposition 4a. *The positive effect of human–AI/intelligent technologies configurations will be stronger when employees have fusion skills and AI literacy.*

Proposition 4b. *The positive effect of AI-assisted talent applications is likely to provide a positive employee experience for talents through hyper-personalised talent development opportunities.*

AI-mediated social exchanges. Thirdly, we note that studies on employee-level outcomes as a result of human–AI interplay at work show positive empirical effects or conceptual viewpoints regarding the benefits through such exchanges (e.g. Hohenstein & Jung, 2020; Metcalf et al., 2019; Wilson & Daugherty, 2018), adverse effects (e.g. Brougham & Haar, 2020; Li et al., 2019) or mixed-effects (e.g. Henkel et al., 2020; Prentice et al., 2020a, Prentice et al., 2020b). The studies selected for this review examine employee outcomes such as perceived trust, performance, job satisfaction, affective well-being, turnover intention/retention, and job insecurity.

Research on frontline services can be found in a dominant context concerning human-social robot/intelligent machines that found a range of employee level outcomes, including customers' perspective of service performances. For example, Henkel et al. (2020) found mixed outcomes of service employees in two centralised call centres in the Netherlands, augmenting service employees with AI emotion recognition tool improved the effectiveness of controlling customer emotions and subsequently elevated their affective well-being. Nevertheless, it causes a higher level of stress at the initial phase of the technology. Further evidence suggests that despite employees integrating with AI and related technologies, a range of social support and inducement is needed to cope well with the nature and extent of changes in organisational workplaces. Li et al. (2019) provide evidence that though the relationship between AI and robotic awareness and employee turnover intention is related, the strength of the relationships may moderate from the perceived organisational support and competitive psychological climate from a sample of hospitality employees of China. Investigating the extant literature, we build on a collective term – social-technical interventions, wherein scholars have noted the presence of flexible organisational structures, supportive leadership, opportunities for upskilling, job redesign, change management training and overcoming their fear and anxieties (e.g. Aleksander, 2017; Dwivedi et al., 2021; Li et al., 2019; Lu et al., 2020; Robert et al., 2020). Further, the high quality of AI-mediated exchanges can lead to high levels of EX, which can trigger the norm of reciprocity, such that positive EX of employees of such applications can result in greater employee commitment and job satisfaction (Malik et al., 2021; Nguyen & Malik, 2021). This approach can potentially elevate positive employee outcomes when using AI/intelligent technologies at work. Accordingly, we propose the following:

Proposition 5a. *The positive effect of AI and intelligent technologies on employee outcomes will be strengthened in the presence of supportive social-technical interventions at work.*

Proposition 5b. *The quality of AI applications can positively affect EX, thus triggering a norm of reciprocity by employees in the form of high levels of employee commitment and job satisfaction.*

Some AI scholars assert that employees are considered the most critical assets and can react better than machines (Agrawal et al., 2017; Wirtz, 2019). Moreover, researchers argue that personal factors, such as employees' personality traits, affect people's cognitive, affective, and behavioural outcomes (Abubakar et al., 2019). This is because most employment actions affect the socio-psychological status of employees, such as personal status and perceived fairness (Tambe et al., 2019). Moreover, some scholars argue that employees must emphasise their work's empathetic and emotional dimensions (Huang et al., 2019).

Although service robots can perform cognitive and analytical tasks which require low emotional or social complexity, services connected with high emotional or social complexity require emotional authenticity, which a human can only display. Moreover, tasks that are highly complex and need high emotional-social skills need to be performed by humans and augmented by robots and AI. Henkel et al. (2020) argue that when service employees augment with an AI emotion recognition tool lead to regulating emotions in customers and enhancing customer relation- ships. However, augmentation with AI technology leads to extra stress and requires roles changes.

Agrawal et al. (2017) emphasise that demand for employees increases in the workplace, as they can engage well with customers using emotional intelligence and creating new opportunities. Thus, we put forward the following proposition: developing emotional intelligence and sup- porting specific employee personality types can lead to effective and productive customer interactions.

Proposition 6. Developing emotional intelligence and identifying and supporting certain personality traits of employees can lead to effective perceptions of AI-enabled HRM functions and leads to positive and productive engagement of customers.

Many new relationships need to explore what contextual factors cause employee outcomes to turn into a positive or negative state, what boundary conditions would change the attitudinal and behavioural outcomes in human–AI interplays, and what perceptions are evolving in the use of human–AI collaborations in different industry settings. Future research could explore these emerging issues to expand the depth of extant literature.

Theme 4: ethical and legal challenges in using AI and intelligent technologies in an international HRM context

Ethical and moral issues. Beyond the increasing popularity of adopting AI-enabled intelligent applications and technologies in organisations worldwide, a central theme in the extant literature is to address the vital aspect concerning *ethics, accountability, trust, fairness* and *legal implications* of using AI-driven technologies and autonomous systems at workplaces. The issue of equity, diversity and inclusion (EDI) is also vital, as early applications of AI by large technology corporates such as Amazon revealed biases against women in hiring. In other tech firms, biases against people of colour in the promotion and career advancement decisions are also noted. A lot more work is needed to reduce biases by making high-quality AI applications.

Recent research by Nguyen and Malik (2021, 2022) points to the importance of AI service quality and knowledge sharing in organisations to improve the experience of employees' service quality and customer satisfaction. Subsequently, Malik, Nguyen and Budhwar (2022d) developed a conceptual model of the antecedents and outcomes of AI-mediated knowledge sharing social exchange. However, very few review studies have identified the above topics, such as reviews by Dwivedi et al. (2021) and others (De Stefano, 2019; Glikson & Woolley, 2020; Robert et al., 2020; Tambe et al., 2019). Firstly, the responsibility of decisions made by AI/intelligent technologies and the gravity of such decisions against human value judgement remains a challenge, as discussed by Dwivedi et al. (2021). Secondly, there are instances where moral values come into consideration that could be missing in the radar of AI-driven decision making. To further explain, Tambe et al. (2019) discussed two associated challenges on accountability concerns and possible adverse employee outcomes in reaction to management decisions by algorithms. In particular, employee resistance to AI-driven decisions may be caused when the decision could be biased to certain groups of organisations based on data patterns and frequencies that AI captures may raise concerns in a diverse employee base in a multi-cultural organisation setting. However, AI/intelligent technologies perform better than human judgements in repetitive situations rather than heterogeneous case-based scenarios (Tambe et al., 2019). Thus, a careful delegation of work on what decisions algorithms may be responsible for should be determined to gain a mutual advantage of having accurate and effective decisions without confronting ethical and accountability concerns.

Trust in AI. Researchers have raised the concern of trust as it has been commonly recognised that lack of trust and ethical dimensions of AI/intelligent technologies in data exchange and sharing. Featuring human trust in AI, Glikson and Woolley (2020) proposed a framework that has elements in shaping users' cognitive trust (rational thinking) and emotional trust (affect-based). According to authors, in building human's cognitive trust in AI, role of tangibility (physical presence of robots), transparency (underlying rules of operation and rationale of the technology), reliability (technology trustworthiness for expected behaviour), task characteristics (functional abilities of robots) and immediacy behaviours (extent of physical/psychological closeness – social robots) are said to be important antecedents. For an emotional trust, the role of anthropomorphism (human-like features) and immediacy behaviours (responsiveness) have been identified, in addition to the role of tangibility (Glikson & Woolley, 2020). However, we should note a lack of empirical research on trust issues of adopting AI and autonomous related systems, as it is not investigated how trust could be engendered in different organisational settings (e.g. healthcare, finance, telecommunication and transportation).

Regulation and ethics. Finally, in terms of legal and fairness aspects of AI/ intelligent technologies, the review identifies the studies of De Stefano (2019) and Robert and colleagues (2020). The advent of advancing technologies has increased legal implications in setting new laws, issues related to termination/ redundancies of employment, liabilities to workers (e.g. injuries) caused by bots and protection of personal information. De Stefano (2019, p. 3) asserts on 'jobs of the future', which requires high technical skills, where regulators should allow employees to be equipped with relevant high-tech skills to be employed in modern roles of working and take measures to absorb 'occupational shocks' caused by workplace automation and intrusive business practices which could result from 'management by algorithms'. Thus, studies such as Robert et al. (2020) stress designing AI/BOT systems to support workplace fairness and ethics, ensuring such work organisation is mutually beneficial to humanity and organisational efficiency goals. Theoretical lenses of organisational justice (including three types of fairness: distributive, procedural and interactional) and utilitarian theories have been applied in the discussion of ethical and human aligned-AI/ robotics work settings. (Robert et al., 2020).

Although originally developed for the EU, the establishment of the Global Data Protection Regulation (GDPR) as key legislation dealing with data protection on privacy issues is gradually finding its place in different countries, showing some evidence of harmonisation. Yet, the enforcement is problematic in the context of MNEs and the large IT MNEs who are developers of such AI applications and products, making the accountability of such applications and data ownership and privacy issues a complex problem. Taken together, the findings and conclusions of the studies suggest that potential adverse effects, i.e. ethical concerns on biases in algorithmic decisions, trust and reliability issues and other issues related to employment arise from using AI and intelligence technologies at work, could be minimised using context-specific, transparent guidelines on ethics and accountability. These guidelines should address all possible concerns in HRM functions organising work from human–human and human–machine collaborations that will positively engender individual and organisational level outcomes. Therefore, we propose:

Proposition 7. The presence of transparent, ethical and accountability guidelines for using AI and AI-enabled intelligence technologies at work will positively influence AI-enabled HRM functions, human–AI configurations, and individual and organisational level outcomes.

Implications for theory and practice

Our review analysed the extant literature, presented opportunities and challenges of AI and other automated technologies for HRM, exploring how the automated HRM functions can impact employee and organisational outcomes. From the extant literature, we found that AI and other related automation technologies offer numerous opportunities for HRM functions, particularly in attracting the star performers, enhancing training effectiveness, identifying skill-gaps and recommending any required training and development for employees, assisting in employee payroll, effective decision-making on employees, while reducing the costs and time, cognitive biases made by humans in HRM activities (Karatop et al., 2015; Kshetri, 2021; Pessach et al., 2020; Torres & Mejia, 2017). Thus, AI and related intelligence technologies play a crucial role in strengthening HRM functions and activities.

Moreover, our review highlights that AI-enabled HRM functions can impact both employees and organisations. For this reason, there is a need to study some influential factors which may further strengthen favourable outcomes. Thus, we argue social-technical interventions and employee factors could influence positive consequences at the workplace. Furthermore, literature argued that AI and advanced robot technologies might take human jobs (Wirtz, 2019). However, some arguments of augmentation suggest that instead of automation, it is the importance of AI–human configurations in the effective use of AI-enabled HRM functions that will deliver better outcomes.

Although literature points to AI as an asset, the extent to which it can be classified is questionable and unclear, as AI and other automation technologies always need to adhere to privacy, legal, moral and ethical principles. Further, the service quality of AI applications, their design, and delivery attributes are vital for the ease of use and EX. Hence, further research is needed on developing measurements for AI service quality, AI attributes and AI-mediated knowledge sharing mechanisms. Though some progress has been made in developing measures for AI-service quality and its attributes (Nguyen & Malik, 2021), further work is needed for a range of AI inputs, processes and outputs to advance the field further. Thus, considering clear, transparent legal, ethical, and accountability guidelines are necessary for prompting favourable consequences due to the automation of HRM function at the workplace. Additionally, there is also a need to have sound principles and guidelines on analysing how effectively AI can augment humans and the possible impacts of these configurations. Finally, we believe that the model presented and propositions developed in this review will provide a pathway for future researchers to examine how AI-focused HRM functions enhance positive outcomes in organisations through some interventions and conditions.

In line with the opportunities provided by the intelligence technologies, this review also provides some practical implications for managers, practitioners and policymakers in organisations. As per this review, advanced automated technologies shape, assist and change the handling of HRM activities in organisations. As a result, AI and related automation technologies are not only helping attract and select high calibre, but they also help in providing prompt and effective training and development to employees in handling massive employee data and assisting managers to make better decisions for their employees. The supportive role provided by the technologies in HRM function eventually leads to cultivating favourable employee outcomes such as enhanced employee participation and job satisfaction, commitment and job performance. Thus, it is possible to boost organisational outcomes, such as enhanced performance, productivity, efficiency, cost-effectiveness, and customer satisfaction and service quality. However, on the other hand, it is the responsibility of organisations to ensure all legal, moral, and ethical guidelines on how to use these technologies in HRM, as they can affect workers and the working process.

Most importantly, it is vital to understand how employees perceive and behave in response to technological advancements. Thus, based on this review, we suggest that developing favourable and supportive social-technological interventions such as flexible organisational structure, supportive leadership, ethical workplace culture, change and fear management training, upskilling employees and redesigning job roles will lead to enhanced positive outcomes in the workplace. Moreover, we put forward that creating favourable personal factors of employees, such as personality and emotional intelligence, also assist in creating those positive results for organisations. Finally, our review also greatly recommends the importance of AI–human configurations at the workplace to optimise the benefits offered by technologies.

Despite the increasing attention among scholars on AI and intelligent based technologies in augmenting human potential and elevating organisational outcomes, detailed research concerning its effect, practices/ techniques to effectively use AI–human configurations, and other related topics largely remain unexplored. Nevertheless, this systematic literature review unveiled many potential research areas and developed research propositions. For example, future studies might want to theorise what *a priori* conditions organisations (e.g. cultural and strategical influences) need to adopt for an AI-driven HRM function and then test their effects on employee and organisational level to verify its effectiveness.

We further suggest scholars examine organisational and HRM approaches by making choices regarding delegation of work and decision-making between humans and AI technologies for achieving a better combination between the human–AI interplay at work. Kshetri (2021) provides ten case examples of AI usage in domestic, government and global multinational enterprises covering different aspects of HRM's functional practices, such as recruitment and selection (e.g. in WeChat recruiting, DBS's Jim, Talkpush's Stanley and Ajingas's talent management tool) and other talent management, development and utilisation tools (e.g., EY's Goldie, Supa Agent's DIANE, Leena's AI chatbot and Daeyea's 'brain surveillance device). Therefore, it is crucial to investigate how job redesign and upskilling of employees can be utilised to facilitate changes in future organisational work. Specific areas of HRM functions, for example, predictions of human resource planning via AI-enabled HR analytics, personalised coaching on employee career development, a personalised recommendation for training and upskilling, could be vital applications for producing insights for HR practitioners to organise well in the future world of work. Apart from the positive effects, future studies might also look at potential conflicts at an employee and organisational level. These include conflicts, such as breaches between human and social robots' psychological contract, identity struggles and cognitive dissonance of coping with non-humans and humanoid-based systems at work.

Papers in this special issue

We highlight the current state and potential areas of future research on the very topic from our systematic literature review in the first section that pave the path to this section, where we introduce cutting-edge research of challenges and opportunities of AI in the international HRM context. We received a total of 25 manuscripts but following a rigorous editorial and double-blind reviewing of papers by expert scholars in this emerging field, whom we sincerely thank, we included six exciting and rigorously executed studies relevant to research for an international HRM context.

The contributions span 24 European countries, including data in different papers on subsidiaries of several Canadian, French, Irish, Swiss, the US and UK, multinational corporations (MNCs), including domestic firms and MNCs from India and China. The contributions include quantitative, qualitative and conceptual papers. The focus of these papers was on AI scholarship in IHRM, ranging on aspects such as higher-level debates on automation and augmentation, firm-level productivity and performance, the impact of AI-enabled applications on HR effectiveness and individual-level outcomes, the specific impact of AI-enabled HRM applications on individual outcomes, and the impact of a bundle of HRM practices on skills needed by employees and HR practitioners for managing change. A substantive review of the field is also included in this special issue.

Presented in the order of propositions, the first chapter by Del Giudice et al. (2021) presents data from intercultural contexts (partially supports Proposition 1), analysing data from 24 European countries using the theoretical lens of service robot deployment model and organisational ambidexterity to investigate the impacts of robots in the workplace on firm productivity. Their distinctive contribution lies in analysing the indirect impact of robots deployment on productivity by modifying existing and creating new creative routines. Furthermore, the authors argue the vital role of leaders in managing this transition of automation and adoption of service robots by ensuring they maintain the balance between exploratory and exploitative routines.

The second chapter by Pan et al. (2021) explores AI use adoption in employee recruitment practices. Employing the technology, organisation and environment model and integrating it with transaction cost theory, the authors analyse the enablers and barriers in adopting AI and its usage for employee recruitment practices. The authors analysed data from 297 Chinese firms and found that various technological, organisational and environ- mental elements directly affect AI usage for recruitment in the surveyed sample. The authors found positive moderation effects for the interaction terms between transaction cost theory determinant of asset specificity in examining the relationship between technology competence on AI usage, indicating that the interaction was only significant for firms with high levels of asset-specificity. Similarly, support was also found for the moderation effects of uncertainty in examining the relationship between technical competence and AI usage, such that the interaction was significant for companies facing high uncertainty, thus partly supporting Proposition 3a.

The third chapter by Malik et al. (2021) presents an in-depth qualitative case study data of humongous global information technology consulting MNC with its subsidiary in India, focusing on delivering innovative and cutting-edge AI and disruptive technology solutions for several industries worldwide. The authors analyse the adoption and diffusion of several AI-enabled HRM applications by the global MNC and develop contextually relevant AI applications for its subsidiary operation in India. The case presents self-learning by different AI applications that deliver solutions and respond to HR queries for an Indian context. Other AI Bots addressed the diverse and specific needs of Indian employees for a range of routine, non-routine and somewhat complex HR queries. These HR-focused AI-applications' ability to offer *personalised, hyper-personalised* responses, suggestions and problem-solving helped employees to receive *individualised* solutions. In addition, these bots collectively improved the overall HR cost-effectiveness in terms of the sheer volume of routine queries dealt with by these applications. Such an AI-mediated social exchange helped improve the overall employee experience proposition, leading to more significant commitment, satisfaction and a reduced intention to quit, thus partly supporting Propositions 3a, b, 4b and 5. The fourth chapter by Jaiswal and colleagues (2021) focuses on the crucial issue of upskilling employees to understand and utilise AI technologies, especially in light of the increased adoption and proliferation of AI-enabled applications and technologies at work. Employing the theoretical lens of dynamic skill, neo-human capital, and AI job replacement theories, the authors present qualitative data analysis of 20 experienced technical and managerial professionals working in subsidiaries of Canadian, Danish, French Irish, Indian, Swiss, the UK and US multinational corporations (MNCs) operating in India. Findings from their analysis highlight five critical core skills, including data analysis, digital, complex cognitive, decision making, and continuous learning, thus partly supporting Proposition 4a.

The fifth chapter by Suseno et al. (2021) examines the change readiness of HR managers for AI adoption. Specifically, the authors focused on HR managers' beliefs about AI and their AI anxiety and examined its relation- ship with change readiness for AI adoption. Analysing data from 417 HR managers working in China and employing social cognitive theory, the authors found a significant negative relationship between HR managers' AI anxiety on change readiness for AI adoption, while a positive and significant relationship between AI beliefs and change readiness. In addition, the authors found the moderating role of high-performance work systems (HPWS), such that HPWS attenuates the adverse effects of AI anxiety on change readiness for AI adoption, thus partly supporting Proposition 4.

The final chapter by Vrontis et al. (2021) presents a systematic review of 45 articles on the literature examining the emergent themes around intelligent automation in HRM and how it impacts firm performance and employment conditions and areas for future research. Among several themes, the authors found that the bulk of the intelligent automation research is in the areas of recruitment, training and job performance. Further, the emerging adoption has led to increasing job replacement thesis, human-bot interactions, and decision-making, including evidence of HRM algorithms showing adaptive and self-learning. The above studies point to several benefits to the employees, work processes and organisational effectiveness, leading to an overall more robust climate and culture for innovation, change, as noted in a recent study on elevating talent's experience through AI-mediated social exchange in the presence of a strong culture of innovation (Malik et al., 2021).

Concluding remarks

Through these contributions and supplementing this with our review of the field and framing future research agenda based on a systematic literature review for the recent ten years, we expected to enhance the current knowledge in this emerging field. First, we extend the knowledge base on the drivers and consequences of the adoption of AI and AI-based intelligent technologies in international HRM and inform the research audience on the growing potentiality for further research. This research area is relatively emerging yet timely needed to be further explored through robust conceptual and empirical research keeping up with dynamic changes of technological advancement and changing business environment. Second, we reviewed the extant literature and derived the main focus areas as four key themes—and the propositions that we have developed for each theme can be explored further in future studies. Third, the theoretical framework we have developed from this review explicates the association of constructs in detail and points to new constructs that can be potentially sensible for further research to provide answers of concern under the review's focus. This review and the articles of this special issue will contribute to the literature and lead business organisations and HR professionals towards facilitating dynamic changes to introduce intelligent technologies in gaining and securing competitive advantages.

Disclosure statement

No potential conflict of interest was reported by the authors.

References

Abraham, M., Niessen, C., Schnabel, C., Lorek, K., Grimm, V., Möslein, K., & Wrede, M. (2019). Electronic monitoring at work: The role of attitudes, functions, and perceived control for the acceptance of tracking technologies. *Human Resource Management Journal*, *29*(4), 657–675. https://doi.org/10.1111/1748-8583.12250

Abubakar, A. M., Behravesh, E., Rezapouraghdam, H., & Yildiz, S. B. (2019). Applying artificial intelligence technique to predict knowledge hiding behavior. *International Journal of Information Management*, *49*, 45–57. https://doi.org/10.1016/j.ijinfo- mgt.2019.02.006

Agar, N. (2019). *How to be human in the digital economy*. MIT Press.

Agar, N. (2020). How to treat machines that might have minds. *Philosophy & Technology*, *33*(2), 269–282. https://doi.org/10.1007/s13347-019-00357-8

Agrawal, A., Gans, J., & Goldfarb, A. (2017). What to expect from artificial intelligence. *MIT Sloan Management Review*, *58*(3), 23-26. http://mitsmr.com/2jZdf1Y

Aleksander, I. (2017). Partners of humans: A realistic assessment of the role of robots in the foreseeable future. *Journal of Information Technology*, *32*(1), 1–9. https://doi.org/10.1057/s41265-016-0032-4

Aouadni, I., & Rebai, A. (2017). Decision support system based on genetic algorithm and multi-criteria satisfaction analysis (MUSA) method for measuring job satisfaction. *Annals of Operations Research*, *256*(1), 3–20. https://doi.org/10.1007/s10479-016-2154-z

Azadeh, A., Yazdanparast, R., Abdolhossein Zadeh, S., & Keramati, A. (2018). An intelligent algorithm for optimising emergency department job and patient satisfaction. *International Journal of Health Care Quality Assurance*, *31*(5), 374–390. https:// doi.org/10.1108/IJHCQA-06-2016-0086

Azadeh, A., & Zarrin, M. (2016). An intelligent framework for productivity assessment and analysis of human resource from resilience engineering, motivational factors, HSE and ergonomics perspectives. *Safety Science*, *89*, 55–71. https://doi.org/10.1016/j.ssci.2016.06.001

Bersin, J., & Chamorro-Premuzic, T. (2019). New ways to gauge talent and potential. *MIT Sloan Management Review*, *60*(2), 1. https://mitsmr.com/2QLPcEN

Bharadwaj, N., & Shipley, G. M. (2020). Salesperson communication effectiveness in a digital sales interaction. *Industrial Marketing Management*, *90*, 106–112. https://doi.org/10.1016/j.indmarman.2020.07.002

Bititci, U., Cocca, P., & Ates, A. (2016). Impact of visual performance management systems on the performance management practices of organisations. *International Journal of Production Research*, *54*(6), 1571–1593. https://doi.org/10.1080/00207543.2015.1005770

Botha, A. P. (2019). A mind model for intelligent machine innovation using future thinking principles. *Journal of Manufacturing Technology Management, 30*(8), 1250–1264. https://doi.org/10.1108/JMTM-01-2018-0021

Brougham, D., & Haar, J. (2020). Technological disruption and employment: The influence on job insecurity and turnover intentions: A multi-country study. *Technological Forecasting and Social Change, 161*, 120276. https://doi.org/10.1016/j.tech- fore.2020.120276

Budhwar, P., & Malik, A. (2020). Call for papers for the special issue on Leveraging artificial and human intelligence through Human Resource Management. *Human Resource Management Review*. Retrieved June 24, 2020, from www.journals.elsevier.com/human-resource-management-review/call-for-papers/leveraging-artificial-and-human-intelligence

Bussler, L., & Davis, E. (2002). Information systems: The quiet revolution in human resource management. *Journal of Computer Information Systems, 42*(2), 17–20.

Buxmann, P., Hess, T., & Thatcher, J. (2019). Call for papers, issue 1/2021. *Business & Information Systems Engineering, 61*(4), 545–547. https://doi.org/10.1007/s12599-019-00606-2

Castellacci, F., & Viñas-Bardolet, C. (2019). Internet use and job satisfaction. *Computers in Human Behavior, 90*, 141–152. https://doi.org/10.1016/j.chb.2018.09.001

Charlwood, A., & Guenole, N. (2022). Can HR adapt to the paradoxes of AI? *Human Resource Management Journal, 32*(4), 729–742. https://doi.org/10.1111/1748-8583.12433

Christofi, M., Vrontis, D., & Cadogan, J. W. (2021). Micro-foundational ambidexterity and multinational enterprises: a systematic review and a conceptual framework. *International Business Review, 30*(1), 101625. https://doi.org/10.1016/j.ibus- rev.2019.101625

Connelly, C. E., Fieseler, C., Černe, M., Giessner, S. R., & Wong, S. I. (2020). Working in the digitised economy: HRM theory & practice. *Human Resource Management Review, 31*(1), ahead-of-print. https://doi.org/10.1016/j.hrmr.2020.100762

de Kervenoael, R., Hasan, R., Schwob, A., & Goh, E. (2020). Leveraging human-robot interaction in hospitality services: Incorporating the role of perceived value, empathy, and information sharing into visitors' intentions to use social robots. *Tourism Management, 78*, 104042. https://doi.org/10.1016/j.tourman.2019.104042

De Stefano, V. (2019). 'Negotiating the algorithm': Automation, artificial intelligence and labour protection. *Comparative Labor Law & Policy Journal, 41*(1), 15–46. https://ssrn.com/abstract=3178233

Del Giudice, M., Scuotto, V., Ballestra, L. V., & Pironti, M. (2021, this issue). Humanoid robot adoption and labour productivity: A perspective on ambidextrous product innovation routines. *The International Journal of Human Resource Management*, ahead-of-print. 1–27. https://doi.org/10.1080/09585192.2021.1897643

Duggan, J., Sherman, U., Carbery, R., & McDonnell, A. (2020). Algorithmic management and app-work in the gig economy: A research agenda for employment relations and HRM. *Human Resource Management Journal, 30*(1), 114–132. https://doi.org/10.1111/1748-8583.12258

Dwivedi, Y. K., Hughes, L., Ismagilova, E., Aarts, G., Coombs, C., Crick, T., Duan, Y., Dwivedi, R., Edwards, J., Eirug, A., Galanos, V., Ilavarasan, P. V., Janssen, M., Jones, P., Kar, A. K., Kizgin, H., Kronemann, B., Lal, B., Lucini, B., … Williams, M. D. (2021). Artificial Intelligence (AI): Multidisciplinary perspectives on emerging chal- lenges, opportunities, and agenda for research, practice and policy. *International Journal of Information Management, 57*, 101994. https://doi.org/10.1016/j.ijinfo- mgt.2019.08.002

Ererdi, C., Nurgabdeshov, A., Kozhakhmet, S., Rofcanin, Y., & Demirbag, M. (2021). International HRM in the context of uncertainty and crisis: A systematic review of literature (2000–2018). *The International Journal of Human Resource Management*, 1–39. ahead-of-print. https://doi.org/10.1080/09585192.2020.1863247

Glikson, E., & Woolley, A. W. (2020). Human trust in artificial intelligence: Review of empirical research. *Academy of Management Annals, 14*(2), 627–660. https://doi.org/10.5465/annals.2018.0057

Grønsund, T., & Aanestad, M. (2020). Augmenting the algorithm: Emerging human-in-the-loop work configurations. *The Journal of Strategic Information Systems, 29*(2), 101614. https://doi.org/10.1016/j.jsis.2020.101614

Henkel, A. P., Bromuri, S., Iren, D., & Urovi, V. (2020). Half human, half machine-augmenting service employees with AI for interpersonal emotion regulation. *Journal of Service Management, 31*(2), 247–5818. https://doi.org/10.1108/JOSM-05-2019-0160

Hohenstein, J., & Jung, M. (2020). AI as a moral crumple zone: The effects of AI-mediated communication on attribution and trust. *Computers in Human Behavior, 106*, 106190. https://doi.org/10.1016/j.chb.2019.106190

Houser, K. (2018). Chinese surveillance is literally getting in workers' heads. *Futurism*. https://futurism.com/china-emotional-surveillance

Huang, M. H., & Rust, R. T. (2018). Artificial intelligence in service. *Journal of Service Research, 21*(2), 155–172. https://doi.org/10.1177/1094670517752459

Huang, M. H., & Rust, R. T. (2020). Engaged to a robot? The role of AI in service. *Journal of Service Research, 24*(1), 30-41. https://doi.org/10.1177/1094670520902266

Huang, M. H., Rust, R., & Maksimovic, V. (2019). The feeling economy: Managing in the next generation of artificial intelligence (AI*). California Management Review, 61*(4), 43–65. https://doi.org/10.1177/0008125619863436

Jain, H., Padmanabhan, B., Pavlou, P. A. & Santanam, R.T. (Eds). (2018). Call for papers—Special Issue of Information Systems Research—Humans, algorithms, and augmented intelligence: The future of work, organisations, and society. *Information Systems Research, 29*, 250–251.

Jaiswal, A., Arun, C. J., & Varma, A. (2021, this issue). Rebooting employees: Upskilling for artificial intelligence in multinational corporations. *International Journal of Human Resource Management*, 1–30. ahead-of-print. https://doi.org/10.1080/0958519 2.2021.1891114

Kaplan, A., & Haenlein, M. (2020). Rulers of the world, unite! The challenges and opportunities of artificial intelligence. *Business Horizons, 63*(1), 37–50. https://doi.org/10.1016/j.bus hor.2019.09.003

Karatop, B., Kubat, C., & Uygun, Ö. (2015). Talent management in manufacturing system using fuzzy logic approach. *Computers & Industrial Engineering, 86*, 127–136. https://doi.org/10.1016/j.cie.2014.09.015

Kiron, D., & Spindel, B. (2019). *Rebooting work for a digital era*. MIT Sloan Management Review. https://sloanreview.mit.edu/IBM-case

Kshetri, N. (2021). Evolving uses of artificial intelligence in human resource management in emerging economies in the global South: Some preliminary evidence. *Management Research Review, 44*(7), 970–990. https://doi.org/10.1108/MRR-03-2020-0168

Larivière, B., Bowen, D., Andreassen, T. W., Kunz, W., Sirianni, N. J., Voss, C., Wünderlich, N. V., & De Keyser, A. (2017). 'Service Encounter 2.0': An investigation into the roles of technology, employees and customers. *Journal of Business Research, 79*, 238–246. https://doi.org/10.1016/j.jbusres.2017.03.008

Li, J. J., Bonn, M. A., & Ye, B. H. (2019). Hotel employee's artificial intelligence and robotics awareness and its impact on turnover intention: The moderating roles of perceived organisational support and competitive psychological climate. *Tourism Management, 73*, 172–181. https://doi.org/10.1016/j.tourman.2019.02.006

Li, J., Liu, M., & Liu, X. (2016). Why do employees resist knowledge management systems? An empirical study from the status quo bias and inertia perspectives. *Computers in Human Behavior, 65*, 189–200. https://doi.org/10.1016/j.chb.2016.08.028

Lu, V. N., Wirtz, J., Kunz, W. H., Paluch, S., Gruber, T., Martins, A., & Patterson, P. G. (2020). Service robots, customers and service employees: What can we learn from the academic literature and where are the gaps? *Journal of Service Theory and Practice, 30*(3), 361–391. https://doi.org/10.1108/JSTP-04-2019-0088

Maedche, A., Legner, C., Benlian, A., Berger, B., Gimpel, H., Hess, T., Hinz, O., Morana, S., & Söllner, M. (2019). AI-based digital assistants. *Business & Information Systems Engineering, 61*(4), 535–544. https://doi.org/10.1007/s12599-019-00600-8

Malik, A., Budhwar, P., Patel, C., & Srikanth, N. R. (2020c, this issue). May the bots be with you! Delivering HR cost-effectiveness and individualised employee experi- ences in an MNE. *The International Journal of Human Resource Management*, 1–31. ahead-of-print. https://doi.org/10.1080/09585192.2020.1859582

Malik, A., Budhwar, P., & Srikanth, N. R. (2020a). Gig economy, 4IR and artificial intelli- gence: Rethinking strategic HRM. In P. Kumar, A. Agrawal, & P. Budhwar (Eds.), *Human & technological resource management (HTRM): New insights into revolution 4.0* (pp. 75–88). Emerald Publishing Limited.

Malik, A., De Silva, M. T. T., Budhwar, P., & Srikanth, N. R. (2021). Elevating talents' experi- ence through innovative artificial intelligence-mediated knowledge sharing: Evidence from an IT-multinational enterprise. *Journal of International Management, 27*(4), 100871. https://doi.org/10.1016/j.intman.2021.100871

Malik, A., Sreenivasan, P., & De Silva, T. (2022). Artificial intelligence, employee engage- ment, experience and HRM. In A. Malik (Ed.), *Strategic human resource management and employment relations: An international perspective* (2nd ed.). Springer.

Malik, A., Srikanth, N. R., & Budhwar, P. (2020b). Digitisation, artificial intelligence (AI) and HRM. In J. Crawshaw, P. Budhwar, & A Davis (Eds.), *Human resource management: Strategic and international perspectives* (pp. 88–111). Sage.

Malik, A., Budhwar, P. Mohan, H., & Srikanth, NR (2022c) Employee experience – The missing link: Insights from an MNE's AI-based employee engagement ecosystem, *Human Resource Management*, DOI: https://doi.org/10.1002/hrm.22133

Malik, A., Nguyen, M., & Budhwar, P. (2022d). Antecedents and consequences of an artificial intelligence mediated knowledge-sharing social exchange: Towards a conceptual model *IEEE Transactions on Engineering Management,* DOI: 10.1109/TEM.2022.3163117

Malik, A., Budhwar, P. & Kazmi, B. (2023). Artificial intelligence (AI)-assisted HRM: Towards an extended strategic framework *Human Resource Management Review*, 33(1), 100940.

Manoharan, T. R., Muralidharan, C., & Deshmukh, S. G. (2011). An integrated fuzzy multi- attribute decision-making model for employees' performance appraisal. *The International Journal of Human Resource Management, 22*(3), 722–745. https://doi.org/10.1080/09585 192.2011.543763

McColl, R., & Michelotti, M. (2019). Sorry, could you repeat the question? Exploring video- interview recruitment practice in HRM. *Human Resource Management Journal, 29*(4), 637–656. https://doi.org/10.1111/1748-8583.12249

Mehrabad, M. S., & Brojeny, M. F. (2007). The development of an expert system for effective selection and appointment of the jobs applicants in human resource management. *Computers & Industrial Engineering, 53*(2), 306–312.

Meijerink, J. G., Boons, M., Keegan, A., & Marler, J. (2018). Call for papers for the special issue on Digitization and the transformation of human resource management. *International Journal of Human Resource Management*. https://doi.org/10.1080/09585 192.2018.1503845

Metcalf, L., Askay, D. A., & Rosenberg, L. B. (2019). Keeping humans in the loop: Pooling knowledge through artificial swarm intelligence to improve business decision making. *California Management Review, 61*(4), 84–109. https://doi.org/10.1177/0008125619862256

Moosajee, N. (2019). Fix AI's racist, sexist bias. 14 March, https://mg.co.za/article/20 19-03-14-fix-ais-racist-sexist-bias/

Nguyen, T. M., & Malik, A. (2021). A two-wave cross-lagged study on AI service quality: The moderating effects of the job level and job role. *British Journal of Management*. ahead-of- print. https://doi.org/10.1111/1467-8551.12540

Nguyen, T. M., & Malik, A. (2022). 'Impact of knowledge sharing on employees' service quality: The moderating role of artificial intelligence. *International Marketing Review*, ahead-of-print. https://doi.org/10.1108/IMR-02-2021-0078

Nura, A. A., & Osman, N. H. (2013). Gauging the effect of performance management and technology based human resource management on employee retention: The perspective of academics in higher educational institutions in Sokoto State Nigeria. *Asian Social Science*, *9*(15), 295.

Oesterreich, T. D., Teuteberg, F., Bensberg, F., & Buscher, G. (2019). The controlling profession in the digital age: Understanding the impact of digitisation on the controller's job roles, skills and competences. *International Journal of Accounting Information Systems*, *35*(C), 100432. https://doi.org/10.1016/j.accinf.2019.100432

Pan, Y., Froese, F., Liu, N., Hu, Y., & Ye, M. (2021, this issue). The adoption of artificial intelligence in employee recruitment: The influence of contextual factors. *The International Journal of Human Resource Management*, 1–23. ahead-of-print. https:// doi.org/10.1080/ 09585192.2021.1879206

Paul, J., & Criado, A. R. (2020). The art of writing a literature review: What do we know and what do we need to know? *International Business Review*, *29*(4), 101717. https://doi.org/ 10.1016/j.ibusrev.2020.101717

Pejic-Bach, M., Bertoncel, T., Meško, M., & Krstić, Ž. (2020). Text mining of industry 4.0 job advertisements. *International Journal of Information Management*, *50*, 416–431. https://doi. org/10.1016/j.ijinfomgt.2019.07.014

Pessach, D., Singer, G., Avrahami, D., Chalutz Ben-Gal, H., Shmueli, E., & Ben-Gal, I. (2020). Employees recruitment: A prescriptive analytics approach via machine learning and mathematical programming. *Decision Support Systems*, *134*, 113290. https:// doi.org/10.1016/ j.dss.2020.113290

Prentice, C., Dominique Lopes, S., & Wang, X. (2020a). The impact of artificial intelligence and employee service quality on customer satisfaction and loyalty. *Journal of Hospitality Marketing & Management*, *29*(7), 739–756. https://doi.org/10.1080/193 68623.2020.1722304

Prentice, C., Dominique Lopes, S., & Wang, X. (2020b). Emotional intelligence or artificial intelligence–an employee perspective. *Journal of Hospitality Marketing & Management*, *29*(4), 377–403. https://doi.org/10.1080/19368623.2019.1647124

Prentice, C., & Nguyen, M. (2020). Engaging and retaining customers with AI and employee service. *Journal of Retailing and Consumer Services*, *56*, 102186. https://doi.org/10.1016/ j.jretconser.2020.102186

Prikshat, V., Malik, A., & Budhwar, P. (2021). AI-augmented HRM: Antecedents, assimilation and multilevel consequences. *Human Resource Management Review*, *100860*. ahead-of-print.

Rampersad, G. (2020). Robot will take your job: Innovation for an era of artificial intelligence. *Journal of Business Research*, *116*, 68–74. https://doi.org/10.1016/j.jbus- res.2020.05.019

Ransbotham, S., Kiron, D., Gerbert, P., & Reeves, M. (2017). Reshaping business with artificial intelligence: Closing the gap between ambition and action. *MIT Sloan Management Review*, *59*(1), 1-17. https://search.proquest.com/docview/1950374030?accountid=10499

Robert, L. P., Pierce, C., Marquis, L., Kim, S., & Alahmad, R. (2020). Designing fair AI for managing employees in organisations: A review, critique, and design agenda. *Human–Computer Interaction*, *35*(5-6), 545–575.

Shank, D. B., Graves, C., Gott, A., Gamez, P., & Rodriguez, S. (2019). Feeling our way to machine minds: People's emotions when perceiving mind in artificial intelligence. *Computers in Human Behavior*, *98*, 256–266. https://doi.org/10.1016/j.chb.2019.04.001

Sitzmann, T., & Weinhardt, J. M. (2019). Approaching evaluation from a multilevel perspective: A comprehensive analysis of the indicators of training effectiveness. *Human Resource Management Review*, *29*(2), 253–269. https://doi.org/10.1016/j.hrmr.2017.04.001

Snyder, H. (2019). Literature review as a research methodology: An overview and guidelines. *Journal of Business Research, 104*, 333–339. https://doi.org/10.1016/j.jbusres.2019.07.039

Suen, H.-Y., Chen, M. Y.-C., & Lu, S.-H. (2019). Does the use of synchrony and artificial intelligence in video interviews affect interview ratings and applicant attitudes? *Computers in Human Behavior, 98*, 93–101. https://doi.org/10.1016/j.chb.2019.04.012

Suseno, Y., Chang, C., Hudik, M., & Fang, E. S. (2021, this issue). Beliefs, anxiety and change readiness for artificial intelligence adoption among human resource managers: The moderating role of high-performance work systems. *The International Journal of Human Resource Management*, ahead-of-print. 1–28. https://doi.org/10.1080/09585192.2021.1931408

Tambe, P., Cappelli, P., & Yakubovich, V. (2019). Artificial intelligence in human re- sources management: Challenges and a path forward. *California Management Review, 61*(4), 15–42. https://doi.org/10.1177/0008125619867910

Tarafdar, M., Beath, C. M., & Ross, J. W. (2019). Using AI to enhance business operations. *MIT Sloan Management Review, 60*(4), 37–44.

Torres, E. N., & Mejia, C. (2017). Asynchronous video interviews in the hospitality industry: Considerations for virtual employee selection. *International Journal of Hospitality Management, 61*, 4–13. https://doi.org/10.1016/j.ijhm.2016.10.012

Tranfield, D., Denyer, D., & Smart, P. (2003). Towards a methodology for developing evidence-informed management knowledge by means of systematic review. *British Journal of Management, 14*(3), 207–222. https://doi.org/10.1111/1467-8551.00375

van Esch, P., Black, J. S., & Ferolie, J. (2019). Marketing AI recruitment: The next phase in job application and selection. *Computers in Human Behavior, 90*, 215–222. https://doi.org/10.1016/j.chb.2018.09.009

van Esch, P., Stewart Black, J., Franklin, D., & Harder, M. (2020). AI-enabled biomet- rics in recruiting: Insights from marketers for managers. *Australasian Marketing Journal, 29*(3), 225–234. https://doi.org/10.1016/j.ausmj.2020.04.003

Vrontis, D., Christofi, M., Pereira, V., Tarba, S., Makrides, A., & Trichina, E. (2021, this issue). Artificial intelligence, robotics, advanced technologies and human resource management: A systematic review. *The International Journal of Human Resource Management*, 1–30. ahead-of-print. https://doi.org/10.1080/09585192.2020.1871398

Wilson, H. J., & Daugherty, P. R. (2018). Collaborative intelligence: Humans and AI are joining forces. *Harvard Business Review, 96*(4), 114–123.

Wilson, H. J., Daugherty, P., & Bianzino, N. (2017). The jobs that artificial intelligence will create. *MIT Sloan Management Review, 58*(4), 14. http://mitsmr.com/2odREFJ

Wirtz, J. (2019). Organisational ambidexterity: Cost-effective service excellence, service robots, and artificial intelligence. *Organizational Dynamics, 49*(3), 1–9.

Wirtz, J., Patterson, P. G., Kunz, W. H., Gruber, T., Lu, V. N., Paluch, S., & Martins, A. (2018). Brave new world: Service robots in the frontline. *Journal of Service Management, 29*(5), 907–931. https://doi.org/10.1108/JOSM-04-2018-0119

Wong, S. L., & Liu, Q. (2019). Emotion recognition is China's new surveillance craze. November 1, www.ft.com/content/68155560-fbd1-11e9-a354-36acbbb0d9b6

Humanoid robot adoption and labour productivity: a perspective on ambidextrous product innovation routines

Manlio Del Giudice, Veronica Scuotto, Luca Vincenzo Ballestra and Marco Pironti

ABSTRACT

The increasing presence of humanoid robot adoption has generated a change in explorative and exploitative routines. If the explorative routines provoke creativity and critical thinking which are delivered by humans, exploitative routines induce repetitive actions and mimic activities which are executed by humanoids. This has raised the need for a better balance between both routines involving an ambidextrous dynamic process. Here, product innovations play a relevant role in enhancing such balance and labour productivity. If, from the conceptual standpoint, this phenomenon has already been explored, there is still the need to empirically analyse it. We thus offer a meso-analysis of twenty-four countries located in Europe through the lens of the Service Robot Deployment (SRD) Model and the conceptual lens of organizational ambidexterity. By a regression methodology, the results show that humanoid robot adoption is still not affecting labour productivity which, by contrast, is positively and significantly connected with both radically new and marginally modified/unchanged production of innovative routines.

Our original contribution, which falls in the field of Human Resources Management and Artificial Intelligence, is that humanoids are not directly impacting labour productivity but indirectly through the generation of both new and marginally modified (or unchanged) routines. This situation persuades senior leaders to achieve a balance between exploitative and explorative product innovation routines.

Introduction

As highlighted by the report entitled Industry 4.0 – Adoption Index (Research & Markets, 2020), humanoid adoption will be a step further into industry 4.0, introducing the new era of industry 5.0. This will induce an increasing shift of work by 2022 (World Economic Forum, 2018) thanks to the fact that companies can get benefits such as improving customer services in terms of time and costs, reducing information leakage and deception, and enhancing productivity (Kumar et al., 2019; Wirtz & Zeithaml, 2018).

These new technologies have been classified as artificial intelligences (AIs) since 1942 with the release of a new book entitled "Runaround" where a robot was confined by three laws: "(1) a robot may not injure a human being or, through inaction, allow a human being to come to harm; (2) a robot must obey the orders given to it by human beings except where such orders would conflict with the First Law; and (3) a robot must protect its own existence as long as such protection does not conflict with the First or Second Laws" (Haenlein & Kaplan, 2019, p. 6). A humanoid is recognised as an intelligent machine when an individual is not able to discriminate the machine from a human (Turing, 2009). In fact, the machine can have a physical or virtual presence in the form of a humanoid (Wirtz et al., 2018).

This has been also contextualized in a daily business working day where a humanoid is an artificial intelligence machine aimed at automatizing different levels of employees' activities, yielding both advantages (e.g. more agility to adjust a business model to fast market changes, more requests for fast and agile innovation, and more support for overcoming human constraints, among others) and challenges (e.g. more specialized skills and trainings, a growth in employability but also an increase in job loss) (Manyika, 2017).

Van Doorn et al. (2017) introduced the concept of automated social presence, which refers to the duality of social presence (e.g. human-humanoids) that is perceived by customers. Besides, Wirtz et al. (2018) argue that humanoids can perform tasks in a limited range of situations with fewer emotional and cognitive skills. This so induces a more explorative analysis of the routines that are mostly delivered by humanoids. A company tends to modify routines when offering new products or when maintaining the same routines to exploit existing products (Alos-Simo et al., 2020). This reflects the dynamic process of ambidexterity which relies on the organizational capacity to make a balance between explorative and exploitative routines.

This has spurred our interest in exploring humanoid robot adoption along with explorative and exploitative routines in a product innovation and ambidextrous setting and addressing the research question of *how humanoid robot adoption is affecting labour productivity across the exploitative and explorative ambidextrous organizational routines?*

Hence, through the conceptual organizational ambidexterity lens (Stokes et al., 2019) we offer a meso-analysis (or country level analysis) by employing the Service Robot Deployment (SRD) Model (Wirtz et al., 2018; Paluch et al., 2020).

The model shows that "robots will be able to mimic superficial acting-type emotions to a high level, but deep acting and out-of-box thinking at a human level are not attainable in the foreseeable future" (Wirtz et al., 2018, p. 913). In this regard, when the cognitive and emotional complexity is low, the task can be executed by humanoids; whereas, if such complexity is high, humans need to intervene. Humanoids can mainly perform routines ushering the emotional side of humans. As stated by Wirtz (2020), organizational ambidexterity can make the right balance between the adoption of new technologies with "the expected level of human touch" in the employees' work.

Then, in order to operationalize these concepts, we take into account the production of innovative enterprises, which can consist of either (or both) significantly new outputs with the employment of more cognitive and emotional tasks and incrementally modified/unchanged outputs with more mimicking tasks. We consider the former to be related to explorative routines and the latter related to exploitative routines (Pfeiffer, 2016). Furthermore, we have also investigated the effect of human-humanoid routines on labour productivity in a product innovation context. In fact, as documented by several empirical studies, labour productivity is usually (and positively) associated with product innovation (Brown & Guzmán, 2014, Crépon et al., 1998; Kurt & Kurt, 2015). This task is accomplished by means of a regression analysis that is carried out at the national (aggregate) level and takes into account a set of countries located in Europe.

This analysis enhances the current HRM literature which has offered systematic literature review (Lu et al., 2020; Ivanov et al., 2019) of conceptual or qualitative studies focused on the health (Barrett et al., 2012; Beane, 2019; Green et al., 2016) and service industries (Čaić et al., 2019) and on the domain of human resource management (Haenlein & Kaplan, 2019; Tambe et al., 2019) with the organizational ambidexterity point of a view (Stokes et al., 2019) and individual outlook (Swart et al., 2019). However, a general halo of uncertainty still seems to linger about HRM practices and human-humanoid interactions, and how they affect the ambidextrous context of a company is not fully understood.

Besides, despite the advancements in the field of humanoids and AI, a large part of the existing research seems to be oriented to considering them as domains related to companies' processes and infrastructures only (Chaudhry et al., 2018; Chauhan, 2018). On the contrary, very few contributions have been provided that focus on the role of human resource management (HRM) practices in managing business automation and the decision making processes (Haenlein & Kaplan, 2019; Powell & Dent-Micallef, 1997; Tambe et al., 2019). Results show that humanoid robot adoption is still not affecting labour productivity which, by contrast, is positively and significantly connected with both radically new and marginally modified or unchanged products. Hence, our original contribution states the fact that AIs – with a focus on humanoids – are not impacting labour productivity very much. However, the latter is significantly connected to both explorative and exploitative routines.

Especially, the present study shows that there is still a need to explore new approaches without revolutionizing existing routines and knowledge (e.g. exploitative routines) (Malik et al., 2019a; O'Reilly & Tushman, 2008; Raisch et al., 2009; Tushman & O'Reilly, 1996).

This induces the second contribution which has a managerial connotation. So as to create a balance between explorative and exploitative routines, managers should introduce new rewards and empower a culture of trust and collaboration (Chang et al., 2009; Malik et al., 2019a). Employing a collaborative leadership evokes the third contribution which highlights the significance of prolonged orientation and socialization along with team-based design of labour productivity. In this regard, managers tend to adopt a culture of flexibility and adaptation (Simsek, 2009; Simsek et al., 2009).

Overall, humanoid robot adoption can enhance the effectiveness of HRM practices. These activities can be used by companies for screening candidates, employee engagement and re-engagement, and career development. Such collaborations can also be applied to HR policies, procedures, and the HR perspective, and they can enhance the effectiveness of HRM. This is to make sure they are employing individuals with the right skills in order to work towards the strategic objectives.

2. Literature review and hypotheses development

2.1. Humanoid robot adoption and labour productivity in a contextual ambidextrous (CA) product innovation setting

The evolution of the Industry 4.0 has impacted the whole business world along with the macro-economic areas (e.g. political, economic, societal, and technological). In this scenario, companies – either multinationals or small to medium enterprises – are facing several challenges (Malik, 2019) which are inducing a different way of living, communicating, and working. This involves an ambidextrous approach which combines explorative and exploitive learning in three different ways. Generally speaking, researchers have divided organizational ambidexterity into three categories–namely structural, contextual ambidexterity, and co-evolutionary lock-in (Burgelman, 2002; Carmeli & Halevi, 2009; Gibson & Birkinshaw, 2004; Jansen et al., 2008; Kang & Snell, 2009; O'Reilly & Tushman, 2013).

Structural ambidexterity concerns the organizational environment of a company which seeks to exploit its strengths and explore new knowledge. This implicates an integration of all the business units into the core business along with an efficient allocation of resources (Gibson & Birkinshaw, 2004; Kang & Snell, 2009; O'Reilly & Tushman, 2013). Whereas contextual ambidexterity regards people working within a company and their skills and abilities to explore and exploit routines (Gibson & Birkinshaw, 2004). Co-evolutionary lock-in refers to the ability to connect the previous achievements of a company with the existing "product-market environment". Concerning HRM practices, a CA setting is mostly considered with an examination of employees' skills. In fact, in the scenario where humanoids are introduced into an organizational context, there is a common sense that humanoids will replace people and increase the job loss rate (Jarrahi, 2018). In fact, even though the use of humanoids can improve product performance, it can also rather reduce employability (e.g. Keynes [1930] talked about "technological unemployment") and force the development of new skills (Davenport & Ronanki, 2018; Leontief, 1952).

By contrast, Acemoglu and Restrepo (2017a, 2017b) have recently shown that a robot does not shrink employment but can induce the need for highly skilled people (see also Graetz & Michaels, 2015). For instance, nowadays, there is a need for data scientists and analytics along with a clear understanding of what are the benefits of new technologies. A senior manager from a multinational company analysed by Scuotto and Mueller (2018) pointed out the significance of the benefits of using new technologies. People are reluctant to a change. They tend to conform to their routines – exploiting existing knowledge instead of exploring new knowledge.

Therefore, due to the presence of this reluctance to accept the "new", Davenport and Ronanki (2018) recommended first implementing a pilot project to introduce mechanical automation (or humanoids) and then "roll it out across the entire enterprise" (page 8). Besides, team-based designs need to be re-formed in the search for a more efficient balance between human and humanoids. In this regard, the SRD model better describes this interaction. It shows the involvement of cognitive and emotionally complex tasks which are performed by humans compared with the superficial mimicking actions which are better performed by humanoids. Humanoids usher in human action in their daily business practices (Wirtz et al., 2018; Paluch et al., 2020). This can generate more efficiency in HRM practices (see also Malik et al., 2019a) – "freeing up human workers to be more productive and creative" (Davenport & Ronanki, 2018; p. 10).

Kim et al. (2019) talk about "human–robot collaboration" (HRC) which is associated with robots assisting humans in performing their tasks. This intertwines human agility and machine power (Ajoudani et al., 2018) and enhances productivity (Acemoglu & Restrepo, 2017a, 2017b).

In this regard, we state the following:

H_1: *Labour productivity is positively associated with humanoid robot adoption*

2.2. Labour productivity and CA product innovation routines

As stated by Acemoglu and Restrepo (2017a, 2017b), humanoids can increase the level of labour productivity in a company, but there are also other external factors which influence productivity, such as interest rates, imports, and offshoring.

As far as labour productivity is concerned, several studies have documented its positive association with innovation. Although it is universally accepted that innovation increases firm performance by enhancing the productivity of capital, empirical evidence has been provided which shows that innovation increases the productivity of labour too. For instance, Brown and Guzmán (2014), by using a mixed analytical and empirical approach based on a Cobb-Douglas production function, find that innovation has a positive effect on labour productivity. In addition, Kurt and Kurt (2015), by applying panel causality and cointegration techniques, obtained a positive relationship between innovation and labour productivity. Finally, Crépon et al. (1998) developed a structural model that explains firms' productivity in terms of innovation output, finding that the former correlates positively with the latter (a review of papers that examine the relationship between product innovation and labour productivity can be found in Hall, 2011 and in Mohnen & Hall, 2013).

Innovation can have both explorative and exploitative features. Generally speaking, explorative product innovation refers to the development of radically new goods or services in order to meet the needs of emerging customers and markets (Benner & Tushman, 2003); whereas exploitative product innovation entails the repetition and/or incremental refinement of an innovation that already exists (Alos-Simo et al., 2020; Piao & Zajac, 2016). This allows a company "to compete in mature technologies and markets efficiently, where control and incremental improvement are prized, and also to compete in new technologies and markets where flexibility, autonomy, and experimentation are needed" (O'Reilly III & Tushman, 2013; p. 324). In this circumstance, organizations move from a static and risk averse context to a more agile and ambidextrous environment, and employees are stimulated to "undertake cross-functional collaboration" (Fountaine et al., 2019). It has been demonstrated that ambidextrous companies also have high business performance (Campanella et al., 2020) along with the need of an effective senior team who can achieve a balance between exploitative and explorative routines (Halevi et al., 2015; Luo et al., 2018).

In a nutshell, a company needs to be ambidextrous, and intertwine exploitative and explorative routines (Junni et al., 2013, 2015; March, 1991). These routines originate from a mix of practices such as sharing, acquiring, and absorbing new knowledge and combining it with the existing knowledge (Crossan et al., 1999; Scuotto & Mueller, 2018; Scuotto et al., 2017). Especially, exploration routines aim to bring new knowledge within a company; whereas, exploitative routines seek to employ existing domains to work on a daily basis (Galunic & Rodan, 1998; McGrath, 2001).

Researchers have identified the characteristics of ambidexterity in employees' features, offering a variety of studies (Ahammad et al., 2019; Gibson & Birkinshaw, 2004; Patel et al., 2013). The influence of individuals on ambidextrous organizations is defined as contextual ambidexterity which leverages the skills and abilities of employees in order to combine exploitative and explorative routines (Gibson & Birkinshaw, 2004; Jansen et al., 2008; Kang & Snell, 2009; O'Reilly & Tushman, 2013). Basically, business units explore new ideas in a separate context from those that exploit routines (Tushman & O'Reilly, 1996). Along with those skills and abilities, employees' characteristics, such as educational background, career and goal orientation, "goal avoidance orientation", and cognitive features, leverage the capacity of being ambidextrous (Ambos et al., 2008; Jasmand et al., 2012; Stokes et al., 2017; Yu, 2010).

Overall, there is a tendency to preserve existing knowledge and technologies (e.g. exploitative routines) rather than explore new ones. In fact, exploitative routines are enforced by previous achievements. People like to feel familiar with the environment rather take on the risk of the "unknown" (Ahuja & Morris Lampert, 2001; Levinthal & March, 1993; March, 1991; McGrath, 2001; Schön &Argyris, 1996). Exploitative routines serve as the root of a company. They induce a feeling of working in a comfortable zone. People seek to maintain those routines to be more productive (Cohendet & Llerena, 2003; Soosay & Hyland, 2008; Zollo & Winter, 2002). Therefore, we declare the following:

H₂: Labour productivity is positively associated with exploitative product innovation routines

In product innovation, focusing on the domain of HRM practices with the application of new smart intelligence (e.g. humanoids), exploitative routines can be explicated in the sense of being less emotional and more related to mechanical tasks (Huang & Rust, 2018; Malik, 2019); whereas the need for critical thinking and more human actions can be associated with explorative product innovation. The efficient means to capitalize a on routine is to combine exploitative with explorative routines. Winter Sidney and Nelson (1982) define routines as predicable behaviour which should be combined with innovations along with a "culture of trust and empowerment" (Malik et al. (2019a). For instance, in allocating and using companies' resources, the balance between exploitation and exploration routines should come from a senior leader (Gibson & Birkinshaw, 2004; Nemanich & Vera, 2009) (Patel et al., 2013). Along with this, the occupancy time within a company can also impact the level of ambidexterity. In fact, people with a less occupancy time are more prone to generate ambidextrous outcomes (Ambos et al., 2008). Stressing the work of Stoke et al. (2014), career oriented employees are generally inclined to exploit existing routines and explore new ones. This has induced people to be job and assessment oriented (Jasmand et al., 2012) and flexible to market fluctuations. Basically, employees are more skilled to face environmental changes than before. Generally speaking, there are two forms of employees–namely, ambidextrous and goal oriented and "goal avoidance orientated" and ambidextrous. The latter limits the placement of explorative and exploitative routines within a company (Yu, 2010). Nevertheless, along with being goal-oriented, people are ambidextrous if they behave like they are driven by a sense of control and passion (Andriopoulos & Lewis, 2009). Besides, from a cognitive viewpoint, those who are self-confident and open to the change are also favourable to ambidexterity. Alongside this, people characterized by analytical thinking and friendly behaviour are ambidextrous (Good & Michel, 2013; Huang & Kim, 2013). This also occurs when there is a high degree of commitment.

Indeed, it has been demonstrated that businesses' performance depends on employees' skills, commitment, and ability to spot opportunities (Ahammad et al., 2019; Appelbaum et al., 2000; Lepak et al., 2006). Furthermore, it calls for the development of relationships based on agility, control, help, and trust (Ghoshal & Bartlett, 2007; Gibson & Birkinshaw, 2004; Kang & Snell, 2009) and triggers a renewal attitude in a company (Jensen et al., 2010). Although the exploitative routines can constrain innovation, explorative ones can encourage them (Stoke et al., 2017; Swart et al., 2019). On this basis, and also by focusing on explorative routines in product innovation (which, according to the extant literature, is one of the main determinants of labour productivity), we consider the following hypotheses:

H_3: *Labour productivity is positively associated with explorative product innovation routines*

3. Empirical analysis

3.1. Research context

We investigated the effect of the humanoid robot adoption on the productivity of labour in an ambidextrous product innovation setting. Specifically, our goal was to perform a meso (that is country level) analysis. Especially, we assessed the effect of the humanoid robot adoption on national (aggregate) labour productivity. In this respect, it is worth observing that the meso-perspective is often adopted in the literature, since several scholars (see, e.g. Hall, 2011 and Kurt & Kurt, 2015) have found it interesting to investigate the labour productivity of whole (national) economies and also human-humanoid interactions in the domain of HRM (Wirtz et al., 2018).

Therefore, since our goal was to investigate labour productivity and the extent to which it is influenced by humanoid adoption and innovation routines at the national level. We employed a regression model where we considered single countries as statistical units by using data as country-specific. In particular, we have taken into account the EU member countries as well as Norway (which is currently not an EU member). The choice of focusing on Europe was motivated by a number of different reasons. First, as recently documented by the International Federation of Robotics (IFR), the robot adoption in Europe has grown more than in America. Moreover, it has been noted that the use of robots is limited in developing countries (e.g. some African regions). Finally, we also excluded China because it is very different from Europe as far as the political, economic, cultural and labour systems are concerned (see, e.g. Luk & Preston, 2016, Zhongping, 2008). Moreover, it should also be pointed out that in recent years the industrial robotization in China has grown fast, but it has not reached explosive levels. For example, according to the International Federation of Robotics (IFR) in 2017, in China the number of robots in the manufacturing industry per 10,000 human employees was only 97, about one third of the number in Germany (see IFR – International Federation of Robotics. Welcome to the IFR Press Conference, 18 October 2018); whereas "The Robot Report" website (Demaitre, 2019), reports that in 2019 the number of robots per 10,000 human employees was "far behind that of other countries at 140". Additionally, as stated by Haenlein and Kaplan (2019), "While China and, to a certain extent, the United States try to limit the barriers for firms to use and explore AI, the European Union has gone the opposite direction with the introduction of the General Data Protection Regulation (GDPR) that significantly limits the way in which personal information can be stored and processed" (p. 12). Conversely, we include Norway because it is one of the most developed countries in Europe.

Furthermore, to measure explorative and exploitative product innovation routines, we consider the fact that a company is prone to modify routines to create a new product (explorative routines) or to maintain the same routines to exploit an existing product (exploitative routines) (Alos-Simo et al., 2020; Piao & Zajac, 2016). Those routines are also viewed through the lens of the SRD Model (Wirtz et al., 2018; Paluch et al., 2020) which describes humanoid tasks as mimicking activities with less of the critical thinking that is associated with humans. In both cases, humanoids are adopted as a support for the daily basic activities of employees (exploitative routines) or product generation (explorative routines). In a nutshell, explorative routines are considered to be more sophisticated and complex in terms of cognitive and emotional tasks; whereas, exploitative routines are recognised to be more for mimicking and repetitive tasks.

As already mentioned, the involvement of both routines calls for an ambidextrous organizational setting (O'Reilly III & Tushman, 2013).

3.2. Data

All the data were taken from Eurostat, the database of the Statistical office of the EU (see also the websites cited below). We initially collected data concerning the twenty-eight EU countries and Norway. However, the data for Belgium, Cyprus, Denmark, Greece, and Luxemburg were very incomplete, and thus these countries were excluded. So, we ended up with a dataset of twenty-four countries. For each one of the variables employed (which are described below), we considered the average of the data reported by Eurostat over the time-interval from 2014 to 2019, excluding those years in which data were not available (for some variables, data are only available on a single year).

3.3. Model and variables

We tested our hypotheses H_1, H_2, and H_3 by regression analysis. Since our goal is to assess whether labour productivity is associated with humanoid robot adoption, explorative product innovation, and exploitative product innovation routines, we used a baseline regression model (equation

[1]) in which labour productivity was set as the dependent variable, whereas humanoid robot adoption, the amounts of explorative product innovation and exploitative product innovation routines were set as the independent variables. Furthermore, we added the following control variables: a variable related to work meaningfulness (namely the feeling of doing a useful job, see Nikolova & Cnossen, 2020), the working time, and a variable connected with teamwork. These control variables were included because they could have an impact on labour productivity (see, e.g. Bailey et al., 2017; De Spiegelaere & Piasna, 2017; Long & Fang, 2013).

3.3.1 Dependent variable

Labour productivity (*LabProd*) per hour worked was computed by taking the ratio of the real output (the value of all goods and services produced less the value of any goods or services used in their creation) and the total number of hours worked. To have a percentage index, this ratio was further divided by the EU27 average in year 2020 and multiplied by 100 (data are taken from EUROSTAT - Labour productivity per person employed and hour worked).

3.3.2 Independent variables

Humanoid robot adoption (*HumRob*) is the use of humanoid robots for performing "human–robot collaboration" (HRC), i.e. accompanying human tasks, combining human agility and machine power (Ajoudani et al., 2018; Kim et al., 2019). Such adoption can generate "displacement" but also productivity improvement (Acemoglu & Restrepo, 2017a, 2017b).

The IFR classified robots in two main categories, *service* and *industrial* robots. Service robots perform jobs useful for humans, normally in non-manufacturing areas. They mimic and assist humans and usually accomplish tasks that require interaction with people. In contrast, industrial robots fully automate manufacturing tasks and have a limited interaction with people because they perform their tasks in clearly structured environments with external safe-guards.

To measure the humanoid interaction in our baseline regression model we considered service robots because they normally have a larger amount of interaction with people than industrial robots. Specifically, *HumRob* is calculated as the percentage of enterprises that use service robots. Nevertheless, robustness tests were also performed in which *HumRob* was computed based on industrial robots (see Section 4.1) (data are taken from EUROSTAT – 3 D printing and robotics).

Explorative product innovation (*ProdInnExplor*) routines: We measure this by the turnover (per person) of innovative enterprises from new or significantly improved products that were new to the market. Precisely, we consider the product-innovative enterprises according to the 2016 Eurostat classification, i.e. the enterprises who introduced, during 2014–2016, "new or significantly improved goods and/or services with respect to their capabilities, user friendliness, components or sub-systems", quoting from the Eurostat website https://ec.europa.eu/eurostat/cache/metadata/en/inn_cis10_esms.htm). Then, we considered the turnover of innovative enterprises from new or significantly improved products, i.e. the total amount of money that the above enterprises earned in the above three years from the sales of new or significantly improved products that were new to the market. Finally, to obtain the turnover per person, we divided the turnover by the country population (in year 2016). In this way, we obtained an aggregate measure of the radically new production of innovative enterprises, aimed at satisfying the needs of emerging customers and markets, i.e. a measure of the explorative product innovation at the country level.

(The data for the turnover were taken from EUROSTAT - Turnover of product innovative enterprises from new or significantly improved products by NACE Rev. 2 activity and size class. The data for the population were taken from EUROSTAT - Population change - Demographic balance and crude rates at national level).

Exploitative product innovation (*ProdInnExploit*) routines: We measured this by the turnover (per person) of innovative enterprises from only marginally changed or unchanged products. The calculation is analogous to that of *ProdInnExplor* with the only difference being that now we consider the sales of only marginally changed (or unchanged) products. In this way, we obtained an aggregate measure of the only marginally changed or unchanged production of innovative enterprises (i.e. the amount of repetition and/or incremental refinement of innovations that already exist), i.e. a measure of the exploitative product innovation at the country level.

(The data for the turnover were taken from EUROSTAT - Turnover of product innovative enterprises from new or significantly improved products by NACE Rev. 2 activity and size class. The data for the population were taken from EUROSTAT - Population change - Demographic balance and crude rates at national level).

3.3.3 Control variables

As we already mentioned, we controlled for some additional characteristics related to work which could impact labour productivity (see, e.g. Bailey et al., 2017, De Spiegelaere & Piasna, 2017, Long & Fang, 2013):

Feeling of doing a useful work (*UsefulWork*) is the percentage of employed persons who that think that they do useful work.

(Data were taken from EUROSTAT - Employed persons thinking that they do useful work by sex and age)

Working time (TimeWork): This is hours worked in a week. It is the average number of hours worked in a week by a person with full employment. It also includes extra hours, either paid or unpaid.

(Data were taken from EUROSTAT - Hours worked per week of full-time employment)

Team working (TeamWork): This is the attitude towards working in team. It is measured by the percentage of enterprises that consider teamwork as one of the main skills needed for the enterprise development.

(Data are taken from EUROSTAT - Main skills needed for the development of the enterprise by type of skill and size class)

For the reader's convenience, all of the variables employed are listed in Table 1.

3.3. Baseline regression

First of all, we used the following baseline regression model:

$$LabProd = \beta_0 + \beta_1 HumRob + \beta_2 ProdInnExplor + \beta_3 ProdInnExploit$$
$$+ \beta_4 UsefulWork + \beta_5 TimeWork + \beta_6 TimeWork + \varepsilon \qquad (1)$$

where the β coefficients are computed by standard OLS estimation. By computing the so-called VIF (variance inflation factors), we found that there is no multi-collinearity issue (the mean VIF is equal to 1.77, the largest one is equal to 2.93). Moreover, to test the statistical significance of the computed coefficients, we used Huber-White robust standard error estimation (corrected for heteroskedasticity, see Huber, 1967 and White, 1980).

4. Findings

Descriptive statistics for all the variables of model (1) are shown in Table 2. As we may observe, *LabProd* has a rather large variability among

Table 1. Variables' name, description and use.

Variable name	Description	Use
LaborProd	Labour Productivity per hour worked	Baseline regression model
HumRob	Humanoids interaction	Baseline regression model
ProdInnExplor	Explorative product innovation	Baseline regression model
ProdInnExploit	Explorative product innovation	Baseline regression model
UsefulWork	Employees who consider their job useful	Baseline regression model
TimeWork	Time worked	Baseline regression model
TeamWork	Importance of working in team	Baseline regression model
IndRob	Enterprises employing industrial robots	Robustness test
SecondJob	People doing a second job	Robustness test
WorkHome	Employees working from home	Robustness test

Table 2. Descriptive statistics.

	Mean	St.Dev	Min	Max
LaborProd	91.67	32.97	45.67	168.85
HumRob	5.95	2.46	3.00	11.00
ProdInnExplor	1.97	2.14	0.07	10.86
ProdInnExploit	12.81	10.44	0.84	33.54
UsefulWork	85.36	5.05	75.30	95.90
TimeWork	41.19	1.11	38.97	44.21
TeamWork	43.39	12.05	23.20	72.90

Table 3. Pearson's correlations, ** and *** denote significance at the 5% and 1% levels, respectively.

	LaborProd	HumRob	ProdInn Explor	ProdInn Exploit	UsefulWork	Time Work	TeamWork
LaborProd Prod	1						
HumRob	0.3681	1					
ProdInn Explor	0.7370***	0.5616**	1				
ProdInn Exploit	0.9290***	0.2667	0.6141***	1			
UsefulWork Work	0.2640 0.1230 0.0784 0.2937	0.2640 0.1230 0.0784 0.2937	0.2640 0.1230 0.0784 0.2937	0.2640 0.1230 0.0784 0.2937	1		
TimeWork Work	−0.2945	−0.1038	−0.0881	−0.2947	−0.0946	1	
TeamWork Work	−0.1632	−0.0695	0.0596	−0.1967	−0.0133	0.1454	1

the EU countries, since its values range from 45.67 to 168.85. The variables related to the humanoids' interaction and to product innovation show a large variability too. Specifically, *HumRob* ranges from 3.00 to 11.00, *ProdInnExplor* ranges from 0.07 to 10.86, and *ProdInnExploit* ranges from 0.84 to 33.54 (*ProdInnExploit* also has a large standard deviation, 10.44).

Table 3 reports the Pearson's correlations among the variables in model (1). In particular, labour productivity shows a positive and relatively large, albeit not significant, correlation with the humanoids interaction (0.3681) and a positive and large correlation with both explorative product innovation (0.7370) and exploitative product innovation (0.9290).

The results of the regression analysis are reported in Table 4. First of all, we may observe that the regression analysis is statistically significant, as the p-value associated with the F-statistics is smaller than 0.01. Moreover, the proportion of the variance of the dependent variable that the regression is able to predict is rather high, since the adjusted R^2 is equal to 0.829.

As we may observe in Table 4, the coefficients of both *ProdInnExplor* and *ProdInnExploit* are positive and significant (at the 0.01 level), which indicates that labour productivity is positively associated with both

Table 4. Regression results, *** denote significance at the 1% level.

Variable	β
Constant	60.250
HumRob	0.667
ProdInnExplor	10.530***
ProdInnExploit	1.579***
UsefulWork	0.444
TimeWork	−0.898
TeamWork	−0.309
F-stat	20.20***
R^2	0.886
Adjusted R^2	0.829
AIC	149.695
BIC	156.306

explorative and exploitative product innovation. Instead, the coefficient of *HumRob* is not significant (p-value > 0.1), which suggests that humanoid interaction does not affect labour productivity. Therefore, among our research hypotheses H_1, H_2 and H_3, only H_2 and H_3 are supported by the empirical evidence; whereas H_1 is not supported.

Finally, as far as the control variables are concerned, labour productivity is not significantly associated with any of them.

4.1. Robustness tests

We performed some robustness tests to corroborate the results of the baseline regression model (1).

First of all, we re-estimated the model using the standard OLS standard error estimator (without correction for heteroscedasticity), and the results obtained are very similar to those obtained previously. Specifically, *HumRob* is still not significant, whereas *ProdInnExplor* and *ProdInnExploit* are positive and significant (at the 0.05 and 0.01 levels, respectively).

Moreover, we used an econometric specification that generalizes the linear regression (1) and allows for error distributions other than Gaussian. In particular, we employed a generalized linear model (GLM) with the same variables as in (1) and a logarithmic link function (see, e.g. Agresti, 2015). The family function was chosen to be the inverse-Gaussian because, after considering several different kinds of family functions (the Gamma and the power function), we found that the inverse-Gaussian provides the smallest Bayesian information criterion (BIC). The results provided by the GLM, which are reported in Table 5, confirm those of the baseline model (1) because *HumRob* is still not significant whereas *ProdInnExplor* and *ProdInnExploit* are still positive and significant (at the 0.05 0.01 level, respectively). By comparison of Tables 4 and 5, we may see that the GLM yields a relevant improvement

Table 5. GLM results, ** and ***
denote significance at the 5% and 1%
levels, respectively.

Variable	β
Constant	4.252***
HumRob	0.012
ProdInnExplor	0.132**
ProdInnExploit	0.018***
UsefulWork	0.003
TimeWork	−0.012
TeamWork	−0.002
Deviance	0.003
AIC	15.842
BIC	−35.330

with respect to the baseline model, as far as the goodness-of-fit is concerned, since the BIC decreases from 156.306 to −35.330.

Moreover, we also estimated some regression models alternative to the baseline specification (1) in which we used new or additional variables. Specifically, we considered one variable related to the adoption of industrial robots:

Industrial robots (IndRob): the percentage of enterprises that use industrial robots (data taken from EUROSTAT − 3 D printing and robotics) and other two variables related to work (at the country level)

Working from home (WorkHome): the percentage of employed persons that at least in some circumstance worked from home (data taken from EUROSTAT - Employed persons working from home as a percentage of the total employment, by sex, age and professional status)

Second job (SecondJob): the percentage of employed persons who have more than one job

(data taken from EUROSTAT - Percentage of employed adults having a second job by sex, age groups, number of children and age of the youngest child.

Then, as a further robustness test, we replaced *HumRob* with *IndRob* so that the humanoids' interaction is measured by the percentage of enterprises that use industrial robots. That is, we estimated the following model:

$$LabProd = \beta_0 + \beta_1 IndRob + \beta_2 ProdInnExplor + \beta_3 ProdInnExploit$$
$$+ \beta_4 UsefulWork + \beta_5 TimeWork + \beta_6 TimeWork + \varepsilon.$$

The results (which we did not tabulate in order to save space) are perfectly analogous to those yielded by model (1). *IndRob* is still not significant, whereas *ProdInnExplor* and *ProdInnExploit* are still positive and significant, both at the 0.01 level (analogous results would also be obtained if we added *IndRob* in the baseline model (1) as a further regressor instead of simply replacing *HumRob*).

Furthermore, in the baseline model (1) we also included *WorkHome* and *SecondJob* among the regressors:

$$LabProd = \beta_0 + \beta_1 HumRob + \beta_2 ProdInnExplor + \beta_3 ProdInnExploit$$
$$+ \beta_4 UsefulWork + \beta_5 TimeWork + \beta_6 TimeWork$$
$$+ \beta_7 WorkHome + \beta_8 SecondJob + \varepsilon.$$

The results (again, we did not tabulate them in order to save space) are similar to those obtained using model (1). *HumRob* is still not significant, whereas *ProdInnExplor* and *ProdInnExploit* are still positive and significant at the 0.05 and 0.01 levels, respectively.

Thus, in summary, all of the robustness tests performed confirmed the results of the baseline regression model (1).

5. Discussion

As we summarized in Table 6, the empirical evidence indicates that humanoid robot adoption does not impact labour productivity at meso-level. By contrast, labour productivity is positively and significantly associated with exploitative and explorative routines of product innovators.

The positive effect of product innovation on labour productivity, even at the national level, has already been highlighted in previous work (Crépon et al., 1998; Kurt & Kurt, 2015). However, our empirical analysis also shows that the production of radically new outputs is not the only routine that impacts labour productivity at the country level. In fact, we found that the exploitation (i.e. repetition or marginal modification) of existing products made by innovative enterprises is positively associated with labour productivity as well. This is consistent with more general theories according to which exploitative routines are still capable of improving firms' performance (Malik et al., 2019a; O'Reilly & Tushman, 2008; Raisch et al., 2009; Tushman & O'Reilly, 1996).

Innovation can have both explorative and exploitative features, even if the concepts of exploration and exploitation can lead to different definitions and interpretations (see, e.g. Li et al., 2008). According to Benner and Tusthman (2003), we can regard explorative product innovation routines as those related to the development of radically new goods or services in order to meet the needs of emerging customers and

Table 6. Hypotheses tested.

Hypothesis	Evidence
H_1: Labour productivity is positively associated with humanoid robot adoption	Not supported by data
H_2: Labour productivity is positively associated with exploitative product innovation	Supported by data
H_3: Labour productivity is positively associated with explorative product innovation	Supported by data

markets. Whereas, in line with Alos-Simo et al. (2020) and Piao and Zajac (2016) study, exploitative product innovation routines entail repetition and/or incremental refinement of innovations that already exist. This induces an ambidextrous organizational environment aimed at being adaptable to future changes (Junni et al., 2013, 2015; March, 1991). As emerged, the present research has enlarged the debate on humanoid robot adoption in the domain of HRM practices. Looking at this phenomenon from a positive lens (Wilson et al., 2017), there is a need of employing "trainers, explainers, and sustainers" as the new job categories and, accordingly, new HRM practices should be developed so that the use of humanoids can cogitate and absorb new skills (Russell & Norvig, 2016). This is very useful for a long term business orientation (Ramona & Anca, 2013). Moreover, Malik (2019) also examines the effect of the revolution of Industry 4.0 on HRM. He considers a positive value in employing a mechanical automation for labour productivity. Additionally, we highlight the relevance of explorative and exploitative routines that have emerged from the use of robots.

Tambe et al. (2019) affirm that the most complex task is to generate a consensus among employees in interacting with such machines. It asks for a randomized decision making process because humanoids are not able to make fair and valuable decisions even if nowadays some robots can accomplish cognitive and emotional tasks (Avery, 2019; Čaić et al., 2019; Huang & Rust, 2018). Yet, they are very effective in undertaking repetitive activities that are usually defined as routines (Lacity & Willcocks, 2016; Davenport, 2018).

This can usher employees into offering faster and more efficient service (Benmark & Venkatachari, 2016) and dedicating more time to customers' care (Barrett et al., 2012). Yet, humanoids also support data collection and analysis even though this also increases the need for more technologically skilled people (Beck & Libert, 2017). Nevertheless, there are many studies which discuss the negative effects that stem from the new era of AI with a focus on humanoids. Beane (2019) talks about shadow learning which emphasizes the lack of learning opportunities and actions and diminishes the development of a critical thinking. Indeed, Green et al. (2016) have already enforced the need for specialised training. Barrett et al. (2012) noticed the increasing level of frustration among employees and the reduction of autonomy. Alongside this, Beane and Orlikowski (2015) highlight that humanoids can negatively influence work coordination. Other scholars also state that their intelligence will generate a massive level of unemployment (Acemoglu & Restrepo, 2017a). Despite that, our study enforces the positive outcomes derived from humanoid robots' adoption in the organizational ambidexterity context. In fact, such adoption is still not affecting labour productivity which, by contrast, is positively and significantly connected with both radically new and marginally modified/ unchanged production of innovative routines. In this way, organizations make technological advancement; whereas employees have "the expected level of the human touch" (see Wirtz, 2019).

5.1. Production and managerial implications

From the managerial standpoint, this has relevant implications that concern those employees who are reluctant to changes but prefer to work in an existing domain. In fact, a pervasive sense of relying on previous achievements persists, and, as stated by Stokes et al. (2019), people are less prone to change their status quo if they are living in a wealthy condition. Nevertheless, the conservative features of these employees can be profitably exploited as well, because managers can assign them exploitative production tasks, which, according to our findings, would be beneficial to labour productivity.

Yet, explorative and exploitative routines can be separate (Malik et al., 2019a), and senior leaders can pursue both of them and find a suitable balance between them (Gibson & Birkinshaw, 2004; Nemanich & Vera, 2009). The exploitative routines involve the development of creativity and critical thinking (Good & Michel, 2013; Huang & Kim, 2013; Simsek, 2009; Simsek et al., 2009). Jasmand et al. (2012) highlight that employees are job and assessment oriented, and they are flexible and responsive to market changes (see also Ambos et al., 2008). Nevertheless, our findings enforce the presence of "goal avoidance orientation" people. This has resulted in constraining contextual ambidexterity (Yu, 2010). Indeed, it is widely argued that explorative and exploitative routines should coexist in an innovative environment, and the present study confirms this.

Employees are often characterized as being less agile, passionate, self-confident, and open to those who are ambidextrous (Andriopoulos & Lewis, 2009; Good & Michel, 2013; Huang & Kim, 2013). Overall, people tend to preserve exploitative routines, and they are averse to innovations. Working in a comfortable zone in which everything is known and familiar is still considered primary.

Employees should be able to know the relationship between cause and effect in different situations (Ahuja & Morris Lampert, 2001; Levinthal & March, 1993; March, 1991; McGrath, 2001; Schön &Argyris, 1996). This also affects labour productivity (Cohendet & Llerena, 2003; Soosay & Hyland, 2008; Zollo & Winter, 2002). To this aim, it is crucial that HRM "recruits, trains, motivates, and rewards their employees so as to contribute to business growth" (Kelliher & Perrett, 2001, p. 423).

As stated by Levinthal and March (1993) and subsequently by Malik (2019), reluctance creates 'exploration traps'. People desire to justify action and forecast potential outcomes. Nevertheless, referring to Davenport and Ronanki (2018), it is possible to let employees accept new intelligent technologies by introducing a pilot test first and then rolling it out into the whole company. This would gradually gain a sense of acceptance into the organizational environment. Hence, if humanoid robot adoption is still at its infancy, there is a need for better managerial understanding of how to implement it and dramatically improve human resource management.

6. Conclusions

The present research contributes to the existing HRM and management literature by investigating the effect of humanoids' interaction on labour productivity and enforcing the persistent relevance of explorative and exploitative routines in product innovation.

Companies are making efforts to be versatile and adapt to the Industry 4.0 revolution. From a managerial point of view, senior leaders need to intervene to promote the most efficient routines and get the optimal balance among them in an ambidextrous setting. In particular, according to our findings, product innovative companies should pursue explorative innovation by developing significantly new goods and services that fulfil the needs of emerging customers and markets (Benner & Tushman, 2003) as well as exploitative innovation by engaging in the repetition and/or the incremental refinement of innovations that already exist (Alos-Simo et al., 2020; Piao & Zajac, 2016).

More in general, this would encourage new research on the role of senior leaders in an ambidextrous context that incorporates the transforming effect of Industry 4.0 (Malik, 2019). For instance, new rewards or a gradual acceptance can be evaluated as a means for embracing AI introduction into a company (Chang et al., 2009; Davenport & Ronanki, 2018).

Furthermore, there is a general sense of fear and reluctance towards the use of humanoids. The present paper analyses the effect of humanoid interaction on labour productivity, finding no significant association between them. Differently, investigating how robot automatization impacts other firm dimensions (e.g. production costs, product quality and design, process organization and control) could be another interesting line of research. Showing the benefits that stem from robotics (Scuotto & Mueller, 2018) can be an alternative solution for AIs' embracement and acceptance. Qualitative research can be employed because a deep investigation on this new phenomenon is requested. In fact, this theme is so new that new studies are welcome in order to extend our research to different countries or business scenarios (such as family businesses). Alongside this, new analyses can address the need for highly skilled people and how to recruit and engage with them.

To conclude, exploiting the existing domain lingers, and the current business scenario provokes the demand for renewal and a transformative attitude. The research supports a positive opinion of human robot adoption that has the potential to improve human resource management.

Acknowledgement

The article is based on the study funded by the Basic Research Program of the National Research University Higher School of Economics.

Disclosure statement

No potential conflict of interest was reported by the authors.

References

Acemoglu, D., & Restrepo, P. (2017a). Secular stagnation? The effect of aging on economic growth in the age of automation. *American Economic Review*, *107*(5), 174–179. https://doi.org/10.1257/aer.p20171101 [Mismatch]

Acemoglu, D., & Restrepo, P. (2017b). Robots and jobs: Evidence from US labour markets. *Journal of Political Economy*, *128*(6), 2188–2244.

Agresti, A. (2015). *Foundations of linear and generalized linear models*. Wiley-Interscience.

Ahammad, M. F., Glaister, K. W., & Junni, P. (2019). Organizational ambidexterity and human resource practices. *The International Journal of Human Resource Management*, *30*(4), 503–507. https://doi.org/10.1080/09585192.2019.1538651

Ahuja, G., & Morris Lampert, C. (2001). Entrepreneurship in the large corporation: A longitudinal study of how established firms create breakthrough inventions. *Strategic Management Journal*, *22*(6–7), 521–543. https://doi.org/10.1002/smj.176

Ajoudani, A., Zanchettin, A. M., Ivaldi, S., Albu-Schäffer, A., Kosuge, K., & Khatib, O. (2018). Progress and prospects of the human–robot collaboration. *Autonomous Robots*, *42*(5), 957–975. https://doi.org/10.1007/s10514-017-9677-2

Alos-Simo, L., Verdu-Jover, A. J., & Gomez-Gras, J. M. (2020). The dynamic process of ambidexterity in eco-innovation. *Sustainability*, *12*(5), 2023. https://doi.org/10.3390/su12052023

Ambos, T. C., Mäkelä, K., Birkinshaw, J., & d'Este, P. (2008). When does university research get commercialized? Creating ambidexterity in research institutions. *Journal of Management Studies*, *45*(8), 1424–1447. https://doi.org/10.1111/j.1467-6486.2008.00804.x

Andriopoulos, C., & Lewis, M. W. (2009). Exploitation-exploration tensions and organizational ambidexterity: Managing paradoxes of innovation. *Organization Science*, *20*(4), 696–717. https://doi.org/10.1287/orsc.1080.0406

Appelbaum, E., Bailey, T., Berg, P., Kalleberg, A. L., & Bailey, T. A. (2000). *Manufacturing advantage: Why high-performance work systems pay off*. Cornell University Press.

Avery, H. (2019). *Private banking: Wealthtech 2.0 – when human meets robot*. https://www.euromoney.com/article/b1cygh7rdnlqk1/private-banking-wealthtech-20-when-human-meets-robot

Bailey, C., Madden, A., Alfes, K., Shantz, A., & Soane, E. (2017). The mismanaged soul: Existential labor and the erosion of meaningful work. *Human Resource Management Review, 27*(3), 416–430. https://doi.org/10.1016/j.hrmr.2016.11.001

Barrett, M., Oborn, E., Orlikowski, W. J., & Yates, J. (2012). Reconfiguring boundary relations: Robotic innovations in pharmacy work. *Organization Science, 23*(5), 1448–1466. https://doi.org/10.1287/orsc.1100.0639

Beane, M. (2019). Learning to work with intelligent machines. *Harvard Business Review, 97*(5), 140–148.

Beane, M., & Orlikowski, W. J. (2015). What difference does a robot make? The material enactment of distributed coordination. *Organization Science, 26*(6), 1553–1573.

Beck, M., & Libert, B. (2017). The rise of AI makes emotional intelligence more important. *Harvard Business Review, 15*. Retrieved 8 September, 2020, from https://hbr.org/2017/02/the-rise-of-aimakes-emotional-intelligence-more-important

Benner, M. J., & Tushman, M. L. (2003). Exploitation, exploration, and process management: The productivity dilemma revisited. *Academy of Management Review, 28*(2), 238–256. https://doi.org/10.5465/amr.2003.9416096

BenMark, G., & Venkatachari, D. (2016). Messaging apps are changing how companies talk with customers. *Harvard Business Review, 23*. Retrieved 28 September, 2020, from https://hbr.org/2016/09/messaging-apps-are-changing-how-companies-talk-withcustomers

Brown, F., & Guzmán, A. (2014). Innovation and productivity across Mexican manufacturing firms. *Journal of Technology Management & Innovation, 9*(4), 36–52. https://doi.org/10.4067/S0718-27242014000400003

Burgelman, R. A. (2002). Strategy as vector and the inertia of coevolutionary lock-in. *Administrative Science Quarterly, 47*(2), 325–357. https://doi.org/10.2307/3094808

Čaić, M., Mahr, D., & Oderkerken-Schröder, G. (2019). Value of social robots in services: Social cognition perspective. *Journal of Services Marketing, 33*(4), 463–478. https://doi.org/10.1108/JSM-02-2018-0080

Campanella, F., Del Giudice, M., Thrassou, A., & Vrontis, D. (2020). Ambidextrous organizations in the banking sector: An empirical verification of banks' performance and conceptual development. *The International Journal of Human Resource Management, 31*, 272–302.

Carmeli, A., & Halevi, M. Y. (2009). How top management team behavioral integration and behavioral complexity enable organizational ambidexterity: The moderating role of contextual ambidexterity. *The Leadership Quarterly, 20*(2), 207–218.

Chang, Y. C., Yang, P. Y., & Chen, M. H. (2009). The determinants of academic research commercial performance: Towards an organizational ambidexterity perspective. *Research Policy, 38*(6), 936–946. https://doi.org/10.1016/j.respol.2009.03.005

Chaudhry, J., Pathan, A. S. K., Rehmani, M. H., & Bashir, A. K. (2018). Threats to critical infrastructure from AI and human intelligence. *The Journal of Supercomputing, 74*(10), 4865–4866. https://doi.org/10.1007/s11227-018-2614-0

Chauhan, M. S. (2018). Artificial intelligence and parallel cloud role in future modern economies. *Artificial Intelligence, 4*, 16–23.

Cohendet, P., & Llerena, P. (2003). Routines and incentives: The role of communities in the firm. *Industrial and Corporate Change, 12*(2), 271–297. https://doi.org/10.1093/icc/12.2.271

Crépon, B., Duguet, E., & Mairesse, J. (1998). Research, innovation and productivity: An econometric analysis at the firm level. *Economics of Innovation and New Technology, 7*(2), 115–158. https://doi.org/10.1080/10438599800000031

Crossan, M. M., Lane, H. W., & White, R. E. (1999). An organizational learning framework: From intuition to institution. *Academy of Management Review, 24*(3), 522–537. https://doi.org/10.5465/amr.1999.2202135

Davenport, T. H. (2018). From analytics to artificial intelligence. *Journal of Business Analytics, 1*(2), 73–80.

Davenport, T. H., & Ronanki, R. (2018). Artificial intelligence for the real world. *Harvard Business Review, 96*(1), 108–116.

De Spiegelaere, S., & Piasna, A. (2017). *The why and how of working time reduction.* European Trade Union Institute (ETUI). http://hdl.handle.net/1854/LU-8626448

Demaitre, E., (2019, November, 1). *China robotics outlook: A state of the industry 2019.* https://www.therobotreport.com/china-robotics-outlook-state-industry-2019

EUROSTAT - 3D printing and robotics. http://appsso.eurostat.ec.europa.eu/nui/show.do?dataset=isoc_eb_p3d&lang=en

EUROSTAT - Employed persons thinking that they do useful work by sex and age. https://appsso.eurostat.ec.europa.eu/nui/show.do?dataset=qoe_ewcs_7b3&lang=en

EUROSTAT - Employed persons working from home as a percentage of the total employment, by sex, age and professional status. http://appsso.eurostat.ec.europa.eu/nui/show.do?dataset=lfsa_ehomp

EUROSTAT - Hours worked per week of full-time employment. https://ec.europa.eu/eurostat/databrowser/view/tps00071/default/table?lang=en

EUROSTAT - Labour productivity per person employed and hour worked. https://ec.europa.eu/eurostat/databrowser/view/tesem160/default/table?lang=en

EUROSTAT - Main skills needed for the development of the enterprise by type of skill and size class, https://appsso.eurostat.ec.europa.eu/nui/show.do?dataset=trng_cvt_10s&lang=en

EUROSTAT - Percentage of employed adults having a second job by sex, age groups, number of children and age of the youngest child. https://appsso.eurostat.ec.europa.eu/nui/show.do?dataset=lfst_hh2jchi&lang=en

EUROSTAT - Population change - Demographic balance and crude rates at national level. https://appsso.eurostat.ec.europa.eu/nui/show.do?dataset=demo_gind&lang=en

EUROSTAT - Turnover of product innovative enterprises from new or significantly improved products, by NACE Rev. 2 activity and size class. http://appsso.eurostat.ec.europa.eu/nui/show.do?dataset=inn_cis10_prodt&lang=en

Fountaine, T., McCarthy, B., & Saleh, T. (2019). Building the AI-powered organization. *Harvard Business Review, 97*(4), 62–73.

Galunic, D. C., & Rodan, S. (1998). Resource recombinations in the firm. Knowledge structures and the potential for Schumpeterian innovation. *Strategic Management Journal, 19*(12), 1193–1201. https://doi.org/10.1002/(SICI)1097-0266(1998120)19:12<1193::AID-SMJ5>3.0.CO;2-F

Ghoshal, S., & Bartlett, C. A. (1994). Linking organizational context and managerial action: The dimensions of quality of management. *Strategic Management Journal, 15*(52), 91–112. https://doi.org/10.1002/smj.4250151007

Gibson, C. B., & Birkinshaw, J. (2004). The antecedents, consequences, and mediating role of organizational ambidexterity. *Academy of Management Journal, 47*(2), 209–226.

Good, D., & Michel, E. J. (2013). Individual ambidexterity: Exploring and exploiting in dynamic contexts. *The Journal of Psychology, 147*(5), 435–453. https://doi.org/10.1080/00223980.2012.710663

Graetz, G., & Michaels, G. (2015). Robots at work. *CEP Discussion Paper No 1335.*

Green, T., Hartley, N., & Gillespie, N. (2016). Service provider's experiences of service separation: The case of telehealth. *Journal of Service Research, 19*(4), 477–494. https://doi.org/10.1177/1094670516666674

Haenlein, M., & Kaplan, A. (2019). A brief history of artificial intelligence: On the past, present, and future of artificial intelligence. *California Management Review, 61*(4), 5–14. https://doi.org/10.1177/0008125619864925

Halevi, M. Y., Carmeli, A., & Brueller, N. N. (2015). Ambidexterity in SBUs: TMT behavioural integration and environmental dynamism. *Human Resource Management, 54*(S1), S223–S238. https://doi.org/10.1002/hrm.21665

Hall, B. H. (2011). *Innovation and productivity.* National Bureau of Economic Research, Inc.

Huang, J., & Kim, H. J. (2013). Conceptualizing structural ambidexterity into the innovation of human resource management architecture: The case of LG Electronics. *The International Journal of Human Resource Management, 24*(5), 922–943. https://doi.org/10.1080/09585192.2012.743471

Huang, M. H., & Rust, R. T. (2018). Artificial intelligence in service. *Journal of Service Research, 21*(2), 155–172. https://doi.org/10.1177/1094670517752459

Huber, P. J. (1967). The behavior of maximum likelihood estimates under nonstandard conditions. In *Proceedings of the Fifth Berkeley Symposium on Mathematical Statistics and Probability.*

IFR – International Federation of Robotics. (2018, October 18). *Welcome to the IFR Press Conference.* https://ifr.org/downloads/press2018/WR_Presentation_Industry_and_Service_Robots_rev_5_12_18.pdf

Ivanov, S., Gretzel, U., Berezina, K., Sigala, M., & Webster, C. (2019). Progress on robotics in hospitality and tourism: A review of the literature. *Journal of Hospitality and Tourism Technology, 10*(4), 489–421.

Jansen, J. J. P., George, G., Van Den Bosch, F. A. J., & Volberda, H. W. (2008). Senior team attributes and organizational ambidexterity: The moderating role of transformational leadership. *Journal of Management Studies, 45*(5), 982–1007. https://doi.org/10.1111/j.1467-6486.2008.00775.x

Jarrahi, M. H. (2018). Artificial intelligence and the future of work: Human-AI symbiosis in organizational decision making. *Business Horizons, 61*(4), 577–586. https://doi.org/10.1016/j.bushor.2018.03.007

Jasmand, C., Blazevic, V., & De Ruyter, K. (2012). Generating sales while providing service: A study of customer service representatives' ambidextrous behavior. *Journal of Marketing, 76*(1), 20–37.

Jensen, S. H., Poulfelt, F., & Kraus, S. (2010). Managerial routines in professional service firms: Transforming knowledge into competitive advantages. *The Service Industries Journal, 30*(12), 2045–2062. https://doi.org/10.1080/02642060903191082

Junni, P., Sarala, R. M., Taras, V., & Tarba, S. Y. (2013). Organizational ambidexterity and performance: A meta-analysis. *Academy of Management Perspectives, 27*(4), 299–312. https://doi.org/10.5465/amp.2012.0015

Junni, P., Sarala, R. M., Tarba, S. Y., Liu, Y., & Cooper, C. L. (2015). Guest editors' introduction: The role of human resources and organizational factors in ambidexterity. *Human Resource Management, 54*(S1), s1–s28. https://doi.org/10.1002/hrm.21772

Kang, S. C., & Snell, S. A. (2009). Intellectual capital architectures and ambidextrous learning: A framework for human resource management. *Journal of Management Studies, 46*(1), 65–92. https://doi.org/10.1111/j.1467-6486.2008.00776.x

Kelliher, C., & Perret, G. (2001). Business Strategies and approaches to HRM: A Case Study of new developments in the UK restaurant industry. *Personal Review 30*(4), 421–437.

Kim, W., Lorenzini, M., Balatti, P., Nguyen, P. D. H., Pattacini, U., Tikhanoff, V., Peternel, L., Fantacci, C., Natale, L., Metta, G., & Ajoudani, A. (2019). Adaptable workstations for human-robot collaboration: A reconfigurable framework for improving worker ergonomics and productivity. *IEEE Robotics & Automation Magazine*, *26*(3), 14–26. https://doi.org/10.1109/MRA.2018.2890460

Kumar, V., Rajan, B., Venkatesan, R., & Lecinski, J. (2019). Understanding the role of artificial intelligence in personalized engagement marketing. *California Management Review, 61*(4), 135–155. https://doi.org/10.1177/0008125619859317

Kurt, S., & Kurt, Ü. (2015). Innovation and labour productivity in BRICS countries: Panel causality and co-integration. *Procedia - Social and Behavioral Sciences, 195,* 1295–1302. https://doi.org/10.1016/j.sbspro.2015.06.296

Lacity, M. C., & Willcocks, L. P. (2016). A new approach to automating services. *MIT Sloan Management Review, 58*(1), 41–49.

Leontief, W. (1952). Machines and man. *Scientific American, 187*(3), 150–164.

Lepak, D. P., Liao, H., Chung, Y., & Harden, E. E. (2006). A conceptual review of human resource management systems in strategic human resource management research. *Research in Personnel and Human Resources Management, 25*(1), 217–271.

Levinthal, B., & March, J. G. (1993). The myopia of learning. *Strategic Management Journal, 14*(S2), 95–112. https://doi.org/10.1002/smj.4250141009

Li, Y., Vanhaverbeke, W., & Schoenmakers, W. (2008). Exploration and exploitation in innovation: Reframing the interpretation. *Creativity and Innovation Management, 17* (2), 107–126. https://doi.org/10.1111/j.1467-8691.2008.00477.x

Long, R. J., & Fang, T. (2013). Profit sharing and workplace productivity: Does teamwork play a role? IZA Discussion. Paper No. 7869. Available at SSRN: https://ssrn.com/abstract=2377605

Lu, V. N., Wirtz, J., Kunz, W. H., Paluch, S., Gruber, T., Martins, A., & Patterson, P. G. (2020). Service robots, customers and service employees: What can we learn from the academic literature and where are the gaps? *Journal of Service Theory and Practice, 30*(3), 361–391. https://doi.org/10.1108/JSTP-04-2019-0088

Luk, S. C. Y., & Preston, P. W. (2016). *The logic of Chinese politics. Cores, peripheries and peaceful rising.* Edward Elgar.

Luo, B., Zheng, S., Ji, H., & Liang, L. (2018). Ambidextrous leadership and TMT-member ambidextrous behavior: The role of TMT behavioral integration and TMT risk propensity. *The International Journal of Human Resource Management, 29*(2), 338–359. https://doi.org/10.1080/09585192.2016.1194871

Malik, A. (2019). Creating competitive advantage through source basic capital strategic humanity in the industrial age 4.0. *International Research Journal of Advanced Engineering and Science, 4*(1), 209–215.

Malik, A., Pereira, V., & Tarba, S. (2019a). The role of HRM practices in product development: Contextual ambidexterity in a US MNC's subsidiary in India. *The International Journal of Human Resource Management, 30*(4), 536–564. https://doi.org/10.1080/09585192.2017.1325388

Manyika, J. (2017). *A future that works: AI, automation, employment, and productivity.* Tech. Rep 60. McKinsey Global Institute Research.

March, J. G. (1991). Exploration and exploitation in organizational learning. *Organization Science, 2*(1), 71–87. https://doi.org/10.1287/orsc.2.1.71

McGrath, R. G. (2001). Exploratory learning, innovative capacity, and managerial oversight. *Academy of Management Journal, 44,* 118–132.

Mohnen, P., & Hall, B. H. (2013). Innovation and productivity: An update. *Eurasian Business Review, 3* (1), 47–65.

Nemanich, L. A., & Vera, D. (2009). Transformational leadership and ambidexterity in the context of an acquisition. *The Leadership Quarterly, 20*(1), 19–33. https://doi.org/10.1016/j.leaqua.2008.11.002

Nikolova, M., & Cnossen, F. (2020). What makes work meaningful and why economists should care about it. *Labour Economics*, *65*, 101847. https://doi.org/10.1016/j.labeco.2020.101847

O'Reilly, C. A., III, & Tushman, M. L. (2008). Ambidexterity as a dynamic capability: Resolving the innovator's dilemma. *Research in Organizational Behavior*, *28*, 185–206. https://doi.org/10.1016/j.riob.2008.06.002

O'Reilly, C. A., III, & Tushman, M. L. (2013). Organizational ambidexterity: Past, present, and future. *Academy of Management Perspectives*, *27*(4), 324–338. https://doi.org/10.5465/amp.2013.0025

Paluch, S., Wirtz, J., & Kunz, W. H. (2020). Service robots and the future of service. In M. Bruhn, C. Burmann, & M. Kirchgeorg (Eds.), *Marketing Weiterdenken–Zukunftspfade für eine marktorientierte Unternehmensführung* (2nd ed., pp. 423–435). Springer Gabler-Verlag. https://doi.org/10.1007/978-3-658-31563-4_2112

Patel, P. C., Messersmith, J. G., & Lepak, D. P. (2013). Walking the tightrope: An assessment of the relationship between high-performance work systems and organizational ambidexterity. *Academy of Management Journal*, *56*(5), 1420–1442. https://doi.org/10.5465/amj.2011.0255

Pfeiffer, S. (2016). Robots, Industry 4.0 and humans, or why assembly work is more than routine work. *Societies*, *6*(2), 16. https://doi.org/10.3390/soc6020016

Piao, M., & Zajac, E. J. (2016). How exploitation impedes and impels exploration: Theory and evidence. *Strategic Management Journal*, *37*(7), 1431–1447. https://doi.org/10.1002/smj.2402

Powell, T. C., & Dent-Micallef, A. (1997). Information technology as competitive advantage: The role of human, business, and technology resources. *Strategic Management Journal*, *18*(5), 375–405. https://doi.org/10.1002/(SICI)1097-0266(199705)18:5<375::AID-SMJ876>3.0.CO;2-7

Raisch, S., Birkinshaw, J., Probst, G., & Tushman, M. L. (2009). Organizational ambidexterity: Balancing exploitation and exploration for sustained performance. *Organization Science*, *20*(4), 685–695. https://doi.org/10.1287/orsc.1090.0428

Ramona, T., & Anca, Ş. (2013). Human resource management-from function to strategic partner. *Annals of the University of Oradea, Economic Science Series*, *22*(1), 1682–1689.

Research and Markets. (2020). *Industry 4.0 - adoption index*. https://www.researchandmarkets.com/r/k5jts5

Schön, D., & Argyris, C. (1996). *Organizational learning II: Theory, method and practice*. Addison Wesley.

Scuotto, V., Del Giudice, M., Bresciani, S., & Meissner, D. (2017). Knowledge-driven preferences in informal inbound open innovation modes. An explorative view on small to medium enterprises. *Journal of Knowledge Management*, *21*(3), 640–655. https://doi.org/10.1108/JKM-10-2016-0465

Scuotto, V., & Mueller, J. (2018). *ICT Adoption for Knowledge Management: Opportunities for SMEs*. Oxford, UK: RossiSmith Academic Publishing.

Simsek, Z. (2009). Organizational ambidexterity: Towards a multilevel understanding. *Journal of Management Studies*, *46*(4), 597–624. https://doi.org/10.1111/j.1467-6486.2009.00828.x

Simsek, Z., Heavey, C., Veiga, J. F., & Souder, D. (2009). A typology for aligning organizational ambidexterity's conceptualizations, antecedents, and outcomes. *Journal of Management Studies*, *46*(5), 864–894. https://doi.org/10.1111/j.1467-6486.2009.00841.x

Soosay, C., & Hyland, P. (2008). Exploration and exploitation: The interplay between knowledge and continuous innovation. *International Journal of Technology Management*, *42*(1–2), 20–35. https://doi.org/10.1504/IJTM.2008.018058

Stokes, P., Moore, N., Smith, S. M., Larson, M. J., & Brindley, C. (2017). Organizational ambidexterity and the emerging-to-advanced economy nexus: Cases from private higher education operators in the United Kingdom. *Thunderbird International Business Review, 59*(3), 333–348. https://doi.org/10.1002/tie.21843

Stokes, P., Smith, S., Wall, T., Moore, N., Rowland, C., Ward, T., & Cronshaw, S. (2019). Resilience and the (micro-) dynamics of organizational ambidexterity: Implications for strategic HRM. *The International Journal of Human Resource Management, 30*(8), 1287–1322. https://doi.org/10.1080/09585192.2018.1474939

Swart, J., Turner, N., Van Rossenberg, Y., & Kinnie, N. (2019). Who does what in enabling ambidexterity? Individual actions and HRM practices. *The International Journal of Human Resource Management, 30*(4), 508–535. https://doi.org/10.1080/09585192.2016.1254106

Tambe, P., Cappelli, P., & Yakubovich, V. (2019). Artificial intelligence in human resources management: Challenges and a path forward. *California Management Review, 61*(4), 15–42. https://doi.org/10.1177/0008125619867910

Turing, A. M. (2009). Computing machinery and intelligence. In R. Epstein, G. Roberts, & G. Beber (Eds.), *Parsing the Turing test*, (pp. 23–65). Springer.

Tushman, M. L., & O'Reilly, C. A.III, (1996). Ambidextrous organizations: Managing evolutionary and revolutionary change. *California Management Review, 38*(4), 8–29. https://doi.org/10.2307/41165852

Van Doorn, J., Mende, M., Noble, S. M., Hulland, J., Ostrom, A. L., Grewal, D., & Petersen, J. A. (2017). Domo arigato Mr. Roboto: Emergence of automated social presence in organizational frontlines and customers' service experiences. *Journal of service research, 20*(1), 43–58.

White, H. (1980). A heteroscedasticity-consistent covariance matrix and a direct test for heteroscedasticity. *Econometrica, 48*(4), 817–838. https://doi.org/10.2307/1912934

Wilson, H. J., Daugherty, P., & Bianzino, N. (2017). The jobs that artificial intelligence will create. *MIT Sloan Management Review, 58*(4), 14.

Winter Sidney, G., & Nelson, R. R. (1982). *An evolutionary theory of economic change.* Harvard University Press.

Wirtz, J. (2020). Organizational ambidexterity: cost-effective service excellence, service robots, and artificial intelligence. *Organizational Dynamics, 49*, 1–9.

Wirtz, J., Patterson, P. G., Kunz, W. H., Gruber, T., Lu, V. N., Paluch, S. & Martins, A. (2018). Brave new world: service robots in the frontline. *Journal of Service Management, 29*(5), 907–931.

Wirtz, J., & Zeithaml, V. (2018). Cost-effective service excellence. *Journal of the Academy of Marketing Science, 46* (1), 59–80. https://doi.org/10.1007/s11747-017-0560-7

World Economic Forum. (2018). *The future of jobs report 2018.* http://www3.weforum.org/docs/WEF_Future_of_Jobs_2018.pdf

Yu, Y. T. (2010). *Ambidexterity: The simultaneous pursuit of service and sales goals in retail banking* [Doctoral dissertation]. The University of New South Wales Sydney.

Zhongping, F. (2008). A Chinese perspective on China–European relations. In G. Grevi & A. de Vasconcelos (Eds.), *Partnerships for effective multilateralism.* Chaillot Paper No. 109 (pp. 77–87). EU-ISS.

Zollo, M., & Winter, S. (2002). Deliberate learning and the evolution of dynamic capabilities. *Organization Science, 13*(3), 339–351. https://doi.org/10.1287/orsc.13.3.339.2780

The adoption of artificial intelligence in employee recruitment: The influence of contextual factors

Yuan Pan, Fabian Froese, Ni Liu, Yunyang Hu and Maolin Ye

ABSTRACT

Artificial intelligence (AI) has been presented as a powerful tool in human resource management (HRM), but little academic research exists on the topic. The present study introduces the technology, organization, and environment (TOE) model from information systems research and integrates it with the transaction cost theory to better understand the facilitators and the constraints of companies' AI adoption behavior during employee recruitment. Survey results from 297 Chinese companies suggest that companies' perceived complexity toward AI constrains AI adoption, while technology competence and regulatory support encourage AI adoption. Relative advantages of AI technology, company size, and industry have no significant impact on AI usage. The findings also demonstrate the moderating effects of transaction costs on the influential power of technological complexity and organizations' technology competence.

Introduction

The number of strategic IT applications in HRM has burgeoned in recent years (Florkowski & Olivas-Luján, 2006). New digital technologies have challenged traditional HRM practices in various ways (Florkowski & Olivas-Luján, 2006), but in comparison with artificial intelligence (AI), most other technologies can barely keep abreast regarding usage potential and public concern. AI can be defined as systems or algorithms with learning functions and cognitive abilities which can perform tasks that would usually require human intelligence (e.g. Guenole & Feinzig, 2018; Oh et al., 2017). Although AI is still in the early stages of development and implementation (Bughin et al., 2017; Rao & Verweij, 2017), industry experts expect a dramatic increase in AI usage within the coming decade, contributing to a 14% increase in global GDP in 2030, and the greatest gains are likely in China, with a projected 26% boost in

GDP (Rao & Verweij, 2017). AI has shown great potential in changing HRM landscapes. For instance, IBM successfully realized a 107 million dollars reduction in HR costs in 2017 as a result of implementing AI, and the company believes AI will underpin the future of HRM (Guenole & Feinzig, 2018).

Not surprisingly, there is growing academic interest in AI usage in HRM. Nascent research demonstrates that AI can provide great benefits to companies by improving companies' HRM performance (Faliagka et al., 2014). Others argue that companies are not ready for AI in HRM due to a lack of know-how (Tambe et al., 2019). Prior AI research has primarily been conducted in non-HR disciplines, with a focus on IT techniques (e.g. Faliagka et al., 2014). While some studies in the field of management research discuss AI usage in HRM, they are rather descriptive, targeting practical applications rather than theoretical contributions (e.g. Ransbotham et al., 2017; Tambe et al., 2019). In summary, academic research from an HRM perspective lags behind the industry's awareness of AI's importance to the future of HRM. Thus, this study investigates the antecedents and boundary conditions of AI adoption in employee recruiting, as exemplified by the case of China.

This study makes the following contributions. First, it serves to enrich HRM literature by introducing the technology, organization, and environment (TOE) framework (Tornatzky & Fleischer, 1990) from the information system (IS) domain, and by providing empirical evidence regarding the validity of the TOE model in HRM research. The aforementioned TOE model should aid in scholarly understanding of companies' adoption behaviors toward HRM technologies, which is important for effective HRM. Second, we extend the TOE model by integrating it with the transaction cost theory (Williamson, 1989). Prior research based on TOE has produced inconsistent results (Baker, 2011; Wang et al., 2010). We argue that the integration of the transaction cost theory can help explain these inconsistent findings. It is plausible to expect that different levels of transaction costs may change companies' technology usage behavior under the same TOE context. Accordingly, we develop and empirically test a model in which transaction cost moderates the influential power of TOE on AI adoption in employee recruitment. Given the scarcity of literature about AI usage in HRM, this interdisciplinary research will benefit future scholars in achieving further theoretical developments pertaining to high-tech instruments in HRM.

Theory

HR recruitment is under the significant influence of technology (Lee, 2011). Several studies have illustrated AI's implications in HR recruitment, with focuses on candidates' attitudes toward AI (Suen et al., 2019; Van Esch et al., 2019) and the fairness of AI recruitment (Lambrecht & Tucker, 2019; Suen et al., 2019). We failed to find studies pertaining to companies' adoption behaviors toward AI recruitment. Prior literature has provided us some insights into the adoption of HRM practices. Jackson et al. (2014) proposed a theoretical framework to better understand the relationship between contextual factors, HRM systems and HR outcomes, indicating the importance of context in influencing HRM system adoption. Additionally, scholars believe that companies' absorptive capacity, i.e. the ability to recognize, assimilate and apply new knowledge from the external environment, is an important determinant of organizational innovative performance (Cohen & Levinthal, 1990). Absorptive capacity, which is intensively related to companies' prior knowledge and their incentive to learn, also interactively operates with the characteristics of the new knowledge and surrounding context (Cohen & Levinthal, 1990). Therefore, we believe that context may also influence the adoption of AI recruitment.

However, it is difficult to build our study on the above theories, primarily because of the differences between the characteristics of HRM practice adoption and technology adoption. For example, while Jackson et al. (2014) model is comprehensive for HRM system studies, the theoretical constructs are inadequate for AI adoption. The model omits prior internal resources that support the implications of innovative technology. On the other hand, absorptive capacity realizes the importance of existing resources but lacks a focus on external context. Most importantly, existing HRM theories cannot adequately capture the characteristics of AI recruitment, and as a result, they may omit crucial information related to AI adoption. Strohmeier (2007) suggests that HR scholars should borrow established theoretical models from the IS field to study the technology implications specific to HRM (e-HRM). Therefore, this study draws from the well-established TOE model (Tornatzky & Fleischer, 1990) in IS research and integrates it with the transaction cost theory to investigate those factors that influence companies' adoption of AI.

The TOE framework argues that three contextual factors – technology, organization, and environment – influence a company's adoption of new technologies. The explanatory power of the TOE model has been demonstrated in various technological, industrial, and national contexts (e.g. Hsu et al., 2006; Oliveira & Martins, 2010; Wang et al., 2010). Despite of its concurred reliability, the model has several limitations. Primarily, the original constructs of the contextual factors are relatively generic and obsolete (Baker, 2011; Wang et al., 2010). Therefore, researchers usually modify model constructs according to specific research contexts or synthesize the model with other theories, yielding more rigorous research (e.g. Hsu et al., 2006; Oliveira & Martins, 2010; Wang et al., 2010; Zhu, Dong, et al., 2006; Zhu, Kraemer, et al., 2006). Some constructs also demonstrate inconsistent results across different research, indicating the potential existence of other factors. Researchers have already noticed that interaction terms can help improve the overall reliability of the model (Hsu et al., 2006; Wang et al., 2010), although moderation effects remain relatively unaddressed in the existing literature. We believe that some non-contextual factors – namely, transaction costs – may influence a company's technology adoption behaviors by moderating the influential power of contextual variables.

Transaction costs are important non-contextual factors that affect the usage of HR technology, because the implementation of technology in HRM is highly relevant to cost reductions in HR operations (Lee, 2011), requires major reorganization of HR workflows, and thus involves significant transaction costs for information processing (Strohmeier, 2007). The different levels of transaction costs provide a potential explanation for companies' different adoption behaviors under the same contextual conditions. Therefore, transaction costs may moderate TOE constructs and increase the reliability of our model. According to the transaction cost theory, companies strive to minimize total costs (Geyskens et al., 2006). A company has two predominant cost components: transaction cost and production cost. Transaction cost is the cost of all necessary information for coordinating people and machines in production, and production cost refers to the cost of all physical processes necessary for production (Son et al., 2005). In our case, implementing AI can reduce the production costs of recruitment by saving human capital. However, if the transaction costs of introducing AI into recruitment are too high, companies are likely to reject AI adoption.

Scholars have identified several determinants of transaction costs. Among them, asset specificity and uncertainty are highly relevant and are therefore included in most transaction cost models (Aubert et al., 2004; Geyskens et al., 2006; Son et al., 2005). Assets can have different natures, including machines, human capital, company knowledge, etc. (Aubert et al., 2004). Asset specificity refers to organizational assets that are tailored to specific transactions (Geyskens et al., 2006). In this study, asset specificity is a company's specific asset investments in AI technology for HRM services. Companies are locked into certain transactions if the existing asset specificity is higher than the cost of alternatives (Son et al., 2005). In other words, asset specificity represents the switching cost of not using AI. Companies with high asset specificity in AI technology will have low transaction costs for AI and high transaction costs for alternatives.

Uncertainty indicates transaction costs in a different way. Organizations often experience bounded rationality in processing transactions (Geyskens et al., 2006). Bounded rationality, which refers to one's limited ability to acquire all needed information, results in a certain level of uncertainty (Aubert et al., 2004). According to Sutcliffe and Zaheer (1998), there are three main types of uncertainty: primary uncertainty, competitive uncertainty, and supplier uncertainty. We regard AI as a supplier of HR support, so supplier uncertainty fits best with our research design. Supplier uncertainty is derived from the unpredictable situations of service providers (Sutcliffe & Zaheer, 1998). Therefore, here, uncertainty represents the extent to which companies believe the future of AI technology is unpredictable. Many companies believe that AI technology involves significant uncertainty (Bughin et al., 2017; Ransbotham et al., 2017).

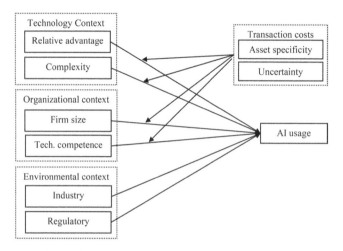

Figure 1. Conceptual model.

High uncertainty increases the transaction cost of processing information (Son et al., 2005), so higher uncertainty in AI may reduce companies' willingness to adopt the technology.

Companies' demands and capabilities for making specific asset investments are related to technology and organization, and the technological knowledge of a company and the nature of AI technology may influence a company's perception regarding the uncertainty of AI. Therefore, both asset specificity and uncertainty may interact with technological and organizational contexts. However, the source of transaction costs in this research does not involve any external party, so we expect no interaction between transaction cost determinants and external contextual factors. Consequently, we propose a theoretical model (see Figure 1) that integrates the TOE model with transaction cost determinants. Detailed hypotheses are developed in the following section.

Hypotheses development

Technological contexts

Technological contexts include the characteristics and availabilities of existing and emerging technologies relevant to a company (Tornatzky & Fleischer, 1990). Although the original TOE model does not offer descriptive details of technological factors, later research has extended the model and introduced reliable constructs (e.g. Zhu, Kraemer, et al., 2006; Zhu, Dong, et al., 2006). In this study, technological factors include relative advantage and technology complexity, as they are highly relevant, representing the most frequently used characteristics in prior research (Rogers, 2003; Wang et al., 2010; Zhu, Dong, et al., 2006).

In general, relative advantage refers to the degree of benefits that innovation can bring to an organization (Rogers, 2003; Zhu, Dong, et al., 2006). Benefits motivate companies to acquire new knowledge and thus increase companies' absorptive capacity to adopt new technology. Consequently, scholars find that relative advantage contributes to higher levels of technology adoption (Hsu et al., 2006; Zhu, Dong, et al., 2006). Relative advantage indicates the perceived usefulness AI can offer to companies in supporting recruitment activities. AI has great potential to earn relative advantage by performing complicated tasks just as human recruiters do, since AI scholars and early adopters in the industry applaud the future of AI for its usefulness in recruitment (Faliagka et al., 2014; Guenole & Feinzig, 2018). Therefore, we argue that the relative advantage of AI is the incentive for companies to use AI recruitment. Thus, we propose the following hypothesis:

H1a. Higher technological relative advantage is associated with a higher level of AI usage in recruitment.

Technological complexity is the perceived difficulty of using certain technology (Rogers, 2003). Greater difficulty demotivates organizations to acquire new knowledge and thus reduces the absorptive capacity of companies to innovate (Cohen & Levinthal, 1990). As a result, complexity is likely to constrain innovative behaviors. The empirical evidence suggests that complexity has a negative impact on technology adoption (Wang et al., 2010). Complexity indicates the extent to which companies believe AI recruitment tools are difficult to use. Because AI is a typical high-tech feature which requires significant IT knowledge to understand and thus is relatively difficult to implement compared to traditional IT, the complexity of AI recruitment tools may be an important concern for many companies due to their technological novelty. Therefore, we argue that complexity may become a significant obstacle for companies in adopting AI technology:

H1b. Higher technological complexity is associated with a lower level of AI usage in recruitment.

The transaction costs of using AI may change companies' attitudes toward technological factors. According to the transaction cost theory, companies ultimately look for a minimum total cost (Geyskens et al., 2006), and AI recruitment has a dual effect on total cost minimization. AI adoption can reduce the production costs of companies by saving on human capital, because it can perform tasks that would usually require HR professionals (Faliagka et al., 2014; Guenole & Feinzig, 2018). However, AI adoption can also result in transaction costs, because implementing AI requires adjustments of HRM structures and procedures (Tambe et al., 2019). The high transaction costs of AI adoption may prevent companies from implementing AI, because companies believe that the potential benefits of AI, which are brought about by the relative advantage of AI, cannot compensate for the higher transaction costs. Therefore, the encouraging effect of AI's relative advantage may be obvious only when transaction costs are low, and the determinants for low transaction costs, i.e. high asset specificity and low uncertainty, may enhance the positive effects of relative advantage. Meanwhile, when the transaction costs of using AI are low, companies are less concerned about AI's complexity, because the potential difficulties, which are brought about by the complexity of AI, cannot undermine the reduction in production costs stemming from AI implementation. Therefore, determinants of low transaction costs, i.e. high asset specificity and low uncertainty, may reduce the influential power of complexity. Therefore, we propose the following assumptions:

H2a/b. Lower transaction costs, i.e. (a) higher asset specificity, and (b) lower uncertainty, will enhance the effect of relative advantage on AI usage in recruitment.

H2c/d. Lower transaction costs, i.e. (a) higher asset specificity, and (b) lower uncertainty, will reduce the effect of complexity on AI usage in recruitment.

Organizational context

Organizational context refers to the characteristics of an organization, including organizational structure, communication processes, organization size, and the availability of internal slack resources (Tornatzky & Fleischer, 1990). Prior IS research uses various proxies to measure organizational context in the TOE model (e.g. Hsu et al., 2006; Oliveira & Martins, 2010; Wang et al., 2010). In the present study, we focus on two of the most common proxies of organizational context, i.e. company size and company technology competence.

Company size refers to a company's size in terms of staff and budget (Rogers, 2003). It is a surrogate measure of various organizational components such as slack resources, capital, organizational structure, and so forth (Hsu et al., 2006; Rogers, 2003). Company size is one of the most frequently discussed organizational contextual factors (Baker, 2011; Oliveira & Martins, 2010; Zhu, Dong, et al., 2006). Although some research has found that company size is not relevant to technology adoption (Oliveira & Martins, 2010), numerous studies have found that company size has positive effects on technology adoption (Baker, 2011; Hsu et al., 2006; Rogers, 2003; Wang et al., 2010). Zhu, Kraemer, et al. (2006) found that although company size is not relevant to technology usage at later stages of technology adoption, large companies have advantages in the early stages of technology adoption due to resource richness. Therefore, we expect larger companies to implement more AI tools related to recruitment, since AI usage in the workplace is still in its infant stages (Bughin et al., 2017; Ransbotham et al., 2017) and large companies enjoy a resource advantage at the initial stages of AI adoption:

H3a. Larger company size is associated with a higher level of AI usage in recruitment.

Technology competence refers to the readiness of existing internal technological resources to support innovation (Zhu, Dong, et al., 2006). Technological resources include prior technological infrastructure, experience, and knowledge employed to support the implementation of innovation without additional investments (Rogers, 2003). Prior knowledge contributes to greater absorptive capacity, thus encouraging companies to innovate (Cohen & Levinthal, 1990). Therefore, technology competence will help companies to implement new technology. Scholars find that technology competence is one of the most influential TOE factors in facilitating technology adoption (Zhu, Kraemer, et al., 2006; Zhu, Dong, et al., 2006). Using AI involves significant IT resources and knowledge (Ransbotham et al., 2017), and highly competent companies will have better resources to support innovation (Hsu et al., 2006; Zhu, Kraemer, et al., 2006; Zhu, Dong, et al., 2006) and stronger absorptive capacity to leverage resource advantages. Therefore, we expect that technology competence will contribute to greater AI usage:

> **H3b**. Higher technology competence is associated with a higher level of AI usage in recruitment.

Both company size and technology competence are proxies of organizational resource richness. Thus, they may engage in similar interactions with transaction cost determinants, i.e. asset specificity and uncertainty. High asset specificity indicates companies' path dependence on specific activities, and path-locked companies tend to further invest their resources in dependent activities (Geyskens et al., 2006), allowing the specific activities to gain greater advantage from company resources in light of the high asset specificity. Therefore, when companies with high AI asset specificity are locked in AI usage, AI recruitment may gain greater advantages from company resources. As a result, high asset specificity can enhance the facilitating effects of company resources in increasing AI usage by locking companies' investments into AI recruitment.

Meanwhile, uncertainty requires extra organizational adjustments and preparations to manage insufficient information (Aubert et al., 2004). Organizational resource richness can reduce the degree of adjustments companies need to make, because companies can use existing resources for preparations with minimum extra adjustments. The richer the resources of companies, the fewer the extra efforts they need to make. Therefore, the privilege of resource richness may be particularly obvious when uncertainty is high and companies need to make vast adjustments. In other words, high uncertainty enhances the facilitating role of company resources. Consequently, companies depend more heavily on existing resources to prepare for AI implementation when AI uncertainty is high (Bughin et al., 2017). As a result, higher AI uncertainty will strengthen the encouraging effects of company resources. We hypothesize as follows:

> **H4a/b**. Higher asset specificity will strengthen the effect of company resources, i.e. (a) company size, and (b) company technology competence, on AI usage in recruitment.

> **H4c/d**. Higher uncertainty will strengthen the effect of company resources, i.e. (a) company size, and (b) company technology competence, on AI usage in recruitment.

Environmental context

Environmental context describes the arena in which an organization operates, including industry characteristics, government regulation, and external innovation infrastructure (Tornatzky & Fleischer, 1990). In this study, we focus on industry and regulatory environment. Both constructs are classic proxies of environmental characteristics and are frequently discussed in the extant literature (Hsu et al., 2006; Oliveira & Martins, 2010).

An industry can indicate industry characteristics and external innovation infrastructure. The industry may significantly influence a company's innovation behaviors (Oliveira & Martins, 2010) and HRM practices (Malik et al., 2020). Some rather traditional industries, such as manufacturing sectors, are less likely to adopt new technology, because they have fewer technology demands (Hsu et al., 2006). On the other hand, some industries are more technology intensive, so the industrial pressure to implement technological advancements may influence companies' innovation initiatives. Experts report industry differences in adopting AI in the workplace, indicating that companies in some industries – namely, IT, telecom, and finance – are more experienced with IT (Bughin et al., 2017; Ransbotham et al., 2017). Correspondingly, we argue that companies in IT-intensive industries may confront higher industry pressure to adopt AI technology:

> *H5a*. IT-intensive industry sectors are associated with a higher level of AI usage in recruitment.

Regulatory environment refers to governmental policies affecting technology diffusion (Zhu, Kraemer, et al., 2006). The regulatory environment may support or constrain a company's technological innovation depending on the nature of regulations (Baker, 2011; Hsu et al., 2006). If the regulatory environment encourages innovation, companies are likely to adopt new technology (Hsu et al., 2006). Regulatory environment is one of the strongest influential environmental factors for technology usage, particularly in developing countries (Zhu, Kraemer, et al., 2006). The Chinese government believes AI to be a strategically important technology and actively promotes AI technology, with massive investments and adoption rates (Bughin et al., 2017; Rao &Verweij, 2017). Therefore, we expect regulatory environment to be a strong incentive for companies to use AI in recruitment:

> *H5b*. A highly supportive regulatory environment is associated with a higher level of AI usage in recruitment.

Methodology

Sample and procedures

We conducted a survey among HR managers and senior managers familiar with HR and IT usage in their companies, relying on the network of a major university in Guangzhou, southern China, to recruit respondents from part-time MBA students and alumni. In addition, a team of research assistants visited companies in Guangzhou, distributed questionnaires, and provided on-site instructions. The high demand for talent in China (Froese et al., 2019; Han & Froese, 2010) and the advancement of IT technology (Zhou et al., 2021) make China a suitable context for the study of our hypotheses. We used both online and paper-based surveys, depending on the convenience of the respondents. All participants completed questionnaires independently, with full acknowledgement of anonymous and ethical codes. We received 416 out of 473 distributed questionnaires and retained 297 complete samples (effective response rate of 62.79%). The quality connections of the network, in conjunction with the personal visits, explain the high response rate.

The number of respondents is relatively equal across different industries, from a low of 10.4% for the commercial and service sectors to high of 17.8% for the education, healthcare and creativity sectors, indicating that the sample achieves strong coverage of companies in different industries. Nearly 27% of the companies are from IT-intensive sectors – namely, 14% from technology and 13% from finance. More than 65% of the companies represented in the survey results have been in business for over ten years. Company size varies from a few employees to over 200,000 employees, with more than 41% of the companies identified as relatively large (more than 1,000 employees).

Measures

We used established multiple-item scales from previous research, rated on a seven-point Likert scale, and modified them to our context as necessary (see Appendix) unless otherwise noted. The original survey was in English. We used the back-translation method to translate the survey into Chinese, and HR professionals provided feedback during pilot tests to help finalize the survey.

Dependent variable

To measure AI usage, we used three items, which followed conventions in IS research, to measure technology usage with percentages of processed services or data according to the focused technological system (Hsu et al., 2006; Zhu, Dong, et al., 2006). We adapted items to the employee recruitment context, focusing on attracting candidates, contacting candidates, and selecting candidates (Armstrong, 2006). Respondents identified a range of percentage points to indicate to what degree AI has helped their company to manage in each of these three domains, on a Likert scale ranging from 1 (below 20 percent) to 5 (over 80 percent). Cronbach's α was 0.89.

Independent variables

We measured *relative advantage* with a three-item scale established by Autry et al. (2010). Cronbach's α was 0.94. We measured *complexity* with a four-item scale from Autry et al. (2010) and reversed scores, so that higher scores imply higher complexity. Cronbach's α was 0.90. The two original scales were for perceived usefulness and perceived ease of use, which are conceptually similar and share similar items. We measured *company size* by the number of employees in the organization and applied a logarithm transformation (Zhu, Kraemer, et al., 2006; Zhu, Dong, et al., 2006). We measured *technology competence* by using three items from Wang et al. (2010). Cronbach's α was 0.88. We measured *industry sector* according to the official industrial classification standard of China, which included 20 industries (NBS & CIS, 2017), and we created a dummy variable to represent IT-intensive industry sectors, including IT, telecom and finance (1 = IT-intensive industry sectors, 0 = other industries). We used a four-item scale to measure *regulatory environment* (Zhu, Kraemer, et al., 2006). Cronbach's α was 0.92.

Moderating variables

The scales for our two moderating variables came from Son et al. (2005). We used four items to measure *asset specificity*. We used three items to measure *uncertainty* and reversed scores, so that higher scores imply higher uncertainty. Cronbach's α for asset specificity and uncertainty were 0.92 and 0.93, respectively.

Control variables

The maturity of an organization may influence organizational structure, strategy and resources (Kulik & Perry, 2008). Older companies often have more established HR practices and thus face difficulties in embracing changes such as AI recruitment, so we controlled for company age. We measured *company age* according to years of operation using five-year intervals (from 1 = 5 years or less, to 4 = over 15 years). Further, we controlled for three HR-related variables, because the nature of HR practices can influence the design of AI recruitment systems (Faliagka et al., 2014). The tendency of HR's strategic role and recruitment effectiveness is likely to be related to innovative HR practices, so we controlled for changes in an HR unit's strategic importance and probation pass rate, as the latter is a proxy for recruitment effectiveness. We measured *changes of HR role over the past five years* with a three-item scale (Kulik & Perry, 2008). Cronbach's α was 0.91. We measured *probation pass rate* by the percentage of probation passed employees, using every 20th percent as an interval (from 1 = less than 20%, to 5 = over 81%). We also controlled for HR department size, because large departments may have more resources to implement AI recruitment. We used the number of HR employees to measure *HR department size*.

Method validity

We conducted confirmatory factor analysis (CFA) to evaluate measurement reliability and validity. The CFA results demonstrate a good model fit ($\chi^2(296)$ = 525.664, CFI = 0.968, $p < 0.001$, RMSEA = 0.051). All factor loadings were over 0.70, except for one item in the asset specificity scale, which still had an acceptable loading (0.64), well above the cut-off of 0.50 (Hair et al., 2014). Average variance extracted (AVE) and composite reliability (CR) were also adequate (AVE > 0.50, CR > 0.70), indicating strong convergent validity of the measurements (Hair et al., 2014). The square roots of AVE were larger than correlations between constructs, confirming the discriminant validity of the measurements (Hair et al., 2014). Table 1 presents the descriptive results, correlations and scale reliabilities.

Both *ex-ante* and *ex-post* approaches (Chang et al., 2010) were taken to avoid common method bias (CMB). First, we strove to avoid the source of CMB in the survey design. We used established scales and carefully organized the item sequence. We included three fact-based variables to reduce respondent bias. Specifically, our dependent variable was primarily based on company facts and applied different scales (five points) with perceptual independent variables (seven points). We also paid attention to the survey administration process. Trained research assistants distributed online and paper questionnaires *via* different channels to increase the representativeness of respondents. The multiple remedies largely reduced CMB. Second, we applied multiple statistical techniques to detect and address the potential problem arising from CMB. The model design included interaction terms, which are less affected by CMB (Chang et al., 2010). In addition, we conducted two statistical tests to detect common variance. The common latent factor test demonstrated that all loading differences between the original model and the common latent factor model were less than 0.04. The Harman's single-factor test revealed that 41.39% of the variance was explained by one factor. Therefore, statistical analyses indicated no serious CMB in our study.

Results

We analyzed data using a hierarchical multiple regression. To reduce multicollinearity concerns, we standardized all variables except for AI usage (dependent variable), and industry (dummy variable) and interaction terms. All independent variables have a variance inflation factor (VIF) lower than 2, indicating no serious multicollinearity problems. Table 2 shows the regression results. We entered control variables in Model 1, independent variables in Model 2, and interaction terms in Model 3.

Hypothesis 1a/b proposed a significant relationship between technology context and AI usage. Relative advantage had no effect on AI usage ($b = 0.10$, $p = 0.208$), thus rejecting hypothesis H1a. Providing support for H1b,

Table 1. Means, standard deviations, correlations, and reliabilities.

	M	SD	1	2	3	4	5	6	7	8	9	10	11	12	13
1. AI usage	2.23	1.09	**.89**												
2. Relative advantage	4.72	1.21	.38**	**.94**											
3. Complexity	3.73	1.19	−.40**	.57**	**.90**										
4. Company size	2.92	1.06	.08	.02	−.01	–									
5. Tech. Competence	4.30	1.34	.42**	.62**	−.52**	.07	**.88**								
6. Industry (IT intensive)	0.37	0.48	−.00	.02	.01	.06	.03	–							
7. Regulatory	3.98	1.34	.33**	.44**	−.39**	−.06	.52**	.01	**.92**						
8. Company age	3.01	1.19	−.04	−.08	.04	.51**	−.01	−.04	−.08	–					
9. HR size	114.69	456.51	.03	−.01	.01	.34**	.03	.02	−.07	.16**	–				
10. HR role	4.87	1.15	.17**	.41**	−.25**	.05	.38**	.04	.27**	−.06	.02	**.91**			
11. Probation rate	4.18	1.01	.04	.06	−.06	.11	.08	.02	−.10	.15**	.05	.17**	–		
12. Asset specificity	3.80	1.41	.43**	.44**	−.42**	.05	.67**	.01	.63**	−.01	.00	.29**	−.09	**.92**	
13. Uncertainty	4.42	1.41	−.36**	−.36**	.33**	−.08	−.55**	.03	−.64**	−.04	.02	−.30**	.07	−.77	**.93**

Note. The diagonal shows Cronbach's Alpha. $n = 297$.

**$p < 0.01$.

*$p < 0.05$.

ARTIFICIAL INTELLIGENCE AND INTERNATIONAL HRM

Table 2. Regression results of AI usage.

	Model 1	Model 2	Model 3
Company age	−0.05	−0.09	−0.15*
Probation rate	0.02	0.03	0.05
HR role	0.18**	−0.05	−0.08
HR size	0.03	0.01	0.02
Relative advantage		0.10	0.18*
Complexity		−0.23**	−0.24**
Company size		0.11	0.12
Tech. competence		0.21**	0.06
Industry (IT intensive)		−0.03	−0.02
Regulatory		0.14*	0.03
Asset specificity			0.13
Uncertainty			−0.13
Advantage*asset specificity			−0.12
Advantage*uncertainty			−0.15
Complexity*asset specificity			−0.20*
Complexity*uncertainty			0.01
Company size*asset specificity			0.12
Company size*uncertainty			0.01
Competence* asset specificity			0.24*
Competence*uncertainty			0.33**
R^2	0.03	0.25**	0.34**
ΔR^2		0.22**	0.09**

Note. $n = 297$.
*$p < 0.05$.
**$p < 0.01$.

complexity was negatively related with AI usage (b = −0.23, $p = 0.002$). Hypothesis 2a/b proposed the moderation effect of transaction cost determinants on relative advantage. The interaction term between asset specificity and relative advantage was statistically insignificant (b = −0.12, $p = 0.267$), and the same result was found with the interaction term between uncertainty and relative advantage (b = −0.15, $p = 0.182$), thus rejecting H2a/b. Hypothesis 2c/d proposed a moderation effect of transaction cost determinants on complexity. Providing support for H2c, the interaction term between asset specificity and complexity indicated that asset specificity reduced the effect of complexity on AI usage (b = −0.20, $p = 0.047$). The interaction term between uncertainty and complexity was not significant ($b = 0.01$, $p = 0.874$), rejecting hypothesis H2d. Figure 2 presents the plot for the moderation effect of asset specificity on the complexity-usage relationship. Simple slopes tests showed that the interaction was significant only for companies with high asset specificity (t = −3.520, $p = 0.001$), but not for companies with low asset specificity (t = −0.389, $p = 0.697$).

Hypothesis 3a/b proposed a significant relationship between organizational context and AI usage. Company size had no effect on AI usage ($b = 0.11$, $p = 0.115$), rejecting H3a. Technology competence was positively related to AI usage ($b = 0.21$, $p = 0.008$), thus supporting H3b. Hypothesis 4a/b proposed a moderation effect of asset specificity on organizational context. The interaction term between asset specificity and company size was not significant ($b = 0.12$, $p = 0.155$), thus rejecting H4a. Providing support for H4b, the interaction term between asset specificity and technology competence indicated that asset specificity strengthened the effect of technology competence on AI usage ($b = 0.24$,

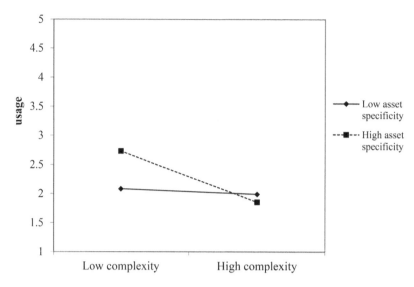

Figure 2. Moderation of asset specificity on complexity-usage.

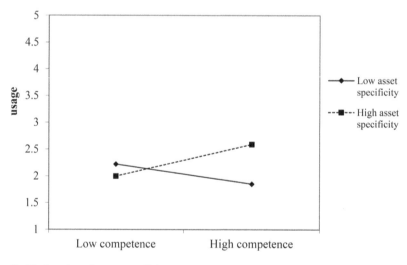

Figure 3. Moderation of asset specificity on competence-usage.

$p = 0.015$). Figure 3 illustrates the moderation effect of asset specificity on the technology competence-usage relationship. Simple slopes tests showed that the interaction was significant only for companies with high asset specificity ($t = 2.212$, $p = 0.028$), but not for companies with low asset specificity (t = −1.385, $p = 0.167$).

Hypothesis 4c/d proposed a moderation effect of uncertainty on organizational context. The interaction term between uncertainty and company size was not significant ($b = 0.01$, $p = 0.909$), thus rejecting H4c. Providing support for H4d, the interaction term between uncertainty and technology competence indicated that uncertainty strengthens the effect of technology competence

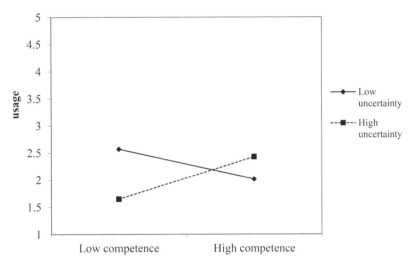

Figure 4. Moderation of uncertainty on competence-usage.

on AI usage ($b = 0.33$, $p = 0.002$). We plotted the moderation effect of uncertainty on the technology competence-usage relationship in Figure 4. Simple slopes tests showed that the interaction was significant only for companies with high uncertainty ($t = 3.197$, $p = 0.002$), but not for companies with low uncertainty (t = −1.803, $p = 0.072$).

Hypothesis 5a/b proposed a significant relationship between environmental context and AI usage. The IT-intensive industry had no effect on AI usage (b = −0.03, $p = 0.828$), thus rejecting H5a. As expected, regulatory environment was positively related to AI usage ($b = 0.14$, $p = 0.049$), supporting H5b.

Discussion

This study investigates the antecedents and boundary conditions of AI adoption in employee recruiting. Our results show that different contextual elements of technology, organization, and environment have an influence on the adoption of AI in employee recruiting, and that transaction costs partially moderate these relationships. For technology context, technology complexity hinders the adoption of AI usage, but high asset specificity can reduce the negative power of complexity. However, technological relative advantage is not associated with AI usage. We discuss this surprising finding later. With regard to organizational context, technology competence has a positive effect on increasing AI usage, as expected. Both high asset specificity and high uncertainty enhance the positive power of technology competence. Company size seems to have little influence on AI usage, probably because large companies do not necessarily dedicate resources toward AI adoption. With regard to environmental context, supportive regulatory environments indeed have a positive effect on AI technology in recruitment, indicating the effectiveness of government initiatives. Meanwhile, companies in IT-intensive industries do not show significant differences in AI usage in terms of recruitment, probably because global standards for IT techniques lead to the convergence of AI systems (Malik et al., 2020). Thus, companies from different sectors may use the same HRM software to conduct similar HRM tasks (Strohmeier, 2007).

Theoretical contributions

Our study contributes significantly to the literature on HR technology and corresponding HRM implications. First, we introduce the TOE framework from IS to HRM research and provide empirical evidence of the model's validity in the HRM domain. Prior scholars continue to report insufficient theoretical foundations to facilitate research in the area of technology implications in HRM (Bondarouk et al., 2017; Marler & Fisher, 2013; Strohmeier, 2007). The strategic HRM literature indicates the importance of context in influencing HRM practices (Jackson et al., 2014) and e-HRM effectiveness (Lee, 2011), but the interdisciplinary nature of HR technology adoption renders it difficult to directly apply management theories on the topic due to a lack of conceptualization of appropriate constructs. While many studies have focused on the effects of AI recruitment approaches largely taken for granted (e.g. Lambrecht & Tucker, 2019), scholars have increasingly called for additional empirical studies that theorize regarding adoption behavior (Bondarouk et al., 2017). Therefore, the introduced TOE model provides a theoretical framework to conceptualize HR technology adoption in context and opens the avenue for the integration of the TOE model with relevant HRM theories (e.g. Jackson et al., 2014) to investigate the strategic outcomes of HRM brought about by adopted technologies.

Empirical evidence is important for maintaining the validity of the TOE framework (Baker, 2011). To the best of our knowledge, we are pioneers in investigating the antecedents of AI usage in HRM using the TOE framework. Our empirical findings have justified the validity of TOE constructs in discussing HR technologies. Interestingly, while previous research has emphasized the advantages of IT in HRM without considering company adoption behaviors (e.g. Faliagka et al., 2014), our results indicate that the relative advantage of IT will not necessarily lead to actual technology usage. Since relative advantage has the highest mean score in our data, the surprising finding does not undermine the advantage of AI. Rather, it illustrates that companies may avoid AI recruitment even though they think AI is useful, since companies seem to concern themselves more with technological complexity over potential advantages.

Additionally, our research extends the TOE model by integrating it with the transaction cost theory and discovering interactions between contextual factors and transaction costs. Theoretical synthesis may further develop the TOE framework and increase overall model validity (Baker, 2011). Some TOE constructs demonstrated inconsistent results in prior studies (Baker, 2011;

Oliveira & Martins, 2010; Wang et al., 2010). Our research confirms that transaction costs change the influential power of TOE constructs, providing a potential explanation for previous inconsistent results. For example, our study suggests that if companies have high asset specificity, complexity will be less important. Therefore, results surrounding complexity may be very different for companies with high asset specificity, and for their counterparts with low asset specificity. Thus, the asset specificity factor may explain the varying influential power of complexity in prior research (e.g. Oliveira & Martins, 2010; Wang et al., 2010).

Practical implications

Our findings provide some important insights that may help experts better understand companies' AI adoption behaviors. Experts believe that AI will bring great potential advantages to companies, and AI development has attracted tremendous levels of investment as a result (Bughin et al., 2017). However, it is AI's complexity, not its relative advantage, which influences companies' AI adoption decisions. Therefore, in comparison to developing useful AI techniques, reducing obstacles is much more important to the future of AI technology. AI developers who provide AI services must realize the difficulty of using AI among non-technological parties. They should place greater effort toward reducing AI complexity and delivering user-friendly AI tools. Otherwise, despite the fact that AI may have greater relative advantages in the future, the development of AI technology may not successfully lead to greater AI adoption, and AI stakeholders will suffer.

Company resources are crucial to AI adoption (Ransbotham et al., 2017), and yet large companies who possess greater general resources show little difference in levels of AI usage. This is because even mature organizations are not strategically ready for the implications of AI (Ransbotham et al., 2017). Instead of emphasizing general company resources, managers should take alternative strategic approaches to increase AI asset specificity and technology competence, which will in turn help to increase AI adoption. For example, companies can provide training for employees to help them better understand AI technology. HR managers can develop specific HRM procedures and routines tailored to the specifications of AI. It is also important for top management to launch specific strategies regarding AI initiatives.

As the country that will benefit most from AI (Rao &Verweij, 2017), China provides evidence of regulatory effectiveness in promoting AI technology. AI is strategically important for all global players to realize economic gains in the future. Others can learn from China's experience and take advantage of regulatory power to boost AI benefits. For example, governments can implement more AI-friendly regulations, integrate AI in procedural requirements, and issue legal protections for AI technology.

Limitations and future research

As with all studies, this study faces several limitations. First, we collected data using a self-reported survey. Although self-reported data represents the best way to capture perceptual information in social science, and we took various actions to address the potential CMB risk, we realize the possible effects of common method variance. We conducted several measures, e.g. survey design and statistical tests, to reduce common method bias. Future studies could conduct multilevel research with additional adoption behavior data from employees, or longitudinal research which follows the full diffusion process of technology, to further advance the results of this study (Rogers, 2003).

Second, we used company size and IT-intensive industry as proxies for the contexts of organization and environment, as seen in prior research (e.g. Hsu et al., 2006; Oliveira & Martins, 2010). However, prior research reported inconsistent findings. Both proxies are rather crude measures and were not significant in our study. Nevertheless, future research is encouraged to further investigate these factors, perhaps applying more specific measures, such as financial resources, industry dynamics, and so forth.

Third, we regard AI as a high-tech tool. However, AI has cognitive abilities that are notably different from other e-HRM instruments. Many people believe that AI is more than a tool (Oh et al., 2017). It would be interesting in future research efforts to seek to discover those factors that influence potential alienation and fear toward AI technology as a human substitute.

Fourth, AI usage may manifest national and cultural differences. Previous research demonstrates cross-cultural differences in technology adoption behaviors (Malik et al., 2020; Zhu, Kraemer, et al., 2006). Our study was conducted in China, and our research points to the effectiveness of regulatory power in influencing AI usage. Given the fact that different countries employ unique governmental initiatives, it would be interesting to research how AI adoption varies across countries, focusing on the role of environmental context.

Conclusion

AI has the potential to significantly influence the workplace and offer companies the chance to gain a competitive advantage (Tambe et al., 2019). Thus, practitioners and researchers need to understand the constraints and the facilitators of AI adoption. Drawing from the TOE model and the transaction cost theory, we developed and empirically tested a model of antecedents and boundary conditions for AI usage in employee recruitment. Survey findings from China demonstrate that various elements in the contexts of technology, organization, and environment have direct effects on AI usage, and that transaction costs partially moderate these relationships. The study confirms the importance of government support and relevant technological resources in AI adoption and encourages IT developers to reduce the technological complexity of AI. This integrated theoretical framework will inspire future scholars to seek to better understand technology adoption behaviors in HRM.

Data availability statement

The data that support the findings of this study are available from the corresponding author, upon reasonable request.

Disclosure statement

No potential conflict of interest was reported by the authors.

References

Armstrong, M. (2006). *A handbook of human resource management practice*. Kogan Page Publishers.

Aubert, B. A., Rivard, S., & Patry, M. (2004). A transaction cost model of IT outsourcing. *Information & Management, 41*(7), 921–932.

Autry, C. W., Grawe, S. J., Daugherty, P. J., & Richey, R. G. (2010). The effects of technological turbulence and breadth on supply chain technology acceptance and adoption. *Journal of Operations Management, 28*(6), 522–536. https://doi.org/10.1016/j.jom.2010.03.001

Baker, J. (2011). The technology-organization-environment framework. In Y. K.Dwivedi, M. R.Wade, & S. L. Schneberger (Eds.), *Information systems theory: Explaining and predicting our digital society* (Vol. 1, pp. 231–245). Springer Science & Business Media.

Bondarouk, T., Parry, E., & Furtmueller, E. (2017). Electronic HRM: Four decades of research on adoption and consequences. *The International Journal of Human Resource Management, 28*(1), 98–131. https://doi.org/10.1080/09585192.2016.1245672

Bughin, J., Hazan, E., Ramaswamy, S., Chui, M., Allas, T., Dahlström, P., Henke, N., & Trench, M. (2017). *Artificial intelligence: The next digital frontier?* McKinsey Global Institute, McKinsey & Company.

Chang, S. J., Van Witteloostuijn, A., & Eden, L. (2010). From the Editors: Common method variance in international business research. *Journal of International Business Studies, 41*(2), 178–184. https://doi.org/10.1057/jibs.2009.88

Cohen, W. M., & Levinthal, D. A. (1990). Absorptive capacity: A new perspective on learning and innovation. *Administrative Science Quarterly, 35*(1), 128–152. https://doi.org/10.2307/2393553

Faliagka, E., Iliadis, L., Karydis, I., Rigou, M., Sioutas, S., Tsakalidis, A., & Tzimas, G. (2014). On-line consistent ranking on e-recruitment: Seeking the truth behind a well-formed CV. *Artificial Intelligence Review, 42*(3), 515–528. https://doi.org/10.1007/s10462-013-9414-y

Florkowski, G. W., & Olivas-Luján, M. R. (2006). The diffusion of human-resource information-technology innovations in US and non-US companies. *Personnel Review, 35*(6), 684–710. https://doi.org/10.1108/00483480610702737

Froese, F. J., Sutherland, D., Lee, J. Y., Liu, Y., & Pan, Y. (2019). Challenges for foreign companies in China: Implications for research and practice. *Asian Business & Management, 18*(4), 249–262.

Guenole, N., & Feinzig, S. (2018). *The business case for AI in HR: With insights and tips on getting started*. IBM Smarter Workforce Institute, IBM.

Geyskens, I., Steenkamp, J. B. E., & Kumar, N. (2006). Make, buy, or ally: A transaction cost theory meta-analysis. *Academy of Management Journal, 49*(3), 519–543. https://doi.org/10.5465/amj.2006.21794670

Hair, J. F., Black, W. C., Babin, B. J., & Anderson, R. E. (2014). *Multivariate data analysis* (7th ed.). Pearson Education.

Han, Z., & Froese, F. J. (2010). Recruiting and retaining R&D professionals in China. *International Journal of Technology Management, 51*(2//3/4), 387–408.

Hsu, P. F., Kraemer, K. L., & Dunkle, D. (2006). Determinants of e-business use in US companies. *International Journal of Electronic Commerce, 10*(4), 9–45. https://doi.org/10.2753/JEC1086-4415100401

Jackson, S. E., Schuler, R. S., & Jiang, K. (2014). An aspirational framework for strategic human resource management. *Academy of Management Annals, 8*(1), 1–56. https://doi.org/10.5465/19416520.2014.872335

Kulik, C. T., & Perry, E. L. (2008). When less is more: The effect of devolution on HR's strategic role and construed image. *Human Resource Management, 47*(3), 541–558. https://doi.org/10.1002/hrm.20231

Lambrecht, A., & Tucker, C. (2019). Algorithmic bias? An empirical study of apparent gender-based discrimination in the display of stem career ads. *Management Science, 65*(7), 2966–2981. https://doi.org/10.1287/mnsc.2018.3093

Lee, I. (2011). Modeling the benefit of e-recruiting process integration. *Decision Support Systems, 51*(1), 230–239. https://doi.org/10.1016/j.dss.2010.12.011

Malik, A., Pereira, V., & Budhwar, P. (2020). HRM in the global information technology (IT) industry: Towards multivergent configurations in strategic business partnerships. *Human Resource Management Review*, 100743. doi.org/10.1016/j.hrmr.2020.100743. https://doi.org/10.1016/j.hrmr.2020.100743

Marler, J. H., & Fisher, S. L. (2013). An evidence-based review of e-HRM and strategic human resource management. *Human Resource Management Review, 23*(1), 18–36. https://doi.org/10.1016/j.hrmr.2012.06.002

National Bureau of Statistics (NBS) & China Institute of Standardization (CIS). (2017). *GB/T 4754-2017: Industrial classification for national economic activities*. National Standardization Administration Committee.

Oh, C., Lee, T., Kim, Y., Park, S., Kwon, S., & Suh, B. (2017, May). Us vs. Them: Understanding artificial intelligence technophobia over the Google deepmind challenge match [Paper presentation]. *Proceedings of the 2017 CHI Conference on Human Factors in Computing Systems*, (pp. 2523–2534). ACM.

Oliveira, T., & Martins, M. F. (2010). Understanding e-business adoption across industries in European countries. *Industrial Management & Data Systems, 110*(9), 1337–1354.

Ransbotham, S., Kiron, D., Gerbert, P., & Reeves, M. (2017). Reshaping business with artificial intelligence: Closing the gap between ambition and action. *MIT Sloan Management Review, 59*(1), 1–17.

Rao, D. A. S., & Verweij, G. (2017). *Sizing the prize: What's the real value of AI for your business and how can you capitalise?* PwC Publication.

Rogers, E. (2003). *The diffusion of innovations* (5th ed.). The Free Press.

Son, J. Y., Narasimhan, S., & Riggins, F. J. (2005). Effects of relational factors and channel climate on EDI usage in the customer-supplier relationship. *Journal of Management Information Systems, 22*(1), 321–353. https://doi.org/10.1080/07421222.2003.11045839

Strohmeier, S. (2007). Research in e-HRM: Review and implications. *Human Resource Management Review, 17*(1), 19–37. https://doi.org/10.1016/j.hrmr.2006.11.002

Suen, H. Y., Chen, M. Y. C., & Lu, S. H. (2019). Does the use of synchrony and artificial intelligence in video interviews affect interview ratings and applicant attitudes?*Computers in Human Behavior, 98*, 93–101. https://doi.org/10.1016/j.chb.2019.04.012

Sutcliffe, K. M., & Zaheer, A. (1998). Uncertainty in the transaction environment: An empirical test. *Strategic Management Journal, 19*(1), 1–23. https://doi.org/10.1002/(SICI)1097-0266(199801)19:1<1::AID-SMJ938>3.0.CO;2-5

Tambe, P., Cappelli, P., & Yakubovich, V. (2019). Artificial intelligence in human resources management: Challenges and a path forward. *California Management Review, 61*(4), 15–42. https://doi.org/10.1177/0008125619867910

Tornatzky, L., & Fleischer, M. (1990). *The process of technology innovation.* Lexington Books.

Van Esch, P., Black, J. S., & Ferolie, J. (2019). Marketing AI recruitment: The next phase in job application and selection. *Computers in Human Behavior, 90*, 215–222. https://doi.org/10.1016/j.chb.2018.09.009

Wang, Y. M., Wang, Y. S., & Yang, Y. F. (2010). Understanding the determinants of RFID adoption in the manufacturing industry. *Technological Forecasting and Social Change, 77*(5), 803–815. https://doi.org/10.1016/j.techfore.2010.03.006

Williamson, O. E. (1989). Transaction cost economics. In R.Schmalensee & R. D.Willig (Eds.), *Handbook of industrial organization* (Vol. 1, pp. 135–182). Elsevier Science.

Zhou, Y., Liu, G., Chang, X., & Hong, Y. (2021). Top-down, bottom-up or outside-in? An examination of triadic mechanisms on firm innovation in Chinese firms. *Asian Business & Management, 20*, 131–162. https://doi.org/10.1057/s41291-019-00085-z

Zhu, K., Kraemer, K. L., & Xu, S. (2006). The process of innovation assimilation by companies in different countries: A technology diffusion perspective on e-business. *Management Science, 52*(10), 1557–1576. https://doi.org/10.1287/mnsc.1050.0487

Zhu, K., Dong, S., Xu, S. X., & Kraemer, K. L. (2006). Innovation diffusion in global contexts: Determinants of post-adoption digital transformation of European companies. *European Journal of Information Systems, 15*(6), 601–616. https://doi.org/10.1057/palgrave.ejis.3000650

Appendix: Multi-item measures

		Items	Source
AI usage	AI1	Attract candidates	Hsu et al. (2006); Zhu, Dong, et al. (2006)
	AI2	Communicate with candidates	
	AI3	Evaluate candidates	
Relative advantage	RA1	Using AI technology improves our recruitment performance	Autry et al. (2010)
	RA2	Using AI technology enhances our recruitment effectiveness	
	RA3	Using AI technology increases our recruitment ability	
Complexity	CO1	AI tools are clear and understandable	Autry et al. (2010)
	CO2	Interacting with AI tools does not require much mental effort	
	CO3	The AI tool we use in our company is easy to use	
	CO4	It is easy to get AI technology to do what we want it to do	
Technology competence	TC1	The technology infrastructure of our company is available for supporting AI tools.	Wang et al. (2010)
	TC2	Our company is dedicated to ensuring that HR employees are familiar with AI tools.	
	TC3	Our company contains a high level of AI tool knowledge.	
Regulatory environment	RE1	The use of the AI was driven by incentives provided by the government.	Zhu, Kraemer, et al. (2006)
	RE2	The use of the AI was required by government procedure	
	RE3	Business laws support AI usage.	
	RE4	There is adequate legal protection for AI usage	
Asset specificity	AS1	Our company has made significant investments in resources dedicated to conduct recruitment with AI	Son et al. (2005)
	AS2	Our operating process has been tailored to meet the requirements of dealing with AI recruitment	
	AS3	The procedures and routines we have developed as part of our AI recruitment are tailored to AI's particular situation.	
	AS4	Training our people to deal with AI recruitment has involved substantial commitments of time and money.	
Uncertainty	UN1	We can accurately predict the company budget spending on AI technologies for the next year.	Son et al. (2005)
	UN2	We can accurately predict the technological feature of AI tools for the next year.	
	UN3	We can accurately predict the volume of AI usage for the next year.	
The degree of change for HR involvement	HR1	HR function/unit in overall responsibility.	Kulik and Perry (2008)
	HR2	The degree of HR practices' integration with the operation of the organization's units.	
	HR3	HR's involvement in organizational strategic planning.	

May the bots be with you! Delivering HR cost-effectiveness and individualised employee experiences in an MNE

Ashish Malik, Pawan Budhwar, Charmi Patel and N. R. Srikanth

ABSTRACT

Using an in-depth qualitative case study design, focusing on a significant global technology consulting multinational enterprise's (MNEs) subsidiary in India, this research analyses interview, documentary and observational data for insights on the proliferation of artificial intelligence (AI) in human resource management (HRM). By developing HRM-focused, AI-enabled applications, the MNE improved HR cost-effectiveness and offered a hyper-personalised and individualised employee experiences. Employing the theoretical lenses of individualisation of HRM practices, AI-mediated social exchange, job signalling and person-organisation fit theories, this research explains employees' experience of HRM practices and its impact on their attitudes and behaviours. Ten interviews were conducted with global technology leaders, champions of innovation, senior HR leaders and employees, including those engaged in the design and implementation of HR-focused AI applications. Findings suggest the use of AI-enabled bots, virtual, digital and personal assistants for carrying out a range of HRM tasks, such as routine, analytical, interactional and communicative tasks involving employees. A diverse set of HRM-focussed AI applications operant at this MNE contributed to its HR cost-effectiveness and enhanced the overall employee experience, thereby resulting in improved levels of employee commitment, satisfaction and reduced employee turnover behaviour. Implications for research and practice are also discussed.

Artificial intelligence (AI) and new technologies are disrupting the way work, worker and the workplace are conceptualised (Malik et al., 2020; Reinhard et al., 2016). This research focuses on the nature and extent of AI usage in HRM and its impact on work, worker and the workplace.

In simple terms, AI, "in business refers to the development of intelligent machines or computerised systems that can learn, react and perform activities like humans for a range of tasks" (Malik et al., 2020, p. 3). The proliferation of AI-based solutions in business processes, reducing employee costs, enhancing customer engagement, job satisfaction, and employee experience is increasingly gaining prominence (Bughin et al., 2017; Faliagka et al., 2014; Guenole & Feinzig, 2018).

This interest has led to a proliferation of scholarship on AI in HRM in the recent call for papers in premier HRM journals (Budhwar & Malik, 2020a, 2020b). This increasing uptake of AI-focused HRM scholarship has pervaded the sub-functional domains of HRM, such as using AI in talent acquisition (Upadhyay & Khandelwal, 2018), video interviews (McColl & Michelotti, 2019), human-and-robot psychological contracts (Bankins & Formosa, 2020), training and development (Maity, 2019), team composition and performance evaluation (Andrejczuk, 2018), talent predictions (Jantan et al., 2010) and coaching (Stavrou et al., 2007).

Despite the above interest and claims regarding the extent to which AI adoption in HRM will impact work, worker and the workplace, scholars have noted limitations, such as 'complexity of the HR phenomena, small data, ethical and legal constraints, and employee reactions to AI management' (Tambe et al., 2019: p.21). This concern is often attributed to the small data size, a limited number of data points and lack of diversity in data, which leads to issues of biases and ethical issues. Nevertheless, a promising stream of research at the interface of AI-HRM has begun exploring how AI can enable higher levels of employee engagement (Hughes et al., 2019) and return significant savings in HRM costs through interactive AI applications. This line of thinking is evident as employees are experiencing HRM practices through a range of HR-focussed AI applications.

Despite the intuitive logic and appeal, there is limited understanding of how employees experience HRM practices through an AI-mediated exchange using AI applications, such as intelligent Bots, humanoids or indeed some other AI-enabled HRM applications. It is also not clear whether such an exchange is cost-effective and improves employee and HR business outcomes. It is, therefore, essential to undertake further research in this currently neglected area of scholarship. Given the emerging nature of scholarship, this study contributes by engaging in an in-depth, qualitative case analysis of a large global technology consulting MNE. This MNE is engaged in the design and delivery of AI applications and technology solutions. Therefore, we analyse how an AI-mediated exchange between humans and machines affects employee experience of

HR practices and impacts HR and employee outcomes. In doing so, this study contributes to the current trilogy of human-to-human experience of HRM practices: i.e. the design of intended HRM policy choices, enactment of these HR policy choices by managers and employees' experience of these policies (Nishii & Wright, 2008) to include an AI-mediated social exchange of employees' experience of HRM practices.

Through this research, we analyse how employees experience intended and enacted practices first-hand, through an AI-mediated technology platform and its potential impact on employees' behaviours and attitudes. Extant research suggests there is limited understanding of how this occurs in the context of HRM and AI and how individualisation of work practices is enabled through an AI-mediated exchange. Limited studies have focused on idiosyncratic deals between managers and employees to gain employee differentiation, motivation, commitment and performance through individualised HRM practices (Anand et al., 2010; Hornung et al., 2008). To the best of our knowledge, no prior study has investigated the impact of individualised HRM practices using an AI-mediated social exchange.

Therefore, by focusing on the dyadic and interactive communications between the employees and the HR-focused AI-applications (e.g. through bots, virtual, digital or personal assistants), this research posits that firms may deliver a better employee experience and such research can further improve our understanding of the relationship between the espoused, enacted and technology-mediated experience of HRM practices by employees. The communicative and interactional nature of HRM-focused AI-applications that employees experience, we argue, is well-placed to deliver personalised, hyper-personalised and individualised HRM practices, which, until now were offered as aggregated HRM practices to select talents or talented groups of employees.

In line with calls for adopting a multidisciplinary approach for studying AI and its impact on HRM, to unbundle how social relations and human-technology interface occurs (Fountaine et al., 2019; Tecuci, 2012), this research draws insights from multiple theoretical lenses, such as individualisation of HRM practices (De Leede et al., 2004; Glassner & Keune, 2012), social exchange theory and its newly coined variant, AI-mediated social exchange theory (Blau, 1964; Ma & Brown, 2020), signalling theory (Casper & Harris, 2008) to explain individual differences (Motowildo et al., 1997; Underwood, 1975) and the need to achieve a strong person-organisation fit (Kristof, 1996; Verquer et al., 2003). Such an approach will help understand if and how it leads to HR cost-effectiveness and better attitudinal and behavioural outcomes for employees. This paper argues that through AI-bots and applications, employees receive signals in the form of an organisation's intent to offer personalised, hyper-personalised and individualised HRM experiences. An employee's subjective experience and behaviour is a function of their interactions with the work environment (Fiske & Taylor, 1991). The higher the congruence between an individual's values and goals and their work environment, a stronger person-organisation fit is likely (Kristof, 1996). A high level of person-organisation fit has been associated with higher levels of job satisfaction and commitment and low levels of intention to quit. Thus, in line with the fundamental tenets of social exchange theory (Blau, 1964), or its emerging variant, AI-mediated exchange theory (Ma & Brown, 2020), employees are more likely to reciprocate their positive experience of interacting with AI-enabled HRM applications with an increased level of job satisfaction, commitment and reduced turnover intentions (Bal et al., 2013). Specifically, this paper seeks to answer the following two research questions:

1. What is the nature and extent of influence of AI-enabled HRM applications on HRM cost-effectiveness?
2. How does employees' experience of AI-mediated HRM practices influence employee attitudes and behaviours?

By addressing these questions, this study contributes by being the first to explore employee experiences of AI-mediated HRM practices. Second, it explores whether the move from employee experiences of a policy-oriented and adherence-focused generalised HRM practices to an AI-mediated experience of personalised, hyper-personalised and individualised HRM practices leads to improvements in employee experience and HR effectiveness. Finally, this research contributes by developing a conceptual framework for understanding the relationship between employees' subjective experiences of AI-mediated experience of HRM practices on HR effectiveness and employee's attitudinal and behavioural outcomes.

Given the exploratory nature of research and a relatively underdeveloped state of theory concerning the impact of AI-mediated experiences of HRM practices on HR cost-effectiveness and individual outcomes, an in-depth qualitative case study is considered as an appropriate research strategy. To overcome the limitations highlighted by Tambe et al. (2019), we purposively selected an extensive global technology consulting MNE, which has a significant subsidiary presence in India. Further, most cutting-edge design and development of AI applications is undertaken by sizeable global technology MNEs. Therefore, our choice of an MNE that specialises in developing solutions for numerous industries using disruptive technologies, such as AI, blockchain and augmented and virtual reality is relevant here. The sheer size and diversity of operations of this MNE designed, developed and the number of AI applications it has implemented, not just for its clients globally, but also for its internal HRM function and HR employees, globally and locally has helped overcomes some of the limitations highlighted by Tambe et al. (2019). Further, this MNE also presents a fertile ground for contemporaneously studying the adoption of AI applications at the workplace.

The rest of the paper is organised as follows. First, it begins by reviewing the relevant literature at the interface of AI and HRM, followed by the analysis of literature on individualisation of HRM practices, relevant theories and its impact on the employee experience in terms of their attitudes and behaviours. Next, details of the research methodology, case insights and analysis of employees' experience of HRM practices through AI-enabled applications that were designed, developed and implemented by this large MNE are presented. A discussion of the findings follows, and we conclude with limitations and implications for research and practice.

Literature review

From generalisation to individualisation of HRM practices

Employee's experience of work and HRM varies across sectors and occupations. For example, in the services sector, contextual factors such as work design, age and gender affect employee experience and business outcomes. For instance, high-performance work systems in age care settings had a positive influence on employee experience (Harley et al., 2007). Whereas, it had a negative impact in specific low-skill service contexts (Berg & Frost, 2006), including those involving aesthetic labour in the hospitality service roles (Warhurst & Nickson, 2007) and lean working environments in the healthcare services (Carter et al., 2013). In a related stream of research, employee experience can be significantly enhanced by focusing on personalisation and individualisation of employees' experience of HRM practices.

The HRM function and HR leaders and managers have started focusing on offering personalised and individualised HR practices to individual employees. Such practices are a departure from existing strands of literature on strategic HRM and talent management (Collings & Mellahi, 2009; Narayanan et al., 2019), which focus on offering a differentiated set of HRM practices targeting select groups of employees (Delery & Doty, 1996), or offering a differentiated HR architecture (Becker et al., 2009) to accommodate the differences in values and uniqueness of human capital employed. Individualised HRM, is a form of a personalised or hyper-personalised HRM approach that is defined as "an HR system where managers have the opportunity and actually use the opportunity to individually negotiate agreements about work arrangements with individual employees … approach individualised HRM as HR programmes that are implemented as HR practices in an organisation" (Bal & Dorenbosch, 2015, p. 43). Such HR practices are designed to not only retain and attract talent but also to use individualisation of HRM practices to offer a positive employee experience. An earlier version of individualised HRM approaches focused on idiosyncratic deals and employment contracts offered by managers to individual employees (Hornung et al., 2009). The inconsistency in employee experience levels can be explained, in part, due to the numerous contextual factors at play, such as age, gender, strategy, leader-member exchange quality and design and effectiveness of the HRM practices (Bal et al., 2013; De Leede et al., 2007; Morf et al., 2019). This calls for further research on a range of contextual factors affecting employees' experience of HRM practices. One such emerging contextual factor is the role of disruptive technologies, such as AI, and its impact on the design and implementation of personalised and individualised employee experiences of HRM practices.

Social exchange, person-organisation fit and employee experience

The social exchange theory suggests that a social exchange between people typically leads to economic and social outcomes between two or more parties (Blau, 1964), through the underlying norms of reciprocity. As evidenced in earlier studies on individualised HRM practices, employees tend to exhibit better performance, attitudinal and behavioural outcomes in return for receiving individualised and personalised HRM considerations. This line of thinking overlaps with the ideas espoused in the person-organisation (P-O) fit theory (Kristof, 1996; Verquer et al., 2003). The P-O fit theory suggests that employees' social behaviour at work is a function of employees' interactional psychological experiences based on the congruence or compatibility of their values and goals and an organisation's socio-technical and relational work environment (Morley, 2007). As a sub-set of the P-O fit, person-job fit, person-vocation fit, and person-person and person-group fits are distinct building blocks of employees' alignment and overall fit with the organisation (Morley, 2007). In Kristof's (1996) review, she referred P-O fit as achieving compatibility with the organisation and its environment such that there is a sense of mutuality between the individual and work organisation. Employees' P-O fit can act as an antecedent to their perceived social exchange (Kim et al., 2013). Most organisations aim to influence attitudes and direct employee behaviours, whereas employees tend to employ their values and goals in guiding their choices for participating in an activity or shaping their attitude towards an object (Kim et al., 2013). Several studies have found that P-O fit has a positive impact on job satisfaction, commitment and employees' decreased intention to quit (Kristof-Bowen et al., 2005).

Further, as Argyris (1964) suggested, organisations should try and restructure their work and practices, so employees develop a sense of perceived control over their decision-making, thereby reducing incongruence or enhancing the person-organisation fit. A fundamental logic of social exchange is mutuality and reciprocity, therefore, as recipients of individualised and personalised experiences of HRM practices and increased values and goals congruence of working in a particular type of organisation, employees are likely to exhibit higher levels of job satisfaction, commitment at work and are less likely to engage in quit behaviour. Despite support for the benefits of individualisation of HRM practices, through personalised contracts and idiosyncratic deals, the effects on employee outcomes are equivocal (Hornung et al., 2008). To this end, this research focuses on a recent extension of the social exchange theory, which attempts to explore an AI-mediated interactional exchange, using both generalised and direct exchanges, such that AI applications serve as mediators of the social exchange between humans and machines (e.g. AI applications and Bots). Most AI applications are autonomous, and like humans, can exercise their agency and affect the environment in which they operate (Ma & Brown, 2020). Such an exchange is likely to create a different type of P-O fit wherein the AI applications are part of the socio-technical system.

Individualisation, AI-mediated exchanges and employee experience

Recent developments and advances in the adoption and implementation of AI-enabled HRM applications has led to increases in employee's experience of HRM practices through an AI-mediated exchange, especially in large MNEs. The proliferation of these practices is high within the services industry. For example, in call centres and customer experience management services, many Bots and interactive intelligent virtual assistants have been deployed alongside employees in client-facing roles for boosting productivity, enhancing customer and employee experience by allowing the Bots to focus on routine and rule-based tasks (Gustavsson, 2005; Imrie & Bednar, 2013). Within the HRM function, numerous AI Bots and virtual agents interact with employees or prospective candidates for evaluating and shortlisting candidate profiles. These AI-mediated exchanges offer transparency, objectivity and enhance current and prospective employee's experience of, for example, the recruitment and selection processes (HR Recruiting, 2016). The trend of personalisation is also gaining prominence in other HR sub-domains through a range of AI-enabled HR applications, such as in training and development (Whiteside, 2019), coaching (Barney, 2018), performance management (BasuMallick, 2019) and a range of routine administrative HR query handling tasks (Haak, 2019).

Individualisation, AI and HR cost-effectiveness

The direct and indirect economic benefits of AI adoption in organisations is well documented (Faliagka et al., 2014; Fan et al., 2012). For example, IBM alone saved US$107 million in HR costs through the design and implementation of several AI applications across its network of subsidiaries around the globe (Guenole & Feinzig, 2018). There are many more examples of both Indian and global MNEs such as Hitachi (Takamoto & Owada, 2018), Convergys, Infosys, Wipro, Amazon and Microsoft who have actively designed and implemented a range of AI applications within the sub-domain of HRM and deployed the same across their subsidiary operations. Using deep and cognitive learning algorithms and diversity of data from a range of the subsidiary operations, significant cost savings and improved employee outcomes are among the key benefits that have been realised by large MNEs.

Based on the above analysis of the theoretical streams of literature, we argue that employees' experience of hyper-personalisation and individualisation of HRM practices through HRM focused AI applications creates an AI-mediated social exchange between individuals and the AI applications. If such experiences are positive, the AI-mediated exchange may invoke reciprocity by humans in the form of increased satisfaction at work, more significant commitment towards the organisation and a reduced intention to quit behaviour. Through these attitudinal and behavioural outcomes and overall savings in costs of transactions, the overall HR effectiveness will increase.

Research methodology

Keeping in mind the relatively novel phenomenon of AI adoption in the field of HRM, an in-depth qualitative case study design of an unusually representative and revelatory case was considered appropriate (Yin, 2003). A single-case, in-depth case study allows for a rich exploration of the real-life phenomenon under investigation, especially if the case design involves data collection from multiple sources and levels (Siggelkow, 2007). Such a design is appropriate if the nature of the phenomenon to be investigated is relatively new and focuses on particular groups of employees (Yin, 2003). In this research, interviews, observational and secondary data from multiple hierarchal levels in the case organisation were collected and analysed. Further, for understanding the impact HRM-focused AI applications on employee and HR level outcomes, this in-depth case design is appropriate. Selecting a revelatory and critical case is therefore essential. In this research, we selected the case study of a large IT MNE specialising in the design and development of AI-enabled applications for all functional areas of a business, serving a range of clients globally. Such a case is rich in insights, not just about the development of AI applications, but also its use and users' experiences of these AI applications. Getting access to data from an innovative AI and IT applications MNC subsidiary operating in India, one that actively engages in the co-development of AI applications with clients globally, is unique and revelatory. As such, conducting in-depth interviews and the analysis of other data makes this an exemplary case. Such an approach is also suggested for undertaking theory-building efforts and identifying theoretical contributions (Corley & Gioia, 2011; Malik et al., 2019; Thomas et al., 2011; Whetten, 1989).

Research context and case organisation

This research was undertaken in a massive global IT MNE's subsidiary operation in India's IT industry. The Indian IT and business process management industry has revenues exceeding US$190 billion and is estimated to clock revenues of US$350 billion by 2025. It continues to attract steady foreign direct investment, employs more than 1 million people and serves a formidable list of Fortune 500 global firms (IBEF, 2020). India is a country of extreme diversity in terms of income, education and technology adoption profiles. Even though there are high illiteracy rates in several parts of the country, several schools are utilising emerging technologies, such as AI, robots and humanoids in schools (Ullas, 2019). Indeed the uptake of advanced AI and robotics technologies are not confined to education and technology firms, it is gradually finding its place in social venues such as restaurants, though such novelty is fast wearing out (Raman, 2018).

Doing business in a diverse, fast-growth, and a culturally complex Indian business environment presents a fertile ground for researchers to contemporaneously analyse the contextual influences at play in terms of technological change and industry growth (Budhwar et al., 2019). Specifically, in the last three decades or so, India has consolidated its position as a centre for global innovation hubs and is ranked 57th on

INSEAD's Global Innovation Index, has the most extensive and growing talent pool of technically qualified digital talent pool and is pegged to be the fourth largest applications economy (Malik et al., 2021; NASSCOM, 2020). As an emerging market economy, Indian business and firms and institutions are transitioning to manage the changes and growth imperatives (Malik & Pereira, 2016; Pereira & Malik, 2015). Industry and skill development taskforces established by the businesses associations such as NASSCOM and the Government of India's Digital India initiatives in business and education has ensured a steady supply of technically qualified graduates. However, only time will tell whether the responses can keep up with the rate and scale of skill obsolescence and technological change.

Data were purposively collected from the MNE's subsidiary operation in India. This case organisation is at the cutting-edge of designing and developing AI applications, not just in the HRM domain, but also in services, marketing, finance, customer support and several other functional fields. The MNE's enormous size, a vast global geographical base of subsidiaries and its application and deployment of several AI-enabled HRM applications across multi-country locations makes this case unusually revelatory and suited for an emerging international scenario in the field.

Furthermore, leading innovations in offering AI-applications such as chatbots, smart bots, intelligent assistants, digital and personal assistants for its clients as well as its internal employees places this MNE in a unique position to access data and insights, which otherwise may not have been possible in an end-user or a client organisation. This case is exceptionally unique and revelatory because more than 75% of its employees are individual contributors to the design and development of AI applications for the business and their customers around the globe. So, as active users and designers of AI applications for HRM and other functional areas, this case site offers an opportunity to explore rich contextual data that would have otherwise not been possible. The choice of this case is relevant for international HRM (IHRM) research as it allows us to contemporaneously study the impact of its parent company HRM policies and how these are diffused to global subsidiaries using HRM-focused AI-mediated exchanges between employees and the Bots. From an IHRM perspective, this case also provides evidence of how it incorporates cultural and ideological business diversity in the design and implementation of HRM-focused AI applications seamlessly, through collaborative cross-border, inter-functional co-development teams for building AI applications. Finally, given the size and scale of operations of this MNE, the limitations of small databases and a lack of diversity in input data for developing HRM Bots and applications as highlighted by Tambe et al. (2019) is less of an issue.

Data collection

The primary source of data collection was qualitative interviews of senior technology, functional and business leaders, heads of AI project teams who are intimately involved in the design and implementation of AI-enabled HRM applications, as well as employees who are users and developers of these applications. A total of 10 in-depth interviews, lasting approximately a total of 10 h with employees and managers were conducted in 2019, at various locations of the MNE's subsidiary operations in India. Organisational documents, such as white papers, organisational value and leadership competency framework and case studies of various client testimonials for use and development of AI applications were analysed. Additionally, other publicly available data such as data from the case organisation's website, its HR policies on its intranet and actual visual and audio observation of two HRM-focused AI-applications in use at the MNE were analysed to understand what the end-users see and how they experience the end-user interface. In order to ensure the confidentiality of the case organisation and its proprietary Bots and humanoids, this paper uses pseudonyms. In addition to analysing organisational documents and observing the functionality of two HR-focused AI applications or Bots, the interviews were transcribed using an AI-bot and then edited for accuracy. Approximately 81,000 words of interview data were analysed.

Data analysis

Based on the analysis of transcripts, first-order coding was undertaken for identifying key concepts and themes. Following the identification and verification of the first-order concepts, a theoretically informed manual coding, employing abductive logic was followed (Gioia et al., 2013; Van Maanen et al., 2007). The data analysis was iteratively conducted by going back and forth between the first-order concepts and second-order themes for theoretical understanding, Based on our analysis of the data, we developed a conceptual framework for understanding how employees' experience of AI-mediated exchange of HRM practices leads to better individual and HR outcomes. Following Yin's (2003) replication logic, only themes that had three or more observations in the data have been included in the analysis. Our analysis found that the MNE's framework of espoused HRM practices and employees value congruence with the same sets the tone for a person-organisation fit. However, the employees' perceptions of HRM practices is enabled through an AI-mediated exchange, which offers employees highly personalised and individualised experience. In this study's context, a favourable P-O fit can lead to a positive AI-mediated exchange, given such an exchange allows for

Table 1. Demographic details of interviewees.

Level in the Organisation	Interviewee Code	Gender	Work Experience in years Total Career Experience (Experience at the Case Organisation)
Senior HR Leader	R1	Male	30 (7)
Middle HR Manager	R2	Male	15 (5)
Senior Innovation Leader	R3	Male	28 (18)
Frontline Team Lead	R4	Female	8 (4)
Employee	R5	Female	5 (2)
Employee	R6	Male	4 (1)
Senior Leader	R7	Male	25+(10)
Senior Leader	R8	Male	30+ (5)
Subject Matter Expert	R9	Male	25 (10)
Associate Team Lead	R10	Male	10 (8)

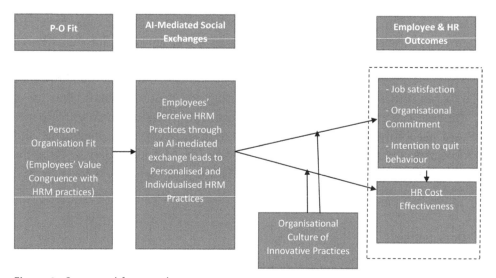

Figure 1. Conceptual framework.

personalisation, hyper-personalisation and individualisation of employees' experience of HRM practices. This AI-mediated social exchange connects the employees P-O fit to their attitudinal and behavioural outcomes. Through better, attitudinal and behavioural outcomes of job satisfaction, organisational commitment, and a reduced intention to quit supported the cost-effectiveness of the HR function. Finally, we also found that the presence of an organisational culture of innovative practices further impacts the relationship between an AI-mediated social exchange and employee and HR outcomes. We specify these relationships in our guiding conceptual framework (see Figure 1). A distinctive contribution of our conceptual framework lies in identifying an AI-mediated exchange as a critical mechanism for explaining the relationship between employees' P-O fit and their attitudinal and behavioural outcomes as well as HR cost-effectiveness. Further, we argue that a culture of innovative work practices moderates this relationship.

Analysis and key findings

Person-organisation fit with HRM practices

There was sufficient evidence of an individual's value and goal congruence with the MNE's espoused HRM practices. Several employees highlighted the fit and alignment they had with the organisational values of innovation and their goals, leading to a good fit.

> It's all about my experience. My experience of a working environment, non-monetary is okay, [it is] something not extrinsic, which is intrinsic, how we perceive it. [R5]

> So, I've never felt like I said that's why I'm happy all here. I've had a very good experience over. [R4]

> ... but I think [this MNE] is pretty innovative and I think is one of the first companies to come up with a facility for innovation ... a state-of-the-art facility like cutting edge and the experience itself is mind-blowing. [R6]

However, this was further mediated by the AI-mediated social exchange of employees' perceived experience of personalised and individualised HRM practices through AI-enabled HRM-focused applications. An example of such interactive and communicative chat experience is illustrated below by observing and recording a human-machine (PBOT) social exchange:

> Employee: When is the next long weekend in Bengaluru?

> PBOT: Let's go over this. Planning a vacation, are we? It is a great thing. The next long weekend begins around Varalakshmi [a festival] for the upcoming holiday, from 9th August in Bangalore, till Monday 12th. Would you like to plan it?

> Employee: Yes, Okay. I can do this.

> PBOT: All right.

> Employee: So PBOT, what is my leave balance

> PBOT: I see you are currently having 33.17 days of leave and is escalating, I've received your fortnightly vacation plan. You have crossed your 30-day [leave] ceiling. Perhaps, you should consider taking a vacation that you always wanted. When? [R1]

AI-mediated social exchanges: better employee experience and HR cost-effectiveness

The MNE has developed several HRM-focused AI applications, such as one-directional and bi-directional chatbots, interactive, smart, virtual or digital assistants and even digital personal assistants, for helping employees experience HRM practices through these AI-mediated social exchanges. From an HR cost-effectiveness perspective, the focus is to free up HR resource time from mundane, routine, high-transaction processing and rule-based information transactions for complex advisory and problem-solving activities. There is a clear focus to from move away from adherence and policy-focused, generic HRM practices to one that can be personalised and individualised to each employee. Through AI, this is possible by integrating existing information from across roles and employee-specific data that is then available for machines to learn from and propose solutions and undertake problem-solving.

Through the use of HRM-focussed AI applications, the MNE has moved away from an adherence-based HRM, which typically focused on the generalisation of HRM practices for the broader set of employees to offer more personalised and hyper-personalised HRM practices through to individualised HRM practices. An example of generalised HRM practice of on-boarding and placing people is where an engineer trainee, typically starts at the introductory level 1 of their employment. However, the Bot or the virtual candidate experience chatbot, through its deep and cognitive learning algorithms, and interactive and communicative approaches can recommend a more personalised HRM experience of the practice in terms of the right staffing level, salary fitment, training and other HRM processes, based on various parameters and attributes that an employee or a trainee may have inputted into the system. From personalisation to hyper-personalisation, it would require going a step further by recommending one or more pathways for further skills training and projects that an employee may be more fitting to, keeping in mind the employee's current profile and interest registered, in an expressed area of future career growth. It depends on employees whether or not they individualise these pathways by exercising their choices. These actions and activities happen in all sub-domains of HRM and through the deployment of various virtual, digital and personal assistants and chatbots, which have varying levels of capabilities.

Given that more than 85% of the population employed at this MNE are Generation Y and Z employees, these employees are required to work on a range of information and communication technologies for developing IT applications for their clients and parent firm locations globally. Given the tech-savvy nature of their work, their uptake of and interactions with AI-enabled applications is significant and, as our data analysis suggests, it leads to a range of positive outcomes, such as improved employee experience through an AI-mediated social exchange. However, some of the more complex human-machine experiences are supported in the back-end, using a human (HR practitioner). The volume of traffic that is handled by a personalised bot or assistant ([PBOT], a pseudonym for a bot) has undoubtedly resulted in significant cost savings through a reduced HR headcount:

> ... close to 1,00,000 employees are on the platform running it and PBOT has dealt with 11,000 questions with 81 per cent accuracy and 500 people are on ... at any given time you have ... . we have received about 19,400 queries per month from 2100 unique users ... if I have a team of 15 people they could see here are the 15 people, and this is Ashish's vacation plans, and then we go back to your Microsoft Project and see what the deliverables are that ... could get impacted if you are going on a vacation. .... [The Bot will prompt] by the way, have you spoken to your supervisor? [R1]

The various AI applications in the form of PBOTs, digital assistants and other conversational and analytical and predictive bots are developed at this Indian subsidiary as well as at different locations, including the MNE's global headquarters. These bots service each of the sub-functional areas of HRM and have received positive employee experiences, which helps in retaining the talent for extended periods. The following section discusses each of the HRM functional areas, for which this research was able to access, collect and analyse data. A generic term 'Bot' is used here to maintain the confidentiality of the AI applications used in this case organisation.

Recruitment and selection bot

Given the global presence of this MNE and significant annual exposure to recruiting more than 10,000 candidates annually, the presence of a digital recruitment and selection bot was not only necessary for HR cost-effectiveness, but it also served as the first point of contact for internal job postings and job applicants or potential new employees coming into the MNEs recruitment ecosystem. For existing employees, this Bot helps them find existing opportunities within the MNE at different locations that fit in with the employee's performance and career conversations, and other personal skills and competency attributes, thereby delivering a hyper-personalised employee experience.

> You have a chatbot that's encouraging you to look at other opportunities; it prompts the user to engage ... the moment you are applying, I have a chatbot that comes up and sees ... if there's a spot. [It would prompt] that these are ten roles for which your CV is best suited for ... If you are based in Hyderabad, you want this role that you are asking for; it is available ... are you okay to relocate here? Then look at these things [other roles], are you only keen on this role, or would look at or explore other opportunities with [the MNE] ... You may be aspiring to get into a project leader role at a certain career level, with ... the number of years of experience, competency and proficiency ... you ought to be posturing to your CV, it may actually put you in a different career level now if you are posturing for a role that is above or below your career aspirations. If it is below, then it will prompt

and ask whether should I engage with you in this conversation? Ask you why? Because, then you are going to be an ambassador of this interactional experience with the Bot... when you talk and see that this is good ... I actually got to know why I fit into that or chose not to take this route. ... So, the expectation is that six months later if I have another opportunity, I will come back for that same role that I was interested in. [R2]

For the external candidates or new potential employees, the Bot helps the candidates navigate through the system and process more than 50% of the recruitment and selection process as well as proposes each candidate based on their attributes, knowledge skills and experience the kinds of competencies and learnings they need to brush up if they are indeed the preferred candidate.

... a seven-step process. Three and a half steps are virtual, ... even more than 50 to 70 per cent of your entire process is virtual. You just come down for an assessment, and you come down for integration and onboarding. Graduates reach to the pool, have smart interviews, [using] video interview platforms. It could also be that a gamified interview process with questions happens, especially, in the BPO [business process outsourcing] area... where you are focusing on a few areas in terms of learning agility, innovation, creativity, ... this smart interviewer actually becomes much more of a consistent evaluator. We use biometrics - its goal is not for elimination; so, it gives you additional insights. You still rely upon to validate that and then do ... a test assessment in the online baskets. [R1]

There are multiple rationales for the use of Bots in the recruitment and selection process. Quite apart from the high-volume and transaction processing activity that it is used for parsing through tens of thousands of CVs, it serves additional purposes for improved HR effectiveness.

Let's put it this way. It's a transparent process which is visible across. ... What happens in that recruiting process is you don't want too much of human interference during the process. This [Bot] increases the objectivity, makes it transparent and tells the candidate, in our case, that we are high volume recruiting numbers. So, you need to have transparency in what is happening in the process. And it has to have traceability. Knowing [that it is] a human-intervened process, there is always a control point, and therefore, it becomes a process-heavy. When you reimagine, the difference between automation and digitisation, it is how you would imagine the existing process when you reimagine the existing processes. [R1]

Coaching assessment and performance management bot

There is a constant interactive discussion and recommendations exchange between the Bot and the employees on aspects, such as critical competencies, skills gaps and career progression concerning dealing with issues of person-organisation and person-occupation fit.

I'm going to evaluate you for the right fit. The recruiter Bot changes from being a recruiter who was interviewing you for skills, to be a Talent coach who will get into a career conversation for you. What is the right kind of fitment for you? Where does the data fit your aspiration, and how do you go about it? [R10]

The conversation can also extend to advisory aspects of performance, and the Bot makes recommendations for making employee's performance planning and analysis easier.

... this is where [the Bot] picks up information and can always come back and say you haven't completed your ethics compliance courses... quarters have lapsed, by the way, this needs to be completed immediately, as it can impact your performance ... So it's prompting this. It's reminding things, ... so we don't want it to be just to be data assisted. ... As an advisor, what you want to do to move to the next level. And then as advisory services, it can also say we want to reach a point where, if it is acceptable for to you to sign-off. [R1]

Training and development bot and new age skills

Conversation on training and development issues focuses on identifying current and future competency gaps and employee's career aspirations. The Bot can recommend different sets of learning pathways for different roles and the likelihood of future opportunities that are coming up in certain areas, including ones where an employee has low visibility.

They engaged through this Chatbot, I understand a lot more about questions and queries and everything the way what my role is going to be, what is the joining date, what is the kind of opportunity. It can also push information here... the latest [updates] about the MNE in media ... and engaging with them on an online platform to keep them prepared in terms of day to go to a bridging program or a course. In terms of training, so that when they come in, they become relevant on day one [of joining]. That is what we are doing with this. [R2]

There are some generic skills and competencies needed by all HR practitioners working with AI and other disruptive technologies. A general flair for new technology and the ability to embrace it, along with and understanding of how analytics and data science operates. Using the new skills, HR practitioners can offer insights and coach staff and leaders on where and how one needs to reinvent and reimagine themselves or re-coach their team members to deliver on better employee and team member experiences in their use of the new AI applications.

[The] HR skill set of the future is focused on three things: digital savviness, data fluency and coaching. ... So how do you imbibe the principles of coaching? And how do you engage with the candidate to provide them with a clear candidate experience that is superlative. [R1]

Talent supply chain bot

For managing this MNE's hundreds of thousands of talent supply chain, an integrated set of Bots and digital assistants were created to keep track of the movements of stocks of talent and its flows locally and globally and tracking their performance and utilisation rates. For an organisation of this size and scale, the business imperative is to maximise talent utilisation rates and keeping it in the 90% range; however, this is not always possible as some of the client deployments are of a shorter-term and this invariably leads to 'bench time' of about 8-9% for the total talent supply chain. The pace and agility required to deploy and redeploy talent across projects and geographies are critical for delivering the HR function's cost-effectiveness.

> So, there are almost two levels of talent management. One is the influx of employees, but then you either recognise or [make] conscious identification.... what is happening in real-time, [gathering] information around various aspects of it. So, what are these metrics at the top, keeping talent lean. Generally, [manage] your attrition. So, you have to continuously keep tracking that. ... in what all different categories, by skill, by career, by business groups, by diversity, employee age, time etc ... visualisations are done by geography, by demographics, etc. So, like a snapshot, it is almost instantly available. At any given point in time, you have this information. We look at in terms of what's the talent heat map, so on year on year, how many people are moving down that? [R9]

Individualised employee experiences

The adoption of AI applications for different HRM practices has had a positive impact in shaping employee experiences and positively influencing their satisfaction and commitment at work, as well as minimising their intention to quit behaviours. As a technology consulting MNE, the case organisation has recorded a lower than average industry employee turnover rates. Overall, the employees have reported positive experiences with the human-computer interaction. The AI-mediated social exchange has been satisfying to the large millennial population employed by this case organisation. Specifically, various Bots serve diverse sets of queries for the employees as well as the clients that visit this technology consulting firm co-creating innovative AI-based solutions (Table 1).

> And it [the AI applications] actually helps in refining the product experience or finding the innovation experience that you bring to the table. Each day it's a learning for us as well. [R4]

Increased levels of human-machine interactions helped strengthen employee experience and their person-organisation fit. The MNE employs hundreds of thousands of employees, as such employees do tend to feel lost, and therefore, value individualised consideration and experience through AI-mediated social exchanges, which may not be possible in the human-human exchanges. The extent of information processed by various interactive Bots about individual employees' attributes allows hyper-personalisation and individualisation opportunities, which is satisfying for employees.

Because then you [are] going to be an ambassador of this interactional experience for the firm with the Bot ... when you talk and see that this is good ... I actually got to know why I fit into that .... [R10]

Depending on the nature and extent of human-machine interactions, the employee experiences also varied. For example, employees who are frequent users, testers and co-designers of the AI-applications, felt significant improvements in their interactional experiences with the Bots.

... so these all these experiences that PBOT, [and other bots and personal assistants], etc., ... in our design itself we have embedded [feedback] .... That actually instantaneously puts into our backlog of where our focus should be now ... [R6]

The constant improvements in the AI-applications' capabilities have helped employees enhance their problem-solving and interactional experience better.

If you feel there is a new problem, let us know that this is what is the basis, so you get plenty to crystallise and figure out what matters to employees because at the end of the day the antidote is to how can we make employee experience better. ... Are we getting enough input for that? Let's look up to the new technology. [R5]

Organisational culture of innovative practices

Sufficient evidence exists for a culture of innovation at this large MNE. As part of employees' work targets and activities, there was an explicit requirement for most roles to deliver technological innovations using a range of disruptive technologies, while others aspired to achieve innovations or claim patents against their names. This culture of innovation was supported by a robust set of intrinsic and extrinsic rewards. Given the organisation's size, gaining visibility by individuals to meet their inherent needs to stand out in this MNE becomes a significant driver for undertaking innovative projects, delivering proofs of concepts and seeking sponsors and resources to carry out these projects. The innovation ecosystem supports multiple forms of activities, such as ranging from individual AI technology teams to co-development and co-creation with the clients.

One is the disruption to create leadership in an area. So, there's pretty clear [mandate for] value co-creation in innovation ... ... Co-innovation with the client, it's a powerful story. ... So, hear me out, a lot of the lay of the land and how it looks like. So, it's good for business. Yes, [its] good for people. There are these two categories ... [We've] got some 40,000 ideas [last year] and get it down to maybe 6 or 7. And it's funny that you also get US$2,000 for those who develop a prototype. So, that's part of the formal extrinsic reward. [R3]

The culture of innovation and the innovation landscape in India has transformed significantly:

> *Look ... look. The world has changed. Initially, most of the offshore centres were more of a cost centre, right? We had to deliver... versus now, where we deliver, but we also sell, end-to-end. And to be fair, that's where most of the offshore centres are today. It's no longer offshore; it's more than nearshore right. So, the way India was 25, 30 years back ... the IT industry itself ... things have changed. Now with the Global Innovation Centres coming in, right, each of our clients has their captive centres [here in India]. ... Right from being a back-end, where you take the requirements, to you deliver. You are now spending more time with your clients.* [R3]

With the changing landscape, the focus at this subsidiary is to empower and enable the clients to co-create in their science and technology labs, look at the ecosystem of other products and services that this MNE has created, and then the clients can see how some of these ideas may be relevant to their workplaces:

> *So, it's about, co-working, right? Humans and machines neither are a threat to anybody. How do you co-exist? Leverage each other... That's where things are progressing, and you would know a lot about how the AI is happening, AI is good for good data and bad for bad data. We keep discussing it, but the reality is people want things to change the world needs to be more open. Need to be more pragmatic, ... more social, ... more networked, in terms of looking ahead into the future.* [R7]

The possibilities for innovation at the Indian subsidiary's innovation hub have provided clients and employees with new ideas and a more profound commitment to developing AI-enabled products and services:

> *Let me quote a use case ... When we bring in our high-stake clientele in our organisation to walk through, what we show them is how a humanoid can do the job of a front office. I'm breaking it down by the use case, which will be easier for you to understand. He walks into the organisation, and there is a humanoid... that welcomes him. In the past, that would be a humanoid, which was only talking one-directional. Well, [now] we have a humanoid which talks bi-directional ... talk to you because they must understand what you're saying... it reciprocates you. ... Clearing your badging process, hands you over [the badge], and then there is a persona which is walking the client through without a human touch within this organisation. I'm just giving you a simple use case of that. So, think about the word when you as Ashish is coming in as a client. ... You have a humanoid walking with you, and after that point forgets the human eye, there is a persona which is walking you through the facility. That's a reality. It's something that's happening right now. We did this for many of our clients.* [R3]

Employees working here have widely expressed excitement (rather than fear) of the opportunities they perceive and the innovations they can develop with their teams and clients at this organisation. Therefore, affiliation motivation and an appreciation of internal AI-based functional applications, including, those for the HRM domain are often looked at as opportunities for teams. People self-nominate and request membership and affiliation for various development teams for working on such AI-applications for the MNE's business needs. It would be interesting to contrast these experiences with a user firm's employee experience of AI-mediated exchange of HRM practices or from a subsidiary or division of the MNE where such high-end innovative work is not undertaken.

Additional theme: AI and ethical issues

The adoption of AI and algorithmic management at the workplace is not free from ethical, moral and legal issues (Duggan et al., 2020). While there was no data that would suggest legal and moral breaches, the informants at the case organisation acknowledged the importance of ethical considerations in the design and implementation of AI applications for HRM focussed applications. They highlighted the importance of an organisational learning approach for successful AI adoption. The case organisation does not claim absolute knowledge or capabilities for an AI application to deliver a flawless system. However, it strives to evolve its developmental efforts and remains open to deal with any ethical issues to the best of its knowledge and capabilities. In order to improve the AI applications, the development teams check these issues as and when they manifest in the implementation stages of various AI applications that are rolled out. The open-mindedness to developing AI applications that are unbiased and socially responsible, the teams were multidisciplinary and continuously sought input from a diverse set of stakeholders

> So, we are saying we don't know everything. Once we think we have something in place. I'll put it across in our systems. We involve in our ecosystem partners, and we also use our audit partners to come and check from time-to-time, and you know, keep us honest about those things. [R3]

The developers and leaders acknowledged the quality and nature of input that goes into the training of the AI applications as fundamental in making these applications more responsible and unbiased in their decision-making. By providing diverse scenarios from a diverse set of people, the biases can be minimised.

> Look, we all need to understand humans and machines, right? The more you train them, the better they get …. But after it is pointed to us, the input that is being fed right now ….those sci-fi movies, which are … really different but I'm sure at some point in time we will be there. But today, we need to understand one thing, which is simply that irrespective of the systems and the language you have used, there is input, which yields an output. [R7]

Discussion

The above analysis and findings confirm that firstly, there is a significant proliferation of AI-enabled applications in the form of Bots, digital, virtual and personal assistants for all the sub-domains of HRM practices including attracting and selecting employees (Upadhyay & Khandelwal, 2018), training and development (Maity, 2019), resource allocation and management (Andrejczuk, 2018; Stavrou et al., 2007) as well as for managing talent (Jantan et al., 2010). Our study's distinctive contribution lies in developing a conceptual framework for understanding the relationship between how a P-O fit connects to employee and HR outcomes through an AI-mediated social exchange. To the best of our knowledge, this is the first study that explicates how employees reciprocate their experience of receiving hyper-personalised and individualised HRM practices with improved attitudinal and behavioural responses as well as the HRM function benefits from increased HR cost-effectiveness. An enhanced experience strengthens their person-organisation fit and engagement with HR practices. In line with the AI-mediated social exchange theory (Ma & Brown, 2020), our interview data finds support for the underlying logic that when employees experience a favourable AI-mediated exchange, they will feel obliged to reciprocate with positive attitudinal and behavioural outcomes. Our interview data further highlights the mechanism of AI-mediated exchange that leads to high levels of job satisfaction, commitment and their weak intention to quit behaviours. Further, the inter-relationships between the themes, especially the moderating role of the organisational culture of innovative practices were also noted as another contextual factor in explaining employee and HR outcomes.

In answering the first research question, there is evidence of HR cost-effectiveness in terms of savings on HR headcount, business value-add, and HR agility realised through AI-mediated social exchanges using HRM-focused bots (Barro & Davenport, 2019; Faliagka et al., 2014; Guenole & Feinzig, 2018; Kiron & Schrage, 2019). The savings are realised in terms of full-time equivalent HR resources and will continue to increase as the AI applications undertake high-volumes of transactional processing HR activities and gradually undertake more complex HR tasks. Additionally, these AI-enabled applications allow the organisation to generate additional insights about its people capabilities and competencies and deploy resources with greater ease and agility to tap into client opportunities as it arises.

The study's second research question focused on the impact of AI-mediated social exchange on employee experience of HR practices. In line with the emerging trends on the personalised, hyper-personalised and individualised experience of HR practices (Haak, 2019; Hughes et al., 2019; Karra, 2019), employees at this MNE too, experienced hyper-personalisation and individualisation of HRM practices through a range of AI-enabled bots, digital, personal and virtual assistants. However, our research identifies the theoretical mechanisms through which this occurs. This form of personalisation and individualisation departs from the existing studies on idiosyncratic deals (Anand et al., 2010; Bal et al., 2013; De Leede et al., 2004; Glassner & Keune, 2012; Hornung et al., 2008; Rosen et al., 2013) on several counts. First, in the traditional forms of social exchange and idiosyncratic deals, personalisation and individualisation of HR practices occur through interactions and negotiations between human-to-human (i.e. between line managers and employees), and it often involved employees in dealing with managers' idiosyncratic approaches and personal preferences. Second, this study departs from the traditional idiosyncratic deals, in that the AI-mediated exchange allows with ease, dealing with issues of perceived fairness as the interactions between human-machine as there are no emotions or subjectivity involved in the exchange creating a higher degree of objectivity in the interactions. Under the new approach to hyper-personalisation and individualisation, the interaction and negotiation occur between the humans and machine-enabled AI application(s) for a range of HR practices. By considering an individual's differences in terms of the congruence in their values, attributes, interests and competencies (Motowildo et al., 1997; Underwood, 1975) with the organisation's environment and practices, a better person-organisation fit is possible (Verquer et al., 2003).

Further, as values drive attitudes and behaviours, the link between P-O fit and attitudes and behaviours is mediated by the interactive nature of human-bot interactions or through the use of AI-mediated applications. It remains to be seen whether this is also due to a perceived lack of power-laden employee experiences between technology and employees, as most employees reported these interactions as positive. Nevertheless, in line with signalling theory, the signals received through the bots (Casper & Harris, 2008). The AI-mediated social exchange (Ma & Brown, 2020), offers a much-nuanced understanding of how employees reciprocate their positive experiences in the form of increased commitment, satisfaction and lower than the industry average, of their intentions to quit behaviours, which then translates into cost savings and help deliver enhanced HR cost-effectiveness (Bal et al., 2013).

Conclusion

Overall, this study demonstrated how the adoption of HRM-focused AI applications in the case organisation had yielded positive outcomes for both the HR function as well as employees, through an AI-mediated social exchange, which offered highly personalised and individualised employee experiences of HR practices. A fundamental limitation of this study is the nature of the case organisation itself, as it does not offer any rival or opposing views. This is so because this MNE is an early adopter and implementor of AI-based HRM and business applications. Further, it is essential to highlight that the core business of this MNE is designing and implementing AI applications for both its internal consumption, as well as for serving its global client base. Therefore, it is not surprising to find high levels of positive experiences.

Implications for research

In terms of implications for future research, the adoption success may yield different results for a client organisation that is only a user and not a producer of such AI applications. Future research should consider evaluating the employee experiences of AI applications that they have purchased from the external marketplace with or without customisations. It would be useful to explore any differences by undertaking comparative research between these two groups, i.e. the developing firms and user firms. Future research should also analyse how AI users that are 'non-designers' of the applications would experience AI-mediated social exchanges. It would be interesting analyse the differences between a user who has transitioned from a human-human exchange to an AI mediated social exchanges experiences the interactions with various AI applications.

Additionally, further research is needed at several levels and in various sub-functional domains of HRM research in domestic and international firms. First, at an individual level, research on the extent of trust, nature of emotions and reactions of employees as they interact with Bots and humanoids will determine the extent of cooperation and leveraging this technology. Second, also at an individual level, scholars can also investigate employees' attitudes towards AI adoption and intention to use their perceptions of trust towards Bots and humanoids as these technologies employ and utilise personal and private data of employees for routine and non-routine decision-making and problem-solving tasks. Third, a related area of future research that this study was not able to thoroughly examine was of legal and ethical issues and biases that may be present in the design and implementation stages of such applications. Although the case organisation indicated the presence of diversity in the development teams, wherein teams from global and local groups of employees participated in the development of AI applications, the differences in the experiences of employees across different global locations of the MNE may persist and presents a future area of inquiry for both AI adoption by HRM in domestic and international firms. Research that explores how the applications deal with biases and local and global differences is timely. Finally, at a functional level, for leveraging the technology, it may require the creation of awareness among employees to engage and share their tacit and explicit knowledge more extensively with AI-mediated technology platforms to create larger databases. Such an approach would require reimagining how to motivate, re-skill and create an ecosystem where employees continue to engage with AI-mediated knowledge sharing platforms.

Implications for practice

There are several implications for practice. First, acquiring the necessary technical and multidisciplinary skills through internal and external training in the design and implementation of HRM-focused AI applications. Adequate training is also critical for the end-users to understand how best to leverage and use the AI-applications for assisting in routine and non-routine tasks. Second, there is a need to put in place higher levels of transparency, consent and information sharing for all employees, so they understand how personal data and information will be used in algorithmic decision-making. Third, developing an appreciation for change to support employees and managers deal with potential issues of resistance to AI-induced change. Fourth, purposively design diverse teams from different geographical and functional areas to minimise data biases that are inherent in a given ecosystem. Fifth, managers and leaders need to evaluate and have an open mind to continuously improve and address potential ethical, moral and legal issues that may creep into an application. Finally, the need to develop a robust business case, one that not only focuses on economic aspects but also incorporates the broader social and relational aspects for multiple users, keeping in mind societal sensitivities may help influence the success of such technology adoptions. To this end, applications that focus on a holistic concept of sustainability using multiple parameters of evaluating a technology are more likely to deliver in the longer term. Employees need to be educated and supported on how they can leverage the technology to improve their skills and competencies in newer areas to help them recreate their career posturing.

Policy level implications

Speculating the impact of AI adoption on HRM on the Indian cultural context, we opine that it will bring several challenges, such as skills development, job displacement, unemployment as well as potentially lead to some digital exclusion and a widening digital divide between those who have access to emerging technologies and the Internet and those who do not. Additionally, the businesses, customers and employees will stand to benefit from an enhanced, personalised and augmented experiences that AI applications have to offer. Some preliminary estimate a strong correlation between AI adoption and total factor productivity growth (TFPG), wherein a one-unit increase in AI intensity can lead to a TFPG of 0.05%, or an estimated contribution of 2.5% to India's GDP (Kathuraia et al., 2020). The impact of AI in HR on work culture is likely to be favourable for those firms that are engaged in the production of IT and knowledge-intensive work, relative to traditional and public sector undertakings. The favourable attitudes towards these new technologies and applications have the potential to affect people with visual and other forms of disabilities. The Indian culture and people management philosophy is oriented more towards collectivism, empathy, harmony and coexistence with all living and non-living objects for achieving holistic well-being. Hopefully, these aspects of people management philosophy are reflected in the interactions humans have with Bots and humanoids.

Acknowledgements

The authors wish to acknowledge the valuable feedback and comments received from the anonymous reviewers for this and an earlier conference version of this paper.

Disclosure statement

No potential conflict of interest was reported by the authors.

Data availability statement

Due to the nature of this research, participants of this study did not agree for data to be shared publicly, so any supporting data collected cannot be made available.

References

Anand, S., Vidyarthi, P. R., Liden, R. C., & Rousseau, D. M. (2010). Good citizens in poor-quality relationships: Idiosyncratic deals as a substitute for relationship quality. *Academy of Management Journal*, 53(5), 970–988. https://doi.org/10.5465/amj.2010. 54533176

Andrejczuk, E. (2018). *Artificial intelligence methods to support people management in organisations* [Unpublished doctoral thesis]. Retrieved January 01, 2020, from http://www.iiia.csic.es/~jar/thesisEwaFinal.pdf

Argyris, C. (1964). *Integrating the individual and the organisation*. John Wiley & Sons, Inc.

Bal, P. M., & Dorenbosch, L. (2015). Age-related differences in the relations between individualised HRM and organisational performance: A large-scale employer survey.

Human Resource Management Journal, 25(1), 41–61. https://doi.org/10.1111/1748-8583.12058

Bal, P. M., Kooij, D. T. A. M., & De Jong, S. B. (2013). How do developmental and accommodative HRM enhance employee engagement and commitment? The role of psychological contract and SOC-strategies. *Journal of Management Studies, 50*(4), 545–572. https://doi.org/10.1111/joms.12028

Bankins, S., & Formosa, P. (2020). When AI meets PC: Exploring the implications of workplace social robots and a human-robot psychological contract. *European Journal of Work and Organizational Psychology, 29*(2), 215–229. https://doi.org/10.1080/1359432X.2019.1620328

Barney, M. (2018). *Artificially intelligent coaching has arrived.* Retrieved February 23, 2020, from https://trainingindustry.com/magazine/may-jun-2018/artificially-intelligent-coaching-has-arrived/

Barro, S., & Davenport, T. H. (2019). People and machines: Partners in innovation. *MIT Sloan Management Review, 60*(4), 22–28.

BasuMallick, C. (2019). *How AI-driven performance feedback can make you a better manager.* Retrieved February 23, 2020, from https://www.hrtechnologist.com/articles/performance-management-hcm/ai-driven-performance-feedback/

Becker, B. E., Huselid, M. A., & Beatty, R. W. (2009). *The differentiated workforce: Transforming talent into strategic impact.* Harvard Business Press.

Berg, P., & Frost, A. (2006). Dignity at work for low wage, low skill service workers. *Relations Industrielles, 60*(4), 657–682. https://doi.org/10.7202/012339ar

Blau, P. M. (1964). *Exchange and power in social life.* Wiley.

Budhwar, P., Varma, A., & Kumar, R. (Eds.). (2019). *Indian business: Understanding a rapidly emerging economy.* Routledge.

Budhwar, P. & Malik, A. (2020a). Special Issue: Leveraging Artificial and Human Intelligence Through Human Resource Management. https://www.journals.elsevier.com/human-resource-management-review/call-for-papers/leveraging-artificial-and-human-intelligence

Budhwar, P. S., & Malik, A. (2020b). Call for papers: Artificial intelligence challenges and opportunities for international HRM. *The International Journal of Human Resource Management.* Retrieved from https://think.taylorandfrancis.com/journal-human-resourcemanagement-artificial-intelligence/

Bughin, J., Hazan, E., Ramaswamy, S., Chui, M., Allas, T., Dahlström, P., Henke, N., & Trench, M. (2017, June). *Artificial intelligence: The next digital frontier?* McKinsey Global Institute. McKinsey & Company.

Carter, B., Danford, A., Howcroft, D., Richardson, H., Smith, A., & Taylor, P. (2013). Stressed out of my box': Employee experience of lean working and occupational ill-health in clerical work in the UK public sector. *Work, Employment and Society, 27*(5), 747–767. https://doi.org/10.1177/0950017012469064

Casper, W. J., & Harris, C. M. (2008). Work-life benefits and organisational attachment: Self-interest utility and signalling theory models. *Journal of Vocational Behavior, 72*(1), 95–109. https://doi.org/10.1016/j.jvb.2007.10.015

Collings, D. G., & Mellahi, K. (2009). Strategic talent management: A review and research agenda. *Human Resource Management Review, 19*(4), 304–313. https://doi.org/10.1016/j.hrmr.2009.04.001

Corley, K. G., & Gioia, D. A. (2011). Building theory about theory building: What constitutes a theoretical contribution? *Academy of Management Review, 36*(1), 12–32. https://doi.org/10.5465/amr.2009.0486

Daugherty, P. R., & Wilson, H. J. (2018). *Human + machine: Reimagining work in the age of AI*. Harvard Business Press.

De Leede, J., Huiskamp, R., Oeij, P., Nauta, A., Goudswaard, A., & Kwakkelstein, T. (2007). Negotiating individual employment relations, evidence from four Dutch organisations. *Revue Interventions Économique, 35*, 1–16.

Delery, J. E., & Doty, D. H. (1996). Modes of theorising in strategic human resource management: Tests of universalistic, contingency, and configurational performance predictions. *Academy of Management Journal, 39*, 802–835.

Duggan, J., Sherman, U., Carbery, R., & McDonnell, A. (2020). Algorithmic management and app-work in the gig economy: A research agenda for employment relations and HRM. *Human Resource Management Journal, 30*(1), 114–132. https://doi.org/10.1111/1748-8583.12258

Faliagka, E., Iliadis, L., Karydis, I., Rigou, M., Sioutas, S., Tsakalidis, A., & Tzimas, G. (2014). Online consistent ranking on e-recruitment: Seeking the truth behind a well-formed CV. *Artificial Intelligence Review, 42*(3), 515–528. https://doi.org/10.1007/s10462-013-9414-y

Fan, C. Y., Fan, P. S., Chan, T. Y., & Chang, S. H. (2012). Using hybrid data mining and machine learning clustering analysis to predict the turnover rate for technology professionals. *Expert Systems with Applications, 39*(10), 8844–8851. https://doi.org/10.1016/j.eswa.2012.02.005

Fiske, S. T., & Taylor, S. E. (1991). *Social cognition* (2nd ed). McGraw-Hill Inc.

Fountaine, T., McCarthy, B., & Saleh, T. (2019). Building the AI-powered organisation. *Harvard Business Review*, 63–73.

Gioia, D. A., Corley, K. G., & Hamilton, A. L. (2013). Seeking qualitative rigor in inductive research: Notes on the Gioia methodology. *Organizational Research Methods, 16*(1), 15–31. https://doi.org/10.1177/1094428112452151

Glassner, V., & Keune, M. (2012). The crisis and social policy: The role of collective agreements. *International Labour Review, 151*(4), 351–375. https://doi.org/10.1111/j.1564-913X.2012.00153.x

Guenole, N., & Feinzig, S. (2018). *The business case for AI in HR: With insights and tips on getting started*. IBM Smarter Workforce Institute, IBM.

Gustavsson, E. (2005). Virtual servants: Stereotyping female front-office employees on the. *Internet. Gender, Work & Organisation, 12*(5), 400–419.

Haak, T. (2019). *Personalisation in HR: Some ideas*. Retrieved February 23, 2020, from https://hrtrendinstitute.com/2019/04/29/personalisation-in-hr/

Harley, B., Allen, B. C., & Sargent, L. D. (2007). High-performance work systems and employee experience of work in the service sector: The case of aged care. *British Journal of Industrial Relations, 45*(3), 607–633. https://doi.org/10.1111/j.1467-8543.2007.00630.x

Hornung, S., Rousseau, D. M., & Glaser, J. (2008). Creating flexible work arrangements through idiosyncratic deals. *The Journal of Applied Psychology, 93*(3), 655–664. https://doi.org/10.1037/0021-9010.93.3.655

Hornung, S., Rousseau, D. M., & Glaser, J. (2009). Why supervisors make idiosyncratic deals: Antecedents and outcomes of I-deals from a managerial perspective. *Journal of Managerial Psychology, 24*(8), 738–764. https://doi.org/10.1108/02683940910996770

HR Recruiting. (2016). *Why personalization matters during the recruitment process*. Retrieved February 23, 2020, from https://thrivetrm.com/personalization-matters-recruitment-process/

Huang, M. H., & Rust, R. T. (2018). Artificial intelligence in service. *Journal of Service Research*, *21*(2), 155–172. https://doi.org/10.1177/1094670517752459

Hughes, C., Robert, L., Frady, K., & Arroyos, A. (2019). Managing people and technology in the workplace. In C. Hughes, L. Robert, K. Frady, & A. Arroyos (Eds.), *Managing technology and middle-and low-skilled employees* (pp. 61–68). Emerald Publishing Limited. https://doi.org/10.1108/978-1-78973-077-720191005

IBEF. (2020). *IT & BPM Industry in India.* https://www.ibef.org/industry/indian-iT-and-iTeS-industry-analysis-presentation

Imrie, P., & Bednar, P. (2013). Virtual personal assistant. In *ItAIS 2013*. AIS Electronic Library (AISeL).

Jantan, H., Hamdan, A., & Othman, Z. (2010). Human talent prediction in HRM using C 4.5 classification algorithms. *International Journal on Computer Science and Engineering*, *2*(8), 2526–2534.

Karra, S. (2019, March 4). The hyper-personalization of HR services. *Forbes.* https://www.forbes.com/sites/forbeshumanresourcescouncil/2019/03/04/the-hyper-personalization-of-hr-services/#b9990ad4b411

Kathuraia, R., Kedia, M., & Kapilavai, S. (2020). *Implications of AI on the Indian economy*. Indian Council for Research on International Economic Relations.

Kim, T. Y., Aryee, S., Loi, R., & Kim, S. P. (2013). Person–organisation fit and employee outcomes: Test of a social exchange model. *The International Journal of Human Resource Management*, *24*(19), 3719–3737. https://doi.org/10.1080/09585192.2013.781522

Kiron, D., & Schrage, M. (2019). Strategy for and with AI. *MIT Sloan Management Review*, *60*(4), 30–35.

Kristof, A. L. (1996). Person–organisation fit: An integrative review of its conceptualisations, measurements, and implications. *Personnel Psychology*, *49*(1), 1–49. https://doi.org/10.1111/j.1744-6570.1996.tb01790.x

Kristof-Brown, A. L., Zimmerman, R. D., & Johnson, E. C. (2005). Consequences of individuals' fit at work: A meta-analysis of person-job, person-organisation, person-group, and person-supervisor fit. *Personnel Psychology*, *58*(2), 281–342. https://doi.org/10.1111/j.1744-6570.2005.00672.x

De Leede, J., Looise, J. K., & Riemsdijk, M. (2004). Collectivism versus individualism in Dutch employment relations. *Human Resource Management Journal*, *14*(1), 25–39. https://doi.org/10.1111/j.1748-8583.2004.tb00110.x

Ma, X., & Brown, T. (2020). AI-mediated exchange theory. In *Extended Abstracts of the 2020 CHI Conference on Human Factors in Computing Systems (Workshop)*. Association for Computing Machinery.

Maity, S. (2019). Identifying opportunities for artificial intelligence in the evolution of training and development practices. *Journal of Management Development*, *38*(8), 651–663.

Malik, A., & Pereira, V. (Eds.). (2016). *Indian culture and work organisations in transition*. Routledge.

Malik, A., Budhwar, P., & Srikanth, N. R. (2020). Gig economy, 4IR and artificial intelligence: Rethinking strategic HRM. In P. Kumar, A. Agarwal, & P. Budhwar (Eds.), *Human & technological resource management (HTRM): New insights into revolution 4.0*. Emerald Publications. pp. 75–88.

Malik, A., Pereira, V., & Tarba, S. (2019). The role of HRM practices in product development: Contextual ambidexterity in a US MNC's subsidiary in India. *The

International Journal of Human Resource Management, 30(4), 536–564. https://doi.org/10.1080/09585192.2017.1325388

Malik, A., Sharma, P., Pereira, V., & Temouri, Y. (2021). From regional innovation systems to global innovation hubs: Evidence of a Quadruple Helix from an emerging economy. *Journal of Business Research* (in press).

Malik, A., Srikanth, N. R., & Budhwar, P. (May 2020). Digitisation, AI and HRM. In J. Crashaw, P. Budhwar, & A. Davis (Eds.), *Strategic human resource management* (pp. 88–110). Sage Publications.

McColl, R., & Michelotti, M. (2019). Sorry, could you repeat the question? Exploring video-interview recruitment practice in HRM. *Human Resource Management Journal, 29*(4), 637–656. https://doi.org/10.1111/1748-8583.12249

Morf, M., Bakker, A. B., & Feierabend, A. (2019). Bankers closing idiosyncratic deals: Implications for organisational cynicism. *Human Resource Management Journal, 29*(4), 585–599. https://doi.org/10.1111/1748-8583.12245

Morley, M. J. (2007). Person-organisation fit. *Journal of Managerial Psychology, 22*(2), 109–117. https://doi.org/10.1108/02683940710726375

Motowildo, S. J., Borman, W. C., & Schmit, M. J. (1997). A theory of individual differences in task and contextual performance. *Human Performance, 10*(2), 71–83. https://doi.org/10.1207/s15327043hup1002_1

Narayanan, A., Rajithakumar, S., & Menon, M. (2019). Talent management and employee retention: An integrative research framework. *Human Resource Development Review, 18*(2), 228–247. https://doi.org/10.1177/1534484318812159

NASSCOM. (2020). *Facts and figures.* https://nasscom.in/knowledge-centre/facts-figures

Nishii, L. H., & Wright, P. (2008). Variability at multiple levels of analysis: Implications for strategic human resource management. In D. B. Smith (Ed.), *The people make the place* (pp. 225–248). Lawrence Erlbaum Associates.

Pereira, V., & Malik, A. (2015). Making sense and identifying aspects of Indian culture (s) in organisations: Demystifying through empirical evidence. *Culture and Organization, 21*(5), 355–365. https://doi.org/10.1080/14759551.2015.1082265

Raman, S. G. (2018, August 20). *Are robots taking over the world? A restaurant in Chennai serves an answer.* https://scroll.in/magazine/8,86,874/are-robots-taking-over-the-world-a-restaurant-in-chennai-serves-an-answer

Ransbotham, S., Kiron, D., Gerbert, P., & Reeves, M. (2017). Reshaping business with artificial intelligence: Closing the gap between ambition and action. *MIT Sloan Management Review, 59*(1), 1–17.

Reinhard, G., Jesper, V., & Stefan, S. (2016). Industry 4.0: Building the digital enterprise. 2016 Global Industry 4.0 Survey. https://doi.org/10.1080/01969722.2015.1007734

Siggelkow, N. (2007). Persuasion with case studies. *Academy of Management Journal, 50*(1), 20–24. https://doi.org/10.5465/amj.2007.24160882

Stavrou, E. T., Charalambous, C., & Spiliotis, S. (2007). Human resource management and performance: A neural network analysis. *European Journal of Operational Research, 181*(1), 453–467. https://doi.org/10.1016/j.ejor.2006.06.006

Strohmeier, S., & Piazza, F. (2015). Artificial intelligence techniques in human resource management—a conceptual exploration. In *Intelligent techniques in engineering management* (pp. 149–172). Springer.

Takamoto, M., & Owada, J. (2018). HR-tech that boosts productivity and makes people shine: New value creation in HR achieved through data analysis. *Hitachi Review, 67*(6), 652–653.

Tambe, P., Cappelli, P., & Yakubovich, V. (2019). Artificial intelligence in human resources management: Challenges and a path forward. *California Management Review*, *61*(4), 15–42. https://doi.org/10.1177/0008125619867910

Tarafdar, M., Beath, C. M., & Ross, J. W. (2019). Using AI to enhance business operations. *MIT Sloan Management Review*, June 2019, pp. 37–44.

Tecuci, G. (2012). Artificial intelligence. *Wiley Interdisciplinary Reviews: Computational Statistics*, *4*(2), 168–180. https://doi.org/10.1002/wics.200

Thomas, D. C., Cuervo-Cazurra, A., & Brannen, M. Y. (2011). Explaining theoretical relationships in international business research: It's about the arrows linking the boxes. *Journal of International Business Studies*, *42*(9), 1073–1078. https://doi.org/10.1057/jibs.2011.44

Ullas, S. S. (2019). *At this Bengaluru school, robots teach, and teachers mentor*. https://timesofindia.indiatimes.com/city/bengaluru/at-this-bengaluru-school-robots-teach-and-teachers-mentor/articleshow/70867664.cms

Underwood, B. J. (1975). Individual differences as a crucible in theory construction. *American Psychologist*, *30*(2), 128–134. https://doi.org/10.1037/h0076759

Upadhyay, A. K., & Khandelwal, K. (2018). Applying artificial intelligence: Implications for recruitment. *Strategic HR Review*, *17*(5), 255–258. https://doi.org/10.1108/SHR-07-2018-0051

Van Maanen, J., Sørensen, J. B., & Mitchell, T. R. (2007). The interplay between theory and method. *Academy of Management Review*, *32*(4), 1145–1154. https://doi.org/10.5465/amr.2007.26586080

Verquer, M. L., Beehr, T. A., & Wagner, S. H. (2003). A meta-analysis of relations between person–organisation fit and work attitudes. *Journal of Vocational Behavior*, *63*(3), 473–489. https://doi.org/10.1016/S0001-8791(02)00036-2

Warhurst, C., & Nickson, D. (2007). Employee experience of aesthetic labour in retail and hospitality. *Work, Employment and Society*, *21*(1), 103–120. https://doi.org/10.1177/0950017007073622

Whetten, D. A. (1989). What constitutes a theoretical contribution? *Academy of Management Review*, *14*(4), 490–495. https://doi.org/10.5465/amr.1989.4308371

Whiteside, E. (2019). *How AI and machine learning enhance personalised learning in the workplace*. Retrieved February 23, 2020, from https://elearningindustry.com/ai-machine-enhance-personalized-learning-workplace

Yin, R. (2003). *Case study research: Design and methods* (3rd ed.). Sage.

§ OPEN ACCESS

Rebooting employees: upskilling for artificial intelligence in multinational corporations

Akanksha Jaiswal ⓘ, C. Joe Arun and Arup Varma

ABSTRACT
Proponents of artificial intelligence (AI) have envisaged a scenario wherein intelligent machines would execute routine tasks performed by humans, thus, relieving them to engage in creative pursuits. While there is widespread fear of corresponding job losses, organizational think tanks vouch for the synergistic culmination of human–machine competencies. Using the dynamic skill, neo-human capital and AI job replacement theories, we contend that the introduction and adoption of AI calls for employees to upskill themselves. To determine the key skills deemed critical for the upskilling of employees, we interviewed 20 experienced professionals in multinational corporations (MNCs) in the information technology sector in India. Deploying Gioia's methodology for qualitative analysis, our investigation revealed five critical skills for employee upskilling: data analysis, digital, complex cognitive, decision making and continuous learning skills.

Introduction

The impact of technology on the global economy, businesses and societies is exponential and has enabled unprecedented advancement, leading experts to predict that the upcoming decade will witness tremendous changes in the nature of work owing to artificial intelligence (AI) (Butler, 2016; Davenport & Kirby, 2016). AI systems extend human capabilities by sensing, comprehending, learning and acting (Daugherty & Wilson, 2018). Not surprisingly, the discourse on the future of work has drawn contrasting views. While critics of AI firmly believe that machines will replace human beings in many jobs, proponents of AI envision new jobs with value creation (Ågerfalk, 2020; Sullivan et al., 2020). Despite

---

This is an Open Access article distributed under the terms of the Creative Commons Attribution-NonCommercial-NoDerivatives License (http://creativecommons.org/licenses/by-nc-nd/4.0/), which permits non-commercial re-use, distribution, and reproduction in any medium, provided the original work is properly cited, and is not altered, transformed, or built upon in any way.

these opposing views, there is agreement on one insight – this wave of technological advancement will disrupt the employment equilibrium, and this disruption of the workforce and displacement of labor is universally applicable as most industries today are enabled by technology (Bughin et al., 2017; Østerlund et al., 2021).

Gradually, artificially intelligent machines are taking over tedious, mechanical and mundane human tasks, such as documenting, scheduling, inspecting equipment, collecting data and conducting preliminary analyses (Huang et al., 2019; Huang & Rust, 2018). As Chaudhuri et al. (2020) note, AI is becoming more commonplace in developing nations such as China and India. In China, 77% of the workforce has employed AI in their work in some shape or form while this number is 71% for India.

These technological advances and achievements are possible due to data science, analytics and machine learning becoming central to the AI functioning – indeed, a key characteristic of artificially intelligent machines is that the intelligence is drawn from a constant learning and adaptation process (Akerkar, 2019; Lecun et al., 2015). AI-powered technologies collaborate with humans towards improved decision making and enhancing the quality of life. Today, multinational corporations (MNCs) are investing heavily in logic and knowledge-based AI-tools that are driven by huge amounts of data, information and rules (Corea, 2019). Tools such as logic-based programming, robotic process automation, expert systems, descriptive and predictive analytics, are helping businesses in transforming the workplace tremendously (Akerkar, 2019; Corea, 2019; Hancock et al., 2020; Wilson et al., 2017). As an example, AI-enabled systems depend on internet-of-things and big data as the main ingredient to facilitate data-driven decision making.[1] Further, AI itself comprises a set of algorithms which depends on data for executing the responses (Jaiswal & Arun, 2021; Portugal et al., 2018). Thus, in this paper, we operationalize *AI as data-driven systems that extend human capabilities by enabling faster and better decision making and problem-solving.*

While sophisticated AI-technologies are reducing the need for human labor in multinationals, linking these technologies to the organizational needs and deliverables requires an in-depth understanding of organizational members' capabilities (Davenport & Kirby, 2016). Clearly, developing competencies related to AI and its applications is extremely important to help employees remain employable in the future. In this study, we operationalize *upskilling as learning new skills to sharpen employee's abilities to understand and utilize AI-based systems.* According to Hancock et al. (2020), roughly 30–40% of employees would need to upgrade their skills significantly, within the next decade. In this connection, several MNCs such as Amazon, Infosys, IBM and Walmart are developing AI-powered products and services, while also investing in developing the required technical and soft skills of the human capital. Given the broad applications of AI, and its potential to affect our day-to-day lives in almost every aspect, it is critical that we study the pros and cons of AI applications, especially in the workplace, as it can have a direct effect on the society, since many jobs might become human-redundant. Accordingly, the present study was designed to address the research question: 'What are the skills that will be deemed critical for the upskilling of employees to remain employable, and thrive, in the era of AI?'

The Indian context

Given the rapid globalization and technological developments, several MNCs have set up operations in emerging economies (Thite et al., 2014). In this connection, India is considered an emerging economic superpower (see Budhwar et al., 2019), not just due to the low cost of operations but also because of its demographic dividend, foreign language skills, intellectual capital and diversity. In 2018, the Indian government think-tank, National Institution for Transforming India (NITI) Aayog, launched a nation-wide programme on AI and its tremendous industrial applications, thus, driving the entire economy towards digitization and AI. By 2035, AI is projected to add US$957 billion, or 15% of India's current gross value (Menon et al., 2017). Recently, the INDIAai website was launched by the government to demonstrate India's journey to global prominence in AI (INDIAai, 2020). Further, since the past three decades, the Indian Information Technology (IT) industry has gained an immense global reputation for deploying the global services delivery model.

Indeed, the global reach of this industry has impacted organizations worldwide as the Indian IT industry powers the digital functioning of major developed and developing nations by providing services in the back-office operations (Jain et al., 2019; Malik et al., 2020; Pereira et al., 2020). Not surprisingly, the practices of the Indian IT industry are benchmarked to global standards (Budhwar & Varma, 2011; Thite et al., 2014). The Indian government's thrust on technology, data and talent to create and use AI-systems across industries has given an extraordinary boost to the IT firms in India. Indeed, this has led to a significant improvement in employment opportunities in India and has led to a corresponding increase in the return of Indian expatriates to contribute to the continuing growth of the Indian economy (see, e.g. Varma & Tung, 2020). Relatedly, the Government of India has issued the National Education Policy (NEP) in July 2020 which has laid out clear procedures to disseminate education, especially in Information Technology and

Computer Science, to all children across different educational levels (NEP, 2020). Accordingly, we decided to conduct our study in the Indian IT sector.

Finally, even though the human resource discipline is replete with studies on the interface between technology and human resources (Bondarouk & Brewster, 2016; Bondarouk et al., 2017; Marler & Boudreau, 2017), recent developments with respect to AI have received scant attention from academicians (Meijerink et al., 2018). Some scholarly work has been initiated towards a better understanding of how, and to what extent, AI impacts HR (Chaudhuri et al., 2020; Malik et al., 2019). These explorations are primarily in the areas of recruitment and selection of applicants and performance management systems (PMS). Further, the neo-human capital theory (NHCT) highlights the increasing demand for technology-induced skills and the development of human capital in times of rapid technological change (Pereira & Malik, 2015). Accordingly, we believe our study is timely and critical, and it makes four key contributions. First, we use the lens of dynamic skill, neo-human capital and AI job replacement theories, to contribute to the understanding of human resource development in the context of AI. Second, we add to the growing literature on the MNCs operating in India in the IT sector. Third, we identify those skill sets which can potentially help IT MNCs and employees prepare themselves for the sustainable design and implementation of AI. Finally, while identification of key skill sets is the starting point, we suggest practical tools for leaders in MNCs to advance employee learning and competencies towards creating value out of human–machine augmented intelligence.

In the following sections, we briefly review the literature on AI, its impact on human resources and the need for upskilling for the era of AI. This is followed by a detailed description of our research design and method, and a discussion of our analyses and findings. We then offer practical and theoretical implications, outline the study limitations and discuss key avenues for further research.

Literature review

In developing the rationale for our study, we employ the theoretical lenses of dynamic skill theory, NHCT and theory of AI job replacement. These theories were specifically chosen, as they help advance the role of skill demand due to technological change in the context of AI.

AI and its impact on human resources (HR)

In present times, technology has proliferated across human lives and industries, and technological change is unprecedented in its pace, scope and magnitude of impact. With game-changing innovations juxtaposed with technological advancements, organizations need to digitally reinvent themselves at an exponential pace to stay relevant and ahead of competitors. AI-systems have the capability to simulate neural networks that train and learn through experiences embedded in massive data sets at a whirlwind speed (Butler, 2016; Jordan & Mitchell, 2015; Mitchell, 2017). In this connection, Tschang and Mezquita (2020) have noted that some scholars argue that AI may lead to unemployment, while others believe AI could be used to augment existing jobs. Clearly, both views have some merit, but both need to be explored further. Not surprisingly, the understanding of how, and to what extent, AI impacts HR is in its nascent stages (Malik et al., 2019).

Two areas of HR where AI has important applications are recruitment and selection of applicants and PMS (Chaudhuri et al., 2020). By using AI-based bots, organizations have expedited the applicant screening and selection processes. Cappelli et al. (2020) explain that algorithms for recruitment are designed based on established predictors and criteria that satisfy a statistically significant relationship. These algorithms are trained on existing recruitment and selection datasets. The prospective candidates are assessed by AI-bots based on the training dataset and screened for the criterion variables. Likewise, PMS determines the rewards (or punishment) for each organizational member based on their competencies, behaviors and task accomplishments. Since the most widely used metric, that is, the performance appraisal score, is subjective and not bias-free, AI-based algorithms can be considered as a suitable HR intervention. With such promising AI applications deployed in organizations, employees need to upskill themselves to understand and appropriately use these tools owing to ethical, legal and contextual considerations that are beyond the scope of this article.

Need for upskilling for AI

The notion that AI will surpass human intelligence is often voiced with advances in AI creating tipping points triggering significant changes in organizational operations and outcomes (Butler, 2016). For instance, there is a shift in demand in the workforce from basic manual and physical work skills to cognitive competencies. This shift has prompted organizations to change the talent mix. Since human beings note rates of change as linear and not exponential, they often find this pace of technological advancement difficult to align with. Not surprisingly, scholars have cited increased attrition rates and unemployment as AI takes up mundane tasks previously performed by humans (Bughin et al., 2018; OECD, 2012). While a technological revolution may eventually be on the cards, the scale and time frames are currently unknown. Thus, the upcoming era necessitates humans to develop appropriate skillsets for redefined jobs and work closely with AI-technologies to progress well in their employment.

Work in today's MNCs is knowledge-intensive and relies heavily on the interface between AI-enabled technology and employees (Bondarouk et al., 2017; Pereira & Malik, 2015). While technology enables organizational deliverables, employees are the key drivers of value creation and source of sustained competitive advantage. Thus, contemporary MNCs not only focus on developing physical and organizational capital but also on developing human capital which is of utmost importance for organizational sustainability and success, more so, in the upcoming era of AI and the changing nature of work. AI is increasingly reshaping work by performing various tasks and is becoming a major source of innovation (Rust & Huang, 2014). Most jobs in MNCs comprise mechanical tasks (such as administering daily routines and tracking attendance), thinking tasks (such as analyzing customer preferences and scheduling logistics) and feeling tasks (such as empathizing with customers and advising therapies to patients). These dimensions of tasks may vary from one job to another and the intelligence required thereof. As AI deemphasized mechanical human labor, humans have to upgrade their focus on tasks that are difficult for AI to assume, that is, tasks requiring thinking and feeling skill sets (Huang et al., 2019; Huang & Rust, 2018).

Theories of upskilling

We draw upon the dynamic skill theory (Fischer et al., 2003), NHCT (Pereira & Malik, 2015) and the theory of AI job replacement (Huang & Rust, 2018) to explicate the need for upskilling. Dynamic skill theory views skill development as a web of activities that is context-specific and outcome-oriented (Kunnen & Bosma, 2003). In a dynamic world, individuals need to be adept in various skills such as social, emotional, technological and physical skills to exhibit good performance or demonstrate appropriate behavior depending upon the context or situation. A web of skills captures the interconnected complexity of skills in diverse contexts. Since dynamic skill theory is a theory for adult cognitive development, we invoked it in the context of skill development for employees in the era of AI.

Further, the NHCT highlights the increasing demand for technology-induced skills and the development of human capital in times of rapid technological change (Pereira & Malik, 2015). Proponents of NHCT argue that individuals with higher levels of human capital concentration (higher level-of-education, experience in training, open to learning and exploration) are more likely to adopt technological changes and develop new skills (Bartel & Lichtenberg, 1987; Wozniak, 1984, 1987). We agree with Pereira and Malik (2015, p. 154) that the need for employee training will not decline with higher levels of technological knowledge. Rather, we believe that with the proliferation of AI-technologies across industries in the near future, there will be a continuous increase in demand for new skillsets and higher levels of human capital concentration.

While AI's ability to increasingly perform various tasks is indeed a major source of innovation and value creation, there is also an increased threat of job loss. The theory of AI job replacement (Huang & Rust, 2018) posits that replacement by AI is primarily at the task-level, rather than at the job-level. More specifically, the changing nature of work is largely for tasks that are easy and repetitive and entail mechanical intelligence. Once AI has accomplished the lower-level and subsequently the higher-level mechanical tasks that comprise a job, it will progress to replace human labor in analytical intelligence, that is, tasks that require rule-based and logical thinking. Soft skills, thus, will assume paramount importance for humans. The future workforce would need to acquire intelligence for higher job complexity including intuitive intelligence (for complex, chaotic and context-specific tasks) and empathetic intelligence (for tasks requiring high levels of emotions and empathy). While AI domain experts are relentlessly developing and training machine-learning algorithms to mimic human capabilities, higher levels of skills such as communication, relationship building, problem-solving, reasoning, empathy and sense-making, are extremely difficult to be emulated by AI (Huang & Rust, 2018). Thus, we contend that in the era of AI, employees need to deconstruct existing skills and cultivate new ones to remain employable and competitive.

Study design

The present study was designed to address a key research question: 'What are the skills that will be deemed critical for the upskilling of employees to remain employable, and thrive, in the era of AI?' In other words, in the era driven by AI, the study aims to identify skills that are considered critical for employees' upskilling. To address our research question, we interviewed 20 seasoned MNC executives in the IT sector in India. These participants were middle to senior-level managers with at least 10 years of total work experience. Further, all participants had an adequate experience of AI implementation and experience in working with AI-enabled services. The IT sector was chosen for our study as technology-led innovations and growth are tightly linked to each other in this industry. Further, among all sectors, IT firms are most likely to expect a high level of role disruption and skill shortage due to AI (Agarwal et al., 2020). Despite the acknowledgment that AI-enabled services are the primary source of innovation in the service industry (Rust & Huang, 2014), there is limited research on human resource development of this workforce (Chaudhuri et al., 2020; Malik et al., 2019; Pereira & Malik, 2015).

In the Indian context, IT firms hold notable significance. From humble beginnings in the 1970s, the Indian IT industry has come a long way (Malik & Rowley, 2015). Today, this sector contributes 7.9% to India's economic growth and is expected to contribute 10% by 2025 (IBEF, 2019). The IT industry is a result of the rapid world of change and technological advancement generating revenue of more than US$180 billion and employing 4.1 million professionals, the highest employment provider in the private sector in India (NASSCOM, 2020).[2] With the Indian government's budget allocation (2020) of US$1.13 billion (spread over five years) for developing technologies and AI-based applications and thrust on deploying AI-powered technologies across other industries, the Indian IT sector has immense scope to grow.

India has also attracted global visibility and gained prominence in terms of intellectual capital with several IT MNCs setting up their major hubs and innovation centres in India (Budhwar, 2012). A key aspect of the present study is the focus on IT organizations with global footprints. Technology-based MNCs are heavily investing and engaging in futuristic AI-powered technologies (Akerkar, 2019; Davenport & Kirby, 2016). Further, MNCs are deploying AI-based products and services developed in one location across varied operations in different countries. While national cultural context plays a crucial role in business decisions, AI-powered data facilitate problem-solving and decision making.

Table 1a summarizes the participants and their company's characteristics. Twenty middle and senior-level employees in both technical and managerial roles were contacted. The participants were employed in different MNCs spread across different locations in India, while their headquarters were based in Canada, the United States of America, Denmark, Ireland, Switzerland, France and India. In India, these MNCs operated from Pune, Chennai, Bangalore, Noida, Kochi, among many other locations. We chose MNCs of varying sizes, determined by the worldwide employment size, to comprehensively assess the need for upskilling in the IT sector. The MNCs were categorized as small, medium and large, based on employee headcount less than 4999, 5000–59,999 and more than 60,000 employees (Lavelle et al., 2012). Thus, five participants each from small and medium-size MNCs and 10 participants from large MNCs comprised the study's dataset.

Table 1a. Participant's and their company's characteristics.

Participant number	Company headquarter	Headcount worldwide	Headcount in India	Gender	Experience (in years)	Job function	Experience of AI implementation	Experience working with AI-enabled services
1	USA	2100	1500	Male	13	Technical	7	7
2	USA	27,000	750	Male	16	Technical	3	3
3	Denmark	100	50	Male	11	Managerial	2	3
4	Ireland	505,000	150,000	Male	20	Managerial	2	2
5	India	243,000	215,000	Male	14	Managerial	2	3
6	USA	500	450	Male	15	Technical	3	3
7	Canada	77,000	13,500	Female	15	Managerial	2	2
8	USA	450,000	140,000	Female	19	Technical	2	2
9	USA	23,000	18,000	Female	10	Managerial	2	3
10	Switzerland	147,000	10,000	Male	12	Technical	2	1
11	Ireland	505,000	150,000	Female	11	Managerial	3	3
12	USA	450,000	140,000	Male	14	Technical	2	4
13	USA	500	450	Male	13	Managerial	2	2
14	USA	800	400	Female	10	Managerial	1	2
15	India	447,000	375,000	Male	42	Managerial	7	7
16	USA	23,000	18,000	Female	20	Managerial	6	6
17	USA	23,000	18,000	Male	26	Managerial	2	2
18	USA	292,000	194,700	Male	28	Managerial	2	4
19	France	122,000	25,000	Female	20	Technical	3	5
20	France	45,000	6,000	Female	13	Technical	2	2

We sought an appointment for conducting the interview after providing the purpose and setting the context of the study. The participants were assured of anonymity and post their informed consent to participate in the study, an in-depth interview was conducted. The interview design was semi-structured in nature (please see Appendix A), and the interviews were guided by an indicative list of questions wherein the interviewees had flexibility in responding, thus, providing deeper insights into the study phenomenon (Banihani & Syed, 2020). While conducting the interview, we refrained from including personal questions/preferences, leading words and kept questions simple to understand. Each interview lasted for 25–30 minutes. Hand-written notes yielded a transcript of roughly 8000 words.

Data analysis

Given the inductive nature of the study, we coded the transcripts manually following the methodology proposed by Gioia et al. (2013).[3] After crafting a well-specified research question, we conducted semi-structured interviews wherein a multitude of informant (participant) terms, codes and categories emerged within the first few interviews. Gioia and colleagues (2013) refer to this stage as *1st-order concepts* in which researchers strictly adhere to the participants' terms, phrases and descriptions, and refrain from drawing specific categories. As we progressed in conducting the interviews, we began recognizing similarities and differences among the categories. We created meaningful clusters of terms and phrases and labelled those categories using the participants' phrases, thus, emerged the *2nd-order themes*. The second-order themes are primarily at the theoretical level and help the researchers in describing and explaining the study phenomenon. The culmination of themes and concepts yielded theoretical saturation (Glaser & Strauss, 1967) and then we proceeded to distill these concepts and themes into *aggregate dimensions*.

The 1st order concepts, 2nd order themes and aggregate dimensions became the basis for building the data structure for the present study (Figure 1). Data structure not only configures the qualitative data into a meaningful visual aid but also provides a graphic representation of the researchers' progress from 1st order raw participants' terms to 2nd order theoretical themes to finally meaningful dimensions that answer the research question. Authors discussed the participants' dialogues, reconciled differing interpretations and finally reached a consensual decision on the themes and dimensions. Constructing the data structure compels researchers to think about the data theoretically and is thus considered as the key component of demonstrating rigor in qualitative research.

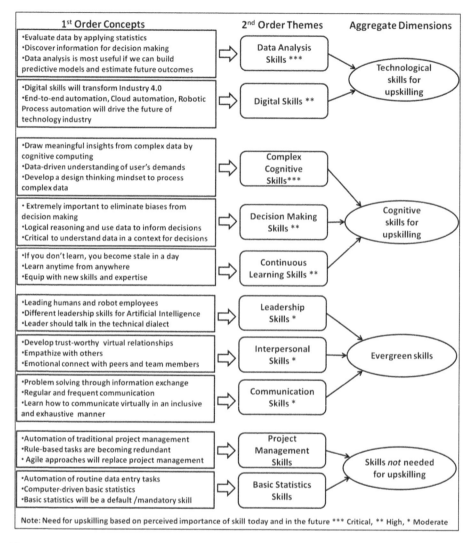

Figure 1. Data structure.

To validate the accuracy of our concepts, themes and dimensions, we conducted five post-study interviews with senior-level managers (different from the dataset participants) working in MNCs in the IT sector in India. Table 1b describes the profile of the post-study participants.

Findings

As a result of the above data analysis, several themes emerged with respect to upskilling the workforce for the era of AI. The present study builds an inductive model grounded in data as exemplified by the data structure model (Figure 1). The data structure demonstrates 1st order concepts, 2nd order themes and aggregate dimensions. The change in

Table 1b. Post-study participants' profile.

Participant number	Company headquarter	Headcount worldwide	Headcount in India	Gender	Experience (in years)	Job function	Experience of AI implementation	Experience working with AI-enabled services
1	USA	23,000	18,000	Male	17	Managerial	7	6
2	India	243,000	215,000	Female	13	Managerial	5	5
3	Canada	77,000	13,500	Male	15	Technical	3	2
4	USA	450,000	140,000	Male	24	Technical	6	6
5	United Kingdom	80,000	20,000	Female	15	Managerial	3	3

perceived importance of the skills in the present and future times is further indicated using asterisks on the 2nd order themes, that is, themes that need upskilling for the future are categorized as Critical, High and Moderate. Table 2 encapsulates additional supporting data in the form of representative quotations for readers to discern and view the evidence for our findings.

Technological skills essential for upskilling

Skill 1: Data analysis skills

The past decade has witnessed the generation of huge amounts of data from varied sources such as the Internet, social media, public sources and interaction with clients. Due to the interconnectedness of technologies, big data are being added to the existing data repository in real-time at high velocity. Further, data are available in different formats and structures such as text, video, audio and image. A participant noted, 'data is the oil' while another said, 'data is gold'. Given the enormous amount of data at their disposal today, data analysis tools extensively used in the IT industry including R programming, Python, Power BI, SAS and Tableau, become highly critical for employee upskilling. Further, expertise in the Hadoop framework that facilitates the processing of big data and Full Stack developers for programming languages such as Java and .Net, are important for upskilling for the future IT workforce. From the narratives, we found that data analysis skills were described in many ways. Broadly, data analysis was viewed as a systematic process of understanding the data and unearthing useful information to inform decision making. Participant 2 *explained, 'Data analysis is basically....applying statistics to describe and evaluate data'.*

Skill 2: Digital skills

Most industries and contemporary organizations are increasingly generating footprints in the digital space. The technology industry aims to connect the physical and digital worlds by creating a robust and secure phygital (physical plus digital) ecosystem. As the economy moves towards

Table 2. Data supporting interpretations of skills identification for upskilling for AI.

Themes	Representative quotations
Technological skills essential for upskilling	
Data analysis skills	'Through data analysis, we discover useful information...use it for [data] interpretation and that provides us a concrete basis for taking decisions' (Participant 19)
	'Data is the key for any business to be successful today...the analysis is useful for predictive modeling' (Participant 3)
	'The current skill needed for professionals is in machine learning and developing models...but the real application is in making better predictions using those models...so data analysis for predictive modeling is the most important skill for the future' (Participant 11)
Digital skills	'The digital skill that is picking up today and will be most important in the future is cloud automation....cloud automation empowers developers and managers to deliver services and meet business demands through end-to-end automation' (Participant 12)
	'Digital skills will enable transformation in Industry 4.0...it's a combination of multiple skills including front-end skills like immersive experience [through] augmented reality/ virtual reality...[and] mobility skills across different devices...and back-end skills like intelligent automation, machine learning, robotic process automation and so on....' (Participant 16).
Cognitive skills essential for upskilling	
Complex cognitive skills	'A design thinking mindset provides an innovative approach to problem-solving....it involves designing, prototyping, and testing out-of-the-box ideas....basically, it's like an ongoing experiment that helps in the decision making process' (Participant 15)
	'We use algorithms to transform data through cognitive computing....our AI-assistant is a smart assistant that runs on big data and Internet-of-Things...as of now, it is about 80-85% accurate in understanding the user's demands and responds accordingly...going forward with improved accuracy, AI-assistants will be of immense support to us for complex data processing' (Participant 4)
	'Humans process information at multiple levels including cognitive, subconscious, and shared cognitive....these also include biases...in future when AI will handle basic data well, complex processing skills for meaningful insights will become very important for humans' (Participant 11)
Decision making skills	'Presently AI's biggest challenge is to overcome biases...data fed into all AI-systems is based on prior experiences of humans which are biased...so, despite all advancements in technology, the AI-based outcomes are also biased... so this awareness is very important for decision-makers' (Participant 1)
	'Decision making is highly contextual...data must be understood in the right context...also there are ethical aspects and human behaviour....all need to be considered for good decision making' (Participant 19)
Continuous learning skills	'As an HR manager, my key role is to identify employees who are stagnant...it is my responsibility to help them transform....equipping [them] with new skills and expertise' (Participant 11)
	'We encourage horizontal movement in the organization across domains...picking up things quickly in different situations or projects shows flexibility and versatility' (Participant 15)
	'Continuous learning was always important and will continue to remain important...else we cannot survive in this industry' (Participant 20)

Evergreen skills for upskilling	
Interpersonal skills	'AI is making everything data-driven...personal judgments and feelings will have no place soon....still as humans, we will continue to understand others and empathize with them' (Participant 2)
Communication skills	'Whatever be the case...personal touch, personal communication is very much needed to maintain a good culture and work environment...if there is a problem, we need humans to solve it....moreover, a chat robot (chatbot) cannot connect with me [psychologically or emotionally] through text messages' (Participant 19)
Leadership skills	'Let's say tomorrow a robot is in your team and is reporting to you....[as a leader] How much of autonomy will you give to the robot and to the human? How will you personalize things for human employees? Leading a mix of robots and humans would be a different ball game altogether' (Participant 16)
Skills not required for upskilling	
Basic statistics skills	'Need for basic skills is there today but diminishing soon... basic statistics will be handled well by AI in the future... humans must do things they are better at' (Participant 11).
	'All routine jobs are being replaced by AI....just knowing statistics is not enough....what is relevant is the application of statistics' (Participant 16)
Project management skills	'Traditional project management is dying now....it was very important a few years back but things like scheduling, resource allocation is being automated now...the only role of project manager remains in handling any crisis kind of a situation...like when a resource suddenly leaves the company...then to find a replacement...Scrum master is replacing project manager as development is happening in short sprints' (Participant 5)
	'Two skills that today's and future managers cannot skip are Agile Coach and Scrum Master....(we sought an explanation of these skills)....agile coach creates [and] facilitates agile processes within an organization....Scrum master is a type of agile coach who implements agility at team level...' (Participant 20)

digitization, processes need to be automated and optimized for efficiency with enhanced security at a reduced cost. Thus, employees must acquire digital skills such as intelligent automation (Blueprism, vision plotting), cloud automation (Slack, Google Cloud Provider), Robotic Process Automation (Kapow, Selenium), cybersecurity (intrusion detection), and runtime applications (Angular, JBOSS). Participant 7 shares, '*The whole IT industry is enabling a digital transformation...there is a move towards a smarter world...with digital metrics, digital strategies, digital tools...so digital will be a core skill...a fundamental skill*'.

Cognitive skills essential for upskilling

Skill 1: Complex cognitive skills

With the enormous amount of data in varied formats and structures, it is becoming challenging to make sense of the data. Complex data must be processed to derive meaningful information, visualization and interpretation. Business intelligence needs convergence of data to design simple solutions and draw relevant insights. Most organizations in the technology industry conduct internal training to develop thinking and higher-order skills for employees. Training in skills such as Watson (Discovery, Studio Dashboard), design thinking, story building and Apache Spark, are being encouraged by organizations to upskill employees for complex information processing, cognition development and critical thinking. Participant 12 quotes, '*Our chatbot ABC[4] is becoming smarter with data...it breaks each sentence into meaningful information, replies to our queries and gets intelligent with every new question asked to her...so humans need to use their higher level of intelligence for much more complex tasks*'.

Skill 2: Decision making skills

Organizations aim to take good decisions for enhancing business performance. Though data are predominantly available for decision making, most contemporary organizations are unable to leverage the power of data. '*Today I have a lot of data and system-generated reports giving me an overview of the data...I should be able to use these [reports] as inputs to inform my decisions*', says Participant 14. Decision making skills are critical for upskilling as decision making is still highly subjective and not as data-driven as it should be. Human biases unconsciously seep into the decisions. Dynamic human behavior, ethical and legal considerations must also be accounted for during decision making. Further, speedy decisions must be taken in real-time such that the decisions reflect current trends and address critical business disruptions. Thus, employees must notably be trained in taking unbiased, rational and evidence-based decisions.

Skill 3: Continuous learning skills

Engaging oneself in an unceasing learning path while responding to the volatile, uncertain, complex and ambiguous business environment (VUCA) is the key ingredient for employee success in the era of AI. Unlike a few decades back when each technology had a lifespan of at least a few years, in contemporary times, the lifespan of technology has reduced to a few months or weeks. In such a dynamically changing technological era, continuous learning is undoubtedly essential for employees to stay relevant and not become obsolete. As a participant said, '*If you don't learn, you become stale in a day in this industry*'. Continuous Improvement, Continual Learning and Troubleshooting are some of the continuous learning programs internally organized by companies while Full Stack development for Java and .NET are some of the domain-specific skills recommended for continuous learning. *'Learning is the DNA of the organization....we have provided access on all platforms to our employees so that they can learn anytime from anywhere'* (Participant 13).

Thus, we found five critical skills for employee upskilling to sustain employment and succeed in the era of AI: data analysis skills, digital skills, complex cognitive skills, decision making skills and continuous learning skills.

Evergreen skills for upskilling

While upskilling in the above-cited technological and cognitive skills is critical for IT sector employees to remain employable and thrive in the era of AI, some other skills were found to be of importance. Social skills, specifically, leadership skills, interpersonal skills and communication skills were mentioned by some participants as important; however, the context will differ. For instance, future leaders must not only be visionaries but also must understand the intricacies of AI and associated technologies. As a participant said, *'the leader should possess algorithmic thinking and talk in the technical dialect in order to drive transformation'*. Further, the need for building strong relationships through trust and interpersonal association would remain essential; however, future employees must also build good virtual relationships without co-locating physically. Likewise, employees will have to become comfortable and conversant in not having in-person communication. A participant notes, *'employees will have to learn how to communicate virtually in an inclusive and exhaustive yet unambiguous manner'*.

Thus, leadership, interpersonal and communication skills were noted to be of importance by most participants. We refer to these skills as 'evergreen skills' because irrespective of time, that is, today or in the future, these skills are deemed crucial for an individual's success. In the present study context of upskilling for AI, the degree to which upskilling in these evergreen skills is needed is not relatively as high as the need for upskilling in technological and cognitive skills.

Skills not required for upskilling

While our primary aim was to identify the skills critical for upskilling in the context of AI, the participants inevitably highlighted skills that have already or will soon become obsolete. Skills needed for delivering routine, mundane and rule-based tasks are not needed as AI-solutions are already adopted for these tasks. For instance, data entry, scheduling, coding, basic statistics, database management and project management are some skills that are gradually losing their lustre. For instance, basic statistics is an important skill in the present for data analysis; however, in the future driven by AI, basic statistics will become a *'default/mandatory/fundamental'* skill as noted by many participants. Further, with changing client demands and faster turnaround times, the role of project management is diminishing exponentially. The Waterfall model for software development life cycle is becoming redundant as the technology industry is moving towards an agile approach. The agile and scrum master processes have stand-up meetings that ensure higher project flexibility, parallel processes, quicker reviews, better product quality, faster delivery, enhanced connectivity with the clients, reduced need for documentation and an integrated development-operations (DevOps) framework. *'SAFe 4.0 is the platform for becoming an Advanced Scrum Master'* shares a participant. Thus, basic skillsets would be managed well by AI-systems; whereas, human beings must elevate to higher-order and complex tasks.

Thus, the key study findings are:

a. Data analysis and digital skills are critical technological skills for employee upskilling.
b. Complex cognitive, decision making and continuous learning are critical cognitive skills for employee upskilling.
c. Leadership, interpersonal and communication are evergreen skills for which the degree of upskilling needed is relatively less than the technological and cognitive skills.
d. Routine skills such as basic statistics and project management will diminish in the future, thus, upskilling is not needed.

The data structure model presented in Figure 1 helped visualize the categorization of the skills into different themes. In the ensuing discussion, the need for upskilling of different skills (2nd order themes) was briefly classified as critical, high and moderate, whereas, some skills were found unimportant for upskilling. To present these findings with more clarity, it is useful to diagrammatically represent the participants' perceptions of the importance of different skills at two points in time: at present and in the future (Figure 2). This representation grounded in data is a dynamic model emerging from the qualitative analysis (Gioia et al., 2013). The figure helps to visualize how the importance of each skill is perceived to 'dynamically' change from present to future and underscores the relative need for upskilling.

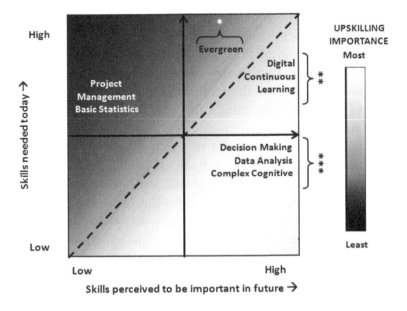

Figure 2. Relative importance of skills for employee upskilling.

Figure 2 schematically represents the relative importance of different skillsets for employee upskilling in the IT industry to remain employable and competitive in the era of AI. The vertical axis is a measure of the importance of a particular skill today, while the horizontal axis represents the skills perceived to be important in the future. The extreme bottom right region in the plot represents the theoretical possibility of a skill that is of slight importance today but has the highest importance in the future and thus qualifies as the most critical zone for upskilling. The grayscale color code (see color bar on the right side of the plot) illustrates the relative importance of any skill for upskilling: skills depicted in the lightest background regions of the figure have the highest importance for upskilling whereas; skills marked in the darker background are of diminishing importance for upskilling. The skills marked on the top left quadrant have diminishing relevance in the future. The importance of skills such as basic statistics and project management is diminishing due to AI-enabled systems, thus, they do not require upskilling. The dotted diagonal line is an 'equipotential' and the skills that hypothetically lie on this line are those for which no change is expected in their *relative* importance between today and in the future. Evergreen skills such as leadership, communication and interpersonal skills are of importance today and will continue to be important in the future. However, the future evergreen skills will be contextualised according to AI and thus, the need for upskilling in these skills exists albeit not to a large extent.

Upon moving further away from the equipotential line towards the bottom right zone, the perceived need for upskilling progressively enhances. The five skills found *critical* for upskilling in the present study are depicted in different quadrants of the figure. The top right quadrant contains one technological skill (i.e. digital) and one cognitive skill (i.e. continuous learning). Participants were unequivocal about their high relevance today as well as their relevance in the future AI-era. These skills are of growing importance for upskilling as we navigate from present to future. Thus, we approximately positioned these skills on the top right quadrant of the diagram to the right of the diagonal. Further, skills including data analysis (technological skills), decision making and complex cognitive (both cognitive skills) were described by the participants to be of moderate importance today but of tremendous importance in the future. The need for upskilling for AI is the highest for these skills which are depicted in the bottom right quadrant of the figure. Thus, Figure 2 represents the skills that are important now, skills that are important in the future and the skills that need the most attention for upskilling for AI.

Discussion

Our study provides important insights regarding how the potential adverse impact of AI in terms of job replacement can be meaningfully redirected into an employee's skill development. The demand for skills due to technological advancement will assume unprecedented importance in the near future. We can broadly map the skills identified in the present study to Huang and Rust (2018) model of four intelligences required for service tasks – mechanical, analytical, intuitive and empathetic. We found that tasks related to mechanical intelligence such as basic statistics will be easily taken over by AI in the near future. Analytical tasks such as data analysis and technology-related digital competence will be difficult to be mimicked by AI. Intuitive tasks such as complex cognitive processing, decision making and continuous learning, and empathetic tasks such as communication, interpersonal and leadership skills will be even more difficult to be emulated by AI. Thus, the changing nature of work in the IT sector necessitates employees to perform jobs that require more of analytical, intuitive and empathetic skills so that they remain employed and create value for the organization.

Corroborating with the dynamic skill theory and recent Mckinsey report (Agarwal et al., 2020), our study participants highlighted that Indian organizations are dynamically engaging employees in building their skills as a priority activity. With the integration of AI across industry types, there is a shrinking need for basic cognitive skills such as data entry, data processing, scheduling and monitoring. Our findings indicate that there is a significant need for upskilling in technological skills including data analysis and digital skills. Concurrently, the demand for cognitive skills is also on the rise especially for skills such as complex information processing, critical thinking, decision making and continuous learning. It should also be noted that our findings were agnostic of the size of the MNC. The participants included managers from small, medium and large-size MNCs operating in the IT sector in India. Irrespective of the size of MNC, the participants responded alike that employees' skills need to be built to address role disruptions and skill gaps created due to AI. This demonstrates that the orientation and understanding of the IT industry are similar with respect to the challenges, opportunities and avenues that the era of AI will unfold for individual contributors and for organizations.

The proponents of AI do not champion the mass replacement of humans by machines. Rather, they indicate organizational think tanks to nurture the workforce with the right skillsets to augment technological advancements. In view of the current and forecasted changes, contemporary organizations are providing several online and offline learning platforms and opportunities for employees to enhance their current skills portfolio. Increasing tech talent requires upskilling in data analysis including knowledge of advanced statistics, application of predictive modeling and time series forecasting, data interpretation, writing algorithms and familiarization with concepts related to big data, analytics, machine learning and deep learning. Advanced digital skills that are deemed to have strategic importance to the business encompass cloud automation, intelligent automation, robotic process automation, cybersecurity and internet-of-things.

The rise in demand for complex cognitive and information processing skills is owing to the rapidly changing market trends, consumer preferences and overall business scenario. Changes in the macro-level industry environment impact internal organizational functioning and its employees. For instance, employees need to understand the technical details of products/services and explain to customers. This requires cognitive skills such as deriving insights from complex data, visualizing and interpreting it in a meaningful manner. Further, AI-powered technology needs to be embedded in the employees' way of thinking. Developing systems thinking, design thinking, enhancing creativity, and data-driven decision making comprise sharpening thinking skills. Big data analytics, decision support systems and contextual sensemaking by AI-technologies are providing insights to managers, thus, enabling them to take decisions in a better, faster and more precise way. Finally, there is an emphasis on enhancing the learning curve in a cross-functional and team-based work environment as the nature of work will be redefined with a heightened need for agility. Thus, flexibility, continuous learning and agile ways of working are foreseen as top-priorities by organizations. Scrum master, agile coach and DevOps are the critical skills enabling organizational sustenance in the era of disruption and AI.

While there is a major need for upskilling employees in cognitive and technological skills, the need for upskilling in social skills such as leadership, communication and interpersonal remains, thus, we refer to these skills as evergreen skills. Leaders' crucial role lies in thoughtfully redesigning existing jobs and encouraging employees to enhance their skills. Across levels, communication is imperative to inspire employees in creating a mindset of continuous learning and skill enhancement. Further, in an era of digitization, there is a threat of treating people as numbers and dehumanizing them. Thus, developing empathetic and interpersonal skills is needed to enable employees' strengths and capabilities.

We believe that upskilling will reap the requisite benefits only if organizations collaborate with schools and colleges to develop appropriate curricula to address the issue of lack of talent and skill mismatches. Relatedly, educators should redesign the curriculum and develop new metrics to measure broad-based skillsets in tandem with industry requirements.

AI has not only impacted organizations but has set the ball rolling to develop a 'learning and feeling economy'. A learning economy is characterized by a workforce that continues to learn, upskill and reskill based on advances in technology and innovation (Bughin et al., 2018). A feeling economy is an economy in which the employment attributable to feeling tasks such as interpersonal and empathy exceeds the employment generated by thinking and mechanical tasks (Huang et al., 2019). While AI-systems continuously learn and perform thinking and mechanical tasks, humans can spend more time on empathetic and feeling tasks. Thus, managers must restructure the jobs to more people-oriented, feeling-conscious and emotionally intelligent. This requires developing employees on feeling intelligence and people skills.

Finally, the present skills scenario in the sampled IT firms does not demand the need for upskilling in routine or rule-based skills such as data entry, scheduling, coding, basic statistics, database management and project management. As data are being generated continuously and voluminously, AI-powered systems are increasingly becoming capable of analyzing data based on algorithms and making sense of structured data in real-time. Rule-based cognitive systems have the ability to learn and improve performance through continuous analysis of real-time data and user feedback. Thus, AI can automate many repetitive, mundane and high-risk tasks giving human beings more scope for engaging in complex tasks. Further, AI's greater power lies in collaborating with humans and complementing human being's capabilities. In today's highly dynamic industry environment, changing decision criteria powered by real-time data and machine-learning approaches are creating immense business value, thus, necessitating the workforce to develop skills to work proficiently alongside AI-enabled machines.

Practical implications

In order to capitalize on the benefits of AI, organizations must proactively re-tool their policies, practices and philosophies to accept AI-enabled mechanisms as partners in their operations. More specifically, leaders must raise the capacity of employees in these skills to prepare and perform well in the era of AI. Advancing the NHCT, we suggest using a high commitment human resource (HCHR) strategy towards creating a firm's competitive advantage by building human capital concentration (Collins, 2020). HCHR is a philosophical approach focusing on investment in employee skill and capability development. HCHR outlines the employer–employee relationship by creating an organizational climate that encourages organizational members to build their resources and human capital. Investment in the intangible human capital presents strategic leverage points that drive an organization's competitive advantage (Chadwick & Flinchbaugh, 2020).

The AI job replacement theory necessitates employees to upskill themselves in skills deemed critical for the future such as analytics, predictive modeling, intelligent automation, agility and digital skills. This investment in human capital will not only preserve the in-house functional knowledge and expertise but also boost employee motivation, loyalty, organizational commitment and citizenship. Organizational support towards upskilling is critical in encouraging employees to develop new skillsets. Changes in context require cognitive development and hence the dynamic skill theory helps explain how an individual can adapt to the changing tasks, needs and environment. Developing a habit of lifelong learning is the most important ingredient to develop oneself for the future of work. But, such learning must be supported and rewarded by the organization, so that employees' learning behavior is reinforced.

The future of work embedded in AI requires a transformational change in an individual's previously accepted worldviews and perspectives. Additionally, leaders should enable agility among organizational members, that is, the ability to renew, adapt and change quickly to facilitate their learning and capacity building while ensuring success in the turbulent business environment. Leaders must help employees understand lifelong employability, that is, continuous adaptation and upskilling as the economy evolves. Upskilling should not be considered as an end in itself, but as a means to grow and remain employable.

As organizations aim to leverage the benefits of AI, a basic understanding of technological advancements and their application is binding across all managerial levels. It is necessary to highlight here that upskilling is not just needed for the large proportion of the workforce but also for the top management and senior executives. Dynamic managerial capabilities (DMC) theory (Augier & Teece, 2009; Helfat & Martin, 2015) highlights the impact of varied characteristics and behaviors of senior leaders on the resource advantages in multinational organizations. DMC theorizes the processes through which organizational leaders acquire, develop, deploy and reconfigure capabilities to drive strategic behavioral change among other organizational members. Organizational leaders' acceptance and adoption of technology is critical as it will help them to orchestrate digital changes in a better manner. This does not necessarily mean that they should become AI-experts; however, process redesigning and organizational transformation towards digitalization can be facilitated by top management only if they equip themselves with adequate and updated skill sets.

Furthermore, our study demonstrates the need for developing a symbiotic relationship between humans and machines. Huang and Rust (2018) suggest human–machine integration towards building collaborative intelligence such that AI will enhance human connectivity. Individual employees have limited intelligence, whereas, collectively employees support each other. Likewise, human intelligence can be augmented by the collective intelligence of machines. While AI has the capability to process large amounts of data, the key to remaining important for humans lies in the understanding of data, interpreting the results and decision making. Since, the human brain processes data in a holistic way and AI processes data in a logical way, computational methods on which AI is built will make humans more powerful (Huang & Rust, 2018). Hence, employee upskilling must emphasize the importance of a collaborative relationship between man and machine to surf the AI revolution.

Theoretical implications

Our findings offer several theoretical implications for future research. As we noted earlier, human resource literature is lagging when it comes to examining the intersection of AI and human resources. While the published literature is fairly advanced in investigating how technology has helped speed human resource processes, there is a need to examine how AI is impacting the practice, process and philosophy of human resources. For example, one critical aspect of AI is that individuals will increasingly deal with robots as colleagues and technological platforms as managers. This will necessitate re-visiting our understanding, and revising theories, of supervisor–subordinate relationships and team cohesiveness, for example. As we noted earlier, the dynamic skill theory proposes that individuals would need to be adept in a whole range of skills including social, emotional, technological and physical skills to survive and thrive in the new workplace. In addition, individuals would now also need to become comfortable with human–machine interactions and be willing to update and/or upgrade their skills in this area, as AI-enabled machines and processes get upgraded/upskilled.

Similarly, NHCT and AI job replacement theory both address the issues involved with how AI will impact the ability of human beings to use their skills for finding gainful employment in the workplace and retaining that employment. Our findings of the need for upskilling offer support for these theories while at the same time suggesting that the theories will need to evolve as AI keeps evolving.

Finally, since AI may eliminate or reduce the need for humans in numerous jobs, academics would need to re-visit the classical theories of work and motivation, for example, to better understand how the growth of AI is impacting how humans see their work. In a recent examination of how the technological platforms impact employee control and motivation, Norlander et al. (2021) found that Uber drivers reported greater intrinsic motivation and enjoyment of work compared to taxi drivers, even though they were subject to higher levels of monitoring and control *via* AI platforms. Clearly, there is a need to further investigate the AI and human resource intersection from various angles.

Limitations and future directions

The limitations of our study highlight new avenues for further research. The preliminary ideas that emerge from the current study prompt further data collection, thus, strengthening the qualitative work. Future researchers may generate hypotheses based on the present study, gather new data, and test the propositions using quantitative research design towards generating an explanatory model for skills upgradation in the context of AI. Further, while AI-systems facilitate problem-solving, it is critical to account for the national cultural context for business decision making. AI-based products and solutions are primarily data-driven and data is highly contextual. As there are cultural differences across countries, this may be interesting to investigate in more depth. The current study focused on employee upskilling for AI in a sample of informational technology multinational corporations in India. Future research could explore the adequate skill needs across different sectors with different types of business ownership. MNCs in the IT sector may have a different orientation as compared to a public limited company in the automobile sector, for example.

Next, given that India has been in the lead of developing AI applications and in AI implementation, it is critical that scholars examine the evolution of AI applications in the Indian context. This is critical since India presents a paradoxical environment – a country with a large population with the need for millions of jobs is also in the forefront of developing AI-enabled applications that can replace human labor – as in the case of a restaurant in Bengaluru using robots as waiters and a school using robot as a teacher.

While our focus in the present study was primarily on the upskilling of employees, future studies may examine other options to build the workforce for the future, for instance, redeploying some employees with specific skills within the organization to make better use of their skill-sets. Alternatively, since redeploying does not upskill employees, recruiting people with the desired skills maybe another worthy option. Several firms are also using the services of freelancers or contract employees than hiring a permanent employee. These independent workers not only bring the necessary expertise but also seamlessly integrate into the organization due to increased agility. Thus, future work may explore what works best for organizations – upskilling existing employees or redeploying existing employees or hiring new employees or outsourcing the task. Finally, scholars should also examine the social and psychological impact of AI on those whose employment is made redundant by these technologies, especially in a developing nation such as India.

Conclusion

The present study aimed to unearth the skills deemed critical for the upskilling of employees to sustain employment and thrive in the era of AI. Contemporary organizations do not consider AI as a competitor to humans, rather they believe in the human–AI complementarity. Technology complements and augments human capabilities towards enhancing business growth. The study highlights five critical skills for employee upskilling including data analysis, digital, complex cognitive, decision making and continuous learning skills. Thus, the proposed shift in skill sets emphasizing the development of higher cognitive and technological skills is a pivotal step towards human–AI collaboration. Completely outsourcing intelligence to machines will neither be useful nor ethical owing to the complex socio-economic-political–cultural milieu in which the organizations are fabricated. Evolving to a higher collective intelligence with techno-cognitive skills deems to be the most promising way forward. We are confident that the present study has provided a roadmap for future research in this nascent yet promising domain.

Notes

1. We thank an anonymous reviewer for this suggestion.
2. NASSCOM (National Association of Software and Services Companies) is the agency responsible for IT and ITeS sector in India).
3. We thank the Editors and an anonymous reviewer for this methodology.
4. Name of the chatbot is disguised to maintain organizational anonymity.

Acknowledgements

The lead author thanks Dr. Manu Jaiswal for his support in this research study and constructive comments on the earlier versions of this paper.

Disclosure statement

The authors have no potential conflict of interest.

Geolocation information

The study was conducted in India (Asia).

ORCID

Akanksha Jaiswal (iD) http://orcid.org/0000-0001-8997-0668

Data availability statement

The authors confirm that the data supporting the findings of this study are available within the article. Further details may not be available as it will compromise the privacy of the research participants. For further clarifications, please contact the lead author.

References

Agarwal, S., Smet, A. D., Poplawski, P., & Reich, A. (2020). *Beyond hiring: How companies are reskilling to address talent gaps*. McKinsey Global Institute.

Ågerfalk, P. J. (2020). Artificial intelligence as digital agency. *European Journal of Information Systems*, *29*(1), 1–8. https://doi.org/10.1080/0960085X.2020.1721947

Akerkar, R. (2019). *Artificial intelligence for business*. Springer.

Augier, M., & Teece, D. J. (2009). Dynamic capabilities and the role of managers in business strategy and economic performance. *Organization Science*, *20*(2), 410–421. https://doi.org/10.1287/orsc.1090.0424

Banihani, M., & Syed, J. (2020). Gendered work engagement: Qualitative insights from Jordan. *The International Journal of Human Resource Management, 31*(5), 611–637. https://doi.org/10.1080/09585192.2017.1355838

Bartel, A. P., & Lichtenberg, F. R. (1987). The comparative advantage of educated workers in implementing new technology. *The Review of Economics and Statistics, 69*(1), 1–11. https://doi.org/10.2307/1937894

Bondarouk, T., & Brewster, C. (2016). Conceptualizing the future of HRM and technology research. *The International Journal of Human Resource Management, 27*(21), 2652–2671. https://doi.org/10.1080/09585192.2016.1232296

Bondarouk, T., Parry, E., & Furtmueller, E. (2017). Electronic HRM: Four decades of research on adoption and consequences. *The International Journal of Human Resource Management, 28*(1), 98–131. https://doi.org/10.1080/09585192.2016.1245672

Budhwar, P. S. (2012). Management of human resources in foreign firms operating in India: The role of HR in country-specific headquarters. *The International Journal of Human Resource Management, 23*(12), 2514–2531. https://doi.org/10.1080/09585192.2012.668404

Budhwar, P. S., & Varma, A. (2011). Emerging HR management trends in India and the way forward. *Organizational Dynamics, 40*(4), 317–325. https://doi.org/10.1016/j.orgdyn.2011.07.009

Budhwar, P., Varma, A., & Kumar, R. (Eds.). (2019). *Indian business: Understanding a rapidly emerging economy.* Routledge.

Bughin, J., Batra, P., Chui, M., Manyika, J., Ko, R., Sanghvi, S., Woetzel, J., & Lund, S. (2017). *Jobs lost, jobs gained: Workforce transitions in a time of automation.* McKinsey Global Institute.

Bughin, J., Hazan, E., Lund, S., Dahlström, P., Wiesinger, A., & Subramaniam, A. (2018). *Skill shift: Automation and the future of the workforce.* McKinsey & Company/ McKinsey Global Institute.

Butler, D. (2016). A world where everyone has a robot: Why 2040 could blow your mind. *Nature, 530*(7591), 398–401. https://doi.org/10.1038/530398a

Cappelli, P., Tambe, & Yakubovich, P. (2020). Can data science change human resources? In J. Canals & F. Heukamp (Eds.), *The future of management in an AI world.* IESE Business Collection. https://doi.org/10.1007/978-3-030-20680-2_5

Chadwick, C., & Flinchbaugh, C. (2020). Searching for competitive advantage in the hrm/firm performance relationship. *Academy of Management Perspectives.* https://doi.org/10.5465/amp.2018.0065

Chaudhuri, K., Varma, A., & Malik, A. (2020). Artificial Intelligence as an antidote for managing people in organizations: How realistic?. *Paper presented at the British Academy of Management Conference 2020.*

Collins, C. J. (2020). Expanding the resource-based view model of strategic human resource management. *The International Journal of Human Resource Management.* https://doi.org/10.1080/09585192.2019.1711442

Corea, F. (2019). AI knowledge map: How to classify AI technologies. In *An introduction to data. Studies in big data.* Springer.

Daugherty, P. R., & Wilson, H. J. (2018). *Human + machine: Reimagining work in the age of AI.* Harvard Business Press.

Davenport, T. H., & Kirby, J. (2016). Just how smart are smart machines?*MIT Sloan Management Review, 57*(3), 21–25.

Fischer, K., Yan, Z., & Stewart, J. (2003). Adult cognitive development: Dynamics in the developmental web. *Handbook of developmental psychology* (pp. 491–516). Sage.

Gioia, D. A., Corley, K. G., & Hamilton, A. L. (2013). Seeking qualitative rigor in inductive research: Notes on the Gioia methodology. *Organizational Research Methods, 16*(1), 15–31. https://doi.org/10.1177/1094428112452151

Glaser, B. G., & Strauss, A. L. (1967). *The discovery of grounded theory. Strategies for qualitative research*. Aldine.

Hancock, B., Lazaroff-Puck, K., & Rutherford, S. (2020). *Getting practical about the future of work*. McKinsey Global Institute.

Helfat, C. E., & Martin, J. A. (2015). Dynamic managerial capabilities: Review and assessment of managerial impact on strategic change. *Journal of Management, 41*(5), 1281–1312. https://doi.org/10.1177/0149206314561301

Huang, M. H., & Rust, R. T. (2018). Artificial intelligence in service. *Journal of Service Research, 21*(2), 155–172. https://doi.org/10.1177/1094670517752459

Huang, M.-H., Rust, R., & Maksimovic, V. (2019). The feeling economy: Managing in the next generation of artificial intelligence (AI). *California Management Review, 61*(4), 43–65. https://doi.org/10.1177/0008125619863436

IBEF. (2019). Retrieved January 10, 202, from https://www.ibef.org/industry/information-technology-india.aspx.

INDIAai. (2020). Retrieved July 20, 2020, from https://indiaai.in/.

Jain, N. K., Celo, S., & Kumar, V. (2019). Internationalization speed, resources and performance: Evidence from Indian software industry. *Journal of Business Research, 95*, 26–37. https://doi.org/10.1016/j.jbusres.2018.09.019

Jaiswal, A., & Arun, C. J. (2021). Potential of artificial intelligence for transformation of education system in India. *International Journal of Education and Development Using Information and Communication Technology, 17*(1), 142–158.

Jordan, M. I., & Mitchell, T. M. (2015). Machine learning: Trends, perspectives, and prospects. *Science (New York, N.Y.), 349*(6245), 255–260. https://doi.org/10.1126/science.aaa8415

Kunnen, E. S., & Bosma, H. A. (2003). Fischer's skill theory applied to identity development: A response to Kroger. *Identity, 3*(3), 247–270. https://doi.org/10.1207/S1532706XID0303_05

Lavelle, J., Turner, T., Gunnigle, P., & McDonnell, A. (2012). The determinants of financial participation schemes within multinational companies in Ireland. *The International Journal of Human Resource Management, 23*(8), 1590–1610. https://doi.org/10.1080/09585192.2012.661991

Lecun, Y., Bengio, Y., & Hinton, G. (2015). Deep learning. *Nature, 521*(7553), 436–444. https://doi.org/10.1038/nature14539

Malik, A., & Rowley, C. (Eds.). (2015). *Business models and people management in the Indian IT industry: From people to profits*. Routledge.

Malik, A., Budhwar, P., Srikanth, N. R., & Varma, A. (2019). May the bots be with you! Opportunities and challenges of artificial intelligence for rethinking human resource management practices. *Paper presented at the British Academy of Management Conference 2019*, Birmingham, UK.

Malik, A., Pereira, V., & Budhwar, P. (2020). HRM in the global information technology (IT) industry: Towards multivergent configurations in strategic business partnerships. *Human Resource Management Review*, 100743. https://doi.org/10.1016/j.hrmr.2020.100743

Marler, J. H., & Boudreau, J. W. (2017). An evidence-based review of HR Analytics. *The International Journal of Human Resource Management, 28*(1), 3–26. https://doi.org/10.1080/09585192.2016.1244699

Meijerink, J., Boons, M., Keegan, A., & Marler, J. (2018). Special issue of the international journal of human resource management: Digitization and the transformation of human resource management. *The International Journal of Human Resource Management*. https://doi.org/10.1080/09585192.2018.1503845

Menon, R. M., Vazirani, M., & Roy, P. (2017). *Rewire for growth: Accelerating India's economic growth with Artificial Intelligence.* Accenture Research.

Mitchell, T. M. (2017). Key ideas in machine learning. In *Machine learning* (pp. 1–11). McGraw Hill.

NASSCOM. (2020). Retrieved February 2, 2020 from https://www.nasscom.in/

New Education Policy. (2020). Ministry of Human Resource Development, Government of India. Retrieved August 30, 2020 from https://www.mhrd.gov.in/relevant-documents

Norlander, P., Jukic, N., Varma, A., & Nestorov, S. (2021). The effects of technological supervision on gig workers: Organizational control and motivation of Uber, taxi, and limousine drivers. *International Journal of Human Resource Management*, https://doi.org/10.1080/09585192.2020.1867614

OECD. Publishing, & Organisation for Economic Co-operation and Development. (2012). *Better skills, better jobs, better lives: A strategic approach to skills policies.* OECD.

Østerlund, C., Jarrahi, M. H., Willis, M., Boyd, K., & Wolf, C. T. (2021). Artificial intelligence and the world of work, a co-constitutive relationship. *Journal of the Association for Information Science and Technology*, *72*(1), 128–135. https://doi.org/10.1002/asi.24388

Pereira, V., & Malik, A. (2015). *Human capital in the Indian IT/BPO industry* (1st ed.). Palgrave Macmillan.

Pereira, V., Budhwar, P., Temouri, Y., Malik, A., & Tarba, S. (2020). Investigating investments in agility strategies in overcoming the global financial crisis – The case of Indian IT/BPO offshoring firms. *Journal of International Management*, 100738. https://doi.org/10.1016/j.intman.2020.100738

Portugal, I., Alencar, P., & Cowan, D. (2018). The use of machine learning algorithms in recommender systems : A systematic review. *Expert Systems with Applications*, *97*, 205–227. https://doi.org/10.1016/j.eswa.2017.12.020

Rust, R. T., & Huang, M. H. (2014). The service revolution and the transformation of marketing science. *Marketing Science*, *33*(2), 206–221. https://doi.org/10.1287/mksc.2013.0836

Sullivan, Y., de Bourmont, M., & Dunaway, M. (2020). Appraisals of harms and injustice trigger an eerie feeling that decreases trust in artificial intelligence systems. *Annals of Operations Research*, 1–24.

Thite, M., Budhwar, P., & Wilkinson, A. (2014). Global HR roles and factors influencing their development: Evidence from emerging Indian IT services multinationals. *Human Resource Management*, *53*(6), 921–946. https://doi.org/10.1002/hrm.21621

Tschang, F. T., & Mezquita, E. A. (2020). Artificial intelligence as augmenting automation: Implications for employment. *Academy of Management Perspectives*. https://doi.org/10.5465/amp.2019.0062

Varma, A., & Tung, R. (2020). Lure of country of origin: An exploratory study of ex-host country nationals in India. *Personnel Review*, *49*(7), 1487–1501. https://doi.org/10.1108/PR-10-2019-0578

Wilson, H. J., Daugherty, P. R., & Morini-Bianzino, N. (2017). The jobs that artificial intelligence will create. *MIT Sloan Management Review*, *58*(4), 13–16.

Wozniak, G. (1984). The adoption of interrelated innovations: A human capital approach. *The Review of Economics and Statistics*, *66*(1), 70–79. https://doi.org/10.2307/1924697

Wozniak, G. (1987). Human capital, information, and the early adoption of technology. *The Journal of Human Resources*, *22*(1), 101–112. https://doi.org/10.2307/145869

APPENDIX A

Interview schedule

1. Which skills according to you are critical for your upskilling to remain employable and succeed in the AI era? What is the relevance of the skills you mentioned today?

2. Within the past 3 years, have you been upskilled/undergoing upskilling to prepare for changes due to AI? Please provide some details such as the nature of the upskilling program, module(s), and keywords.

3. Among the skills of relevance today, which skills will not require upskilling for the AI era?

4. Company's information: Headquarter, worldwide employee headcount, headcount in India.

5. Personal information: Gender, job function, total years of work experience, experience of AI implementation, and experience working with AI-enabled services.

Beliefs, anxiety and change readiness for artificial intelligence adoption among human resource managers: the moderating role of high-performance work systems

Yuliani Suseno 🄳, Chiachi Chang, Marek Hudik 🄳 and Eddy S. Fang

ABSTRACT

This study examines the change readiness for artificial intelligence (AI) adoption among human resource (HR) managers. In particular, it investigates the effects of the three elements of attitudes (cognitive, affective and behavioural elements) related to the HR managers' beliefs about AI, their AI anxiety, and their change readiness for AI adoption. The research also seeks to explore the moderating role of high-performance work systems (HPWS) in the relationships between HR managers' beliefs, AI anxiety, and change readiness. Data were obtained from 417 HR managers working in China, with findings indicating that HR managers' beliefs about AI and their AI anxiety have a significant effect on their change readiness for AI adoption. Specifically, HR managers' beliefs positively influence their change readiness, while their AI anxiety negatively predicts their change readiness. Our results further highlight that HPWS can attenuate the negative effect of AI anxiety on HR managers' change readiness for AI adoption. The study's theoretical and practical implications, limitations and directions for future research are also discussed accordingly.

Introduction

Artificial intelligence (AI) plays an increasingly important role in changing the way organisations do business. The adoption of AI represents a paradigm shift in the way organisations operate their business and manage their employees, with AI promising work efficiency and effectiveness in a wide range of application areas. In the context of our study, we refer to AI as 'any intelligent agent (e.g. device) that distinguishes between different environments and can take a course of action(s) to increase the success of achieving predetermined objectives' (van Esch et al., 2019, p. 215). AI systems help organisations and individuals gather information, analyse data, and also enhance their decision-making in various areas, such as finance, transportation, healthcare and data security.

Despite the huge promise and global emergence of AI technologies, organisations may not be overly proactive in adopting AI as they still view AI as disrupting the work environment. In the context of HRM, AI is often used in the selection and recruitment of employees (van Esch et al., 2019), employee training, performance evaluation as well as matching individuals to tasks and enhancing employee experience (Bondarouk & Brewster, 2016). Albert (2019) found a variety of AI applications used in recruitment, such as chatbots, screening software and task automation tools. For instance, chatbots mimic human conversation tools and provide immediate responses to questions. Another example is the use of the screening software to review a large number of CVs and video interviews, while automation tools are used for scheduling events and activities. Overall, these applications using AI help take over routine work and improve the speed of recruitment (Albert, 2019).

Existing research has highlighted that, in any change process, employees' perceptions of change readiness are critical (Choi, 2011; Rafferty & Jimmieson, 2017). Madsen et al. (2005, p. 216) identified that an individual is ready for change 'when he or she understands, believes, and intends to change because of a perceived need'. Arguably, in the case of organisations undergoing changes such as AI adoption, understanding members' readiness for such change is critical (Armenakis et al., 1993; Rafferty et al., 2013). However, this has not been explored in the broader literature of human resource management (HRM) despite the implications of the changes caused by AI to the future of work (Jarrahi, 2018).

Although the body of research on organisational change readiness has provided insights and understanding, existing studies mainly relate to change readiness in the broader organisational change context (e.g. Bouckenooghe, 2010). For example, Eby et al.'s (2000) study is focused on organisational readiness for change, although the data were derived from employees' perceptions and reactions. As highlighted by Bouckenooghe (2010), it is important to ensure that studies either focus on a single level of analysis or highlight the dynamics of the relationships if these are examined at multiple levels. In this study, we focus on the individual-level conceptualisation and analysis of change readiness (Choi, 2011; Shah et al., 2017).

Bouckenooghe's (2010) review further highlighted that most studies are focused on the change recipients, with only a handful of studies focusing on the change agents. This presents another gap in the organisational change literature. In addressing this gap, we focus on HR managers as the change agents, given that HR, as an organisational function, is most likely to capitalise and adopt AI to optimise internal and external business processes (Guenole & Feinzig, 2018; van Esch et al., 2019). HR managers can be the champions of change (Caldwell, 2001), including in the adoption of new technology. Therefore, their change readiness to adopt AI not only potentially minimises any resistance to change but can also empower sceptical employees at all levels.

Few studies have also directly examined the three distinct elements of attitudes toward technology adoption. In order to address this gap in the literature, our study examines the role of cognitive, affective, and behavioural elements of HR managers' change readiness for AI adoption. Specifically, in this study, we consider change readiness for AI adoption as the HR managers' state of inclination to accept this change (Rafferty & Minbashian, 2019; Shah et al., 2017). Change readiness is a behavioural element of attitude as it is 'an individual's evaluation that they were prepared or ready for change' (Rafferty & Minbashian, 2019, p. 1630). We argue that individuals' change readiness can be influenced by their beliefs about AI (the cognitive element of attitude). In addition, Rafferty and Minbashian (2019, p. 1624) highlighted that most change researchers, while focusing on change beliefs, 'have ignored positive emotions about change'. We thus adopt a similar approach to Rafferty and Minbashian (2019) in including the affective element of change; however, we differ in our focus in this study by incorporating a less positive emotion, AI anxiety (Durndell & Haag, 2002; Kummer et al., 2017). We therefore consider the influence of individual AI anxiety (the affective element of attitude) on an individual's change readiness for AI adoption.

Beyond individual attitudes, we consider how organisational context can potentially enable successful change management (Choi, 2011). Existing studies on organisational change emphasise the role of high-performance work systems (HPWS) to support the change management process (Jeong & Shin, 2019), where HPWS enable collective learning (Jeong & Shin, 2019), build commitment (Chang & Chen, 2011), and facilitate employees to adopt change (Della Torre & Solari, 2013). It is particularly timely to examine HPWS as the condition that facilitates change readiness towards AI adoption, given that this is an area that has not been explored in scholarly research.

Specifically, we address two research questions: (1) To what extent do HR managers' beliefs about AI and their anxiety influence their change

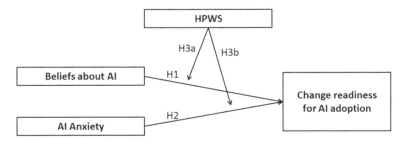

Figure 1. The conceptual model.

readiness for AI adoption?, and (2) To what extent do HPWS influence HR managers' beliefs, their AI anxiety, and their change readiness towards AI adoption? We adopt the tripartite model of attitude (TMA) and social cognitive theory (SCT) in this study to examine the individual and contextual environmental factors that influence change readiness. A conceptual model (Figure 1) was developed based on Rosenberg and Hovland's (1960) and Eagly and Chaiken's (1993) TMA, as our study focuses on examining the relationships between the three elements of attitudes.

The conceptual model was extended using SCT in emphasising the inter-relationships between personal factors (both cognitive and affective), environmental factors, and behavioural outcomes (Bandura, 1986, 2006). This theory highlights that humans are agentic—that is, there is triadic reciprocal determinism in how we make decisions and form judgements based on individual and environmental factors (Bandura, 1986, 2006). These factors may consequently affect the way we feel, and thus the way we act. Underpinned by social cognitive theory, we consider not only the individual's personal factors (beliefs about AI and AI anxiety) but also the HPWS as the environmental factor that influences individual change readiness for AI adoption (the behavioural outcome). Thus, the TMA is used to explain the inter-relationships between the elements of attitude (Ajzen, 2001, 2005), while the SCT is applied to explain the relationships between the personal factors (cognitive and affective), the environmental factor and the behavioural outcome in terms of AI adoption (Bandura, 1986, 2006).

Our study contributes to the literature in several ways. First, we contribute to the literature on organisational change by advancing the theoretical debate on attitudes towards organisational change in the context of AI adoption. Second, we contribute to the emerging literature on AI by exploring individual perceptions of AI adoption and providing insights into how individuals' beliefs and feelings influence their change readiness for AI adoption.

Third, we endeavour to contribute to the strategic HRM literature by considering the role of HPWS as an environmental factor that influences

AI adoption. Most of the research published on HPWS to date has examined macro-level outcomes (e.g. Fu et al., 2017; Zhou et al., 2019). In our study, we explore the individual-level HPWS as this constitutes a significant gap in knowledge on HPWS. Additionally, Boxall and Macky (2009) indicated that the majority of studies on HPWS had been conducted in the American and Western European contexts. As such, an examination of HPWS in another context can provide the contextual perspective of the implementation of HPWS.

Theoretical background and context

Tripartite model of attitudes (TMA)

An attitude is defined as a 'psychological tendency that is expressed by evaluating a particular entity with some degree of favour or disfavour' (Eagly & Chaiken, 1993, p. 1). While many studies have examined attitudes and behaviours, they appear to hold a one-dimensional view when examining attitudes. In this study, we draw upon the TMA, where attitude is portrayed as a tripartite model with three elements—cognitive, affective and behavioural elements (Ajzen, 2001, 2005; Eagly & Chaiken, 1993; Piderit, 2000; Rosenberg & Hovland, 1960). The rationale behind TMA is that even though the three elements of an attitude are manifestations of the same latent variable, they are independent and it is therefore useful to distinguish among them (Ajzen, 2001, 2005).

The cognitive element of an attitude refers to an individual's thoughts, beliefs, ideas or perceptual responses about an object or subject. This can range from an extremely positive response (e.g. useful) to one that is extremely negative (e.g. useless) (Eagly & Chaiken, 1993). The affective element refers to the feelings, moods and emotions that people experience with regard to an object or subject (Avey et al., 2008). These responses also range from extremely positive (e.g. hope and optimism) to extremely negative (e.g. fear and pessimism) (Albarracín et al., 2005; Eagly & Chaiken, 1993). Finally, the behavioural element (or conative element) of an attitude is reflected by an individual's evaluations of the attitude (Ajzen, 2001, 2005) based on his or her past experiences or future intentions (Piderit, 2000).

The TMA has been applied in management (e.g. Piderit, 2000) as well as in the psychology and marketing fields (e.g. Harnish & Roster, 2019), but it is not commonly considered in the scholarly literature on technology adoption. While the three elements of an attitude should be closely aligned, this assumption may not always hold. For example, one may have a positive cognitive and affective attitude towards new technologies such as AI, yet when confronted with having to learn the new technology (particularly without possessing basic knowledge and understanding), the behavioural element to learning this technology can be negative. In this case, there may be inconsistencies in the cognitive, affective and behavioural elements of attitudes. The literature on attitudes indeed shows that the cognitive, affective and behavioural elements may not always align (Olson & Kendrick, 2008).

Piderit (2000) outlined that employees' resistance to organisational changes can be examined through viewing attitudes as multidimensional, comprising emotional, cognitive and intentional elements. Each of these dimensions is a separate continuum, allowing for the 'possibility of different reactions along the different dimensions' (Piderit, 2000, p. 787). Given that there is a potential duality effect of AI - such as labour adjustments, potential unemployment and inequality on the one hand, and increased productivity, automation and efficiency on the other hand, our study can provide a useful platform to examine the inter-relationships of the cognitive element (beliefs about AI), the affective element (AI anxiety), and the behavioural element (change readiness towards AI), representing the three elements of attitudes identified by the TMA. In line with the theory of TMA (Ajzen, 2001, 2005), we consider these three dimensions of attitudes to be distinct and separate.

Social cognitive theory (SCT)

A possible shortcoming of the TMA is that it neglects the effect of contextual or environmental factors on attitudes (e.g. Olson & Kendrick, 2008). Following recent developments in the literature (Ferguson & Fukukura, 2012), attitudes are increasingly perceived as being 'constructed on the spot' (e.g. Gawronski & Bodenhausen, 2006). Thus, attitudes are considered to be constructs that are not innate to individuals but are processed in a specific time and context. The shortcoming of TMA in excluding environmental factors is addressed in this study through the application of the SCT (Bandura, 1986, 2006). This theory views that an individual's behaviour is likely to be influenced by both individual and environmental factors. Individuals are conceived as dynamic planners who anticipate the outcomes of their actions, as self-regulators who correct their plans if necessary, and as social beings who operate in social systems. These actions co-create the social systems, which in turn affect their behaviours (Bandura, 2005).

This theory suggests that there are personal (internal) and external environmental factors that facilitate (or inhibit) an outcome expectation (Otaye-Ebede et al., 2020). These factors are numerous including, but not limited to, social support, training, self-efficacy, self-regulation, and locus of control. The theory has been applied in various contexts, such as in studies about sustainable consumption (e.g. Phipps et al., 2013) or in research on workplace spirituality and ethical climate (Otaye-Ebede et al., 2020).

In the context of technology adoption, several studies using SCT have taken into account the aspect of anxiety in general, or technology anxiety in particular. For example, technology anxiety has been considered in the case of computer use (Conrad & Munro, 2008) and sensor-based technology (e.g. Kummer et al., 2017). Other studies using SCT have highlighted how the environment affects both the cognitive and affective aspects of technology adoption, such as in the use of knowledge management systems (e.g. Hoffman et al., 2015).

Drawing on these studies, we apply SCT to illustrate the role of environmental factors, embodied in HPWS, as a way to manage individual beliefs and feelings towards AI adoption. On the one hand, employees may believe that AI will increase their productivity and efficiency. On the other hand, they may also feel anxious as AI can introduce disruptive changes to their workplace and employment continuity. The theory highlights that there are aspects of the environment that can help individuals, and we argue in this case that organisations can change their environmental conditions through the implementation of HPWS in order to ease their employees' feelings when faced with change.

HPWS are commonly referred to as a group of separate yet coherently interconnected HR practices, including selection, extensive training, internal mobility, employment security, clear job descriptions, appraisal, rewards and participation (Han et al., 2018; Sun et al., 2007). Research on HPWS illustrates the need for organisations to invest in employees and to adopt and implement HR practices that leverage employees' skills and knowledge to create strategic value (Kehoe & Wright, 2013). The SCT is essentially used to understand the effects of personal factors and environmental determinants on an individual's behaviour change. In this study, we apply SCT in exploring the relationships between the personal factors (i.e. individual's beliefs about AI and individual's AI anxiety) and HPWS as the environmental factor in influencing the individual's change readiness towards AI (the behavioural factor).

AI adoption in China

AI changes the workplace in a variety of ways. AI-enabled machines can take over some of the tasks previously performed by human labour (Frey & Osborne, 2017). At the same time AI is expected to create up to 58 million new jobs in the next few years (Chowdhry, 2018), including new types of jobs for programmers, engineers, and other highly skilled specialists. Given the potentially disruptive effects of AI on employees and firm governance, many firms have been reluctant to proceed with its adoption. Moreover, firms may lack the necessary information about the various threats and opportunities provided by AI, limiting their decision-making process to adopt AI. Interestingly, what AI is and what it does is still not well understood even among top managers. Based on a survey of 1,500 senior executives in the United States, only about 15% of the executives who responded to the survey noted that they were familiar with AI and its application in their companies (Deloitte, 2017).

This study focuses on AI adoption in Chinese firms. China presents an interesting context given the pace at which the country is pushing for the development and adoption of AI solutions. A report from the China Institute for Science and Technology (2018) noted that China leads the world in AI paper outputs and AI patents given that the country has the world's second-largest talent pool for AI. China also has the highest venture investment in AI and the highest concentration of AI companies in the world (primarily concentrated in Beijing). Additionally, tangible applications of AI are already part of everyday life among Chinese citizens, with some AI solutions contributing to COVID-19 measures (tracing applications), social credit scores, and even urban robotics and automation (Chen et al., 2020). Organisations such as Tencent and Baidu are also increasingly using AI and big data to manage their staff turnover (Greeven, 2017). With the country's GDP estimated to increase by more than 20% by 2030 through the application of AI (PwC, 2018), China is investing heavily to gain an advantage in AI (PwC, 2018; Sherman, 2019), and aspires to apply AI in surveillance/security, education, healthcare, and agriculture (Deng et al., 2019). Indeed, the country is poised to be in a position to exploit the applications of AI, making this context relevant for this study.

Hypothesis development

Beliefs about AI and change readiness for AI adoption

Given the relatively recent scholarly literature on the topic of AI in the management/HRM discipline, relevant literature examining individual beliefs about AI is rather limited. However, there are studies exploring individual cognitive attitudes towards the Internet (Durndell & Haag, 2002) and technology in general (Au & Enderwick, 2000). The literature on technology adoption highlights that users decide to adopt a new technology based on their attitudes (Au & Enderwick, 2000; Van der Heijden, 2004).

Drawing on the TMA (Ajzen, 2001, 2005), understanding human cognition and the behavioural aspect of attitude is important in the context of new technology adoption (Au & Enderwick, 2000). This is because our beliefs can have an important influence on individual and organisational outcomes. Previous research has shown how technologies combined with human skills can enhance organisational performance (Dubey et al., 2019). Positive beliefs about technology may induce individuals to acquire the necessary skills to use technology effectively. Likewise, negative beliefs about technology may reduce individuals' willingness to develop complementary skills. They may indeed be apprehensive about how technology may disrupt their work or industry.

In applying the notion of the relationship between cognitive and behavioural elements as illustrated in the TMA, Ajzen (2005) highlighted that the correlation between cognition and connation (i.e. the behavioural element) of an attitude is particularly strong. Armenakis et al. (1993) noted that organisational members' cognitive beliefs and intentions could make them ready for organisational change. Rafferty and Minbashian (2019) also found support that one's cognitive belief about change is an important antecedent of change readiness. In this way, we argue that individuals who have positive beliefs about AI tend to be open to the new technology and are more receptive to the likely effects that AI may have in the workplace. They may view AI as complementary to human intelligence and thus, be more likely to 'join forces' for collaborative intelligence between AI and humans (Jarrahi, 2018; Wilson & Daugherty, 2018). They tend to view the positive effects of changes caused by AI, are less likely to resist change, and adapt quickly to new policies and procedures in relation to this change management. Those who do not believe that AI will enhance their productivity in the workplace are arguably more likely to resist the change, given that they are not ready for the disruption that AI would introduce to their daily work life. We thus posit that the elements of attitudes as reflected in the TMA (Ajzen, 2001, 2005), cognition (i.e. the beliefs about AI) and behaviour (i.e. change readiness towards AI adoption) are positively associated in that individuals who have positive beliefs about AI are more likely to be ready and receptive to adopting AI in the workplace AI in the workplace.

Hypothesis 1: *An individual's beliefs about AI are positively related to the individual change readiness towards AI adoption.*

AI anxiety and change readiness for AI adoption

The topic of anxiety has been studied in several contexts of technology adoption, including in studies examining the phenomenon of 'computer anxiety' (Venkatesh, 2000), 'internet anxiety' (Thatcher et al., 2007), and recently among the digital-native generations (Bellini et al., 2016). Given the emerging nature of AI, AI anxiety (Bellini et al., 2016; Johnson & Verdicchio, 2017) is a new topic, which necessitates further research on AI in the field of management in general, and HRM in particular.

Drawing on the TMA, the affective element of an attitude is distinguishable from the cognition and behavioural elements (Ajzen, 2001, 2005; Eagly & Chaiken, 1993). Studies examining change readiness need to consider not only the cognitive elements experienced by individuals but also their emotional influences (Rafferty et al., 2013; Rafferty & Minbashian, 2019). Existing studies are specifically limited in incorporating a less positive emotion that is particularly relevant in the context of technology adoption, i.e. AI anxiety. On a broader level, anxiety has been used as a measure of employee wellbeing (for a review, see Peccei & Van De Voorde, 2019), either in terms of assessing the consequences of anxiety on organisational performance (Jensen et al., 2013) or as a mediator to study job satisfaction (Wood et al., 2012). However, scholars have yet to fully engage with the topic of AI anxiety from the perspective of the individual. Besides studies focusing on the anxiety that AI creates for individuals seeking employment (van Esch et al., 2019), no empirical research to date has addressed the impact of individuals' AI anxiety on their change readiness for AI adoption.

Given that the affective and behavioural elements of an attitude are separate as illustrated in the TMA (Ajzen, 2001, 2005), the underlying nature of anxiety can potentially affect individuals' change readiness for AI adoption. The rise and popularisation of AI contribute to a general increase in the perceptions of uncertainty about the future of work, driven by the fear that smart machines have started to replace humans as information processors and decision-makers (Jarrahi, 2018; Johnson & Verdicchio, 2017). This feeling of anxiety can thus act as a major force in creating apprehension and distress, which may influence employees' readiness to adopt these new technologies. In addition, there have also been ongoing debates related to the trust that people should place in AI-driven technologies, such as autonomous vehicles and medical assistance devices (Hengstler et al., 2016). These patterns of thinking may result in individuals imagining the worst situation, feeling helpless and not knowing what to do about AI.

The underpinning theory of the TMA illustrates the link between the elements of attitudes in that we posit that there is a relationship between the affective element of attitude (AI anxiety) and the behaviour (change readiness towards AI adoption). It is important for employees to view organisational change positively (Rafferty et al., 2013; Rafferty & Minbashian, 2019). Employees should also have positive perceptions of the implications of such change for themselves and the wider organisation (Armenakis et al., 1993; Jones et al., 2005). Given that individuals' feelings about change influence their change readiness (Rafferty & Minbashian, 2019), we argue that AI anxiety is expected to reduce individuals' change readiness to adopt AI in that the individuals who are more anxious about AI are less likely to be ready to adopt this new technology. Thus:

Hypothesis 2: Individuals' AI anxiety is negatively related to their change readiness for AI adoption.

The moderating role of HPWS

Scholarly work on HPWS highlights that the implementation of HPWS results in increased productivity, employee performance, and organisational performance. HPWS contribute to organisational performance (Han et al., 2018) by changing individuals' attitudes and behaviours through influencing their abilities, motivation and opportunities (Appelbaum et al., 2000). First, HPWS can develop and enhance individuals' abilities through practices such as staffing and extensive training (Jiang et al., 2012). Staffing provides organisations with the right people who have the right skills, knowledge and abilities to perform the job well. Similarly, other practices, such as training, participation, communication, internal career opportunities and incentive compensation, enable individuals to execute tasks much more effectively (Wei et al., 2010).

Second, HPWS can enhance employees' motivation through practices such as formal performance appraisal and performance-based rewards (Boxall & Macky, 2009). Such practices of HPWS motivate employees to perform their tasks to the best of their abilities, as they perceive that they will be evaluated positively and compensated fairly. Third, HPWS can provide more opportunities to employees (Kehoe & Wright, 2013), such as by providing autonomy for employees in decision-making and allowing them to have a say in the implementation of organisational change. All these imply that organisations need to provide a favourable work context to enable employees to perform their tasks well.

Underpinned by SCT, which emphasises the reciprocal relationships between personal, environmental and behavioural factors as previously outlined, we consider not only individual's beliefs and affective feeling as personal factors (cognitive and affective) but also the existence of HPWS as the environmental factor, in facilitating a behavioural outcome (i.e. one's change readiness for AI adoption). Organisations that implement HPWS may facilitate more positive beliefs about change—in our case, the adoption of AI. Effective implementation of HPWS enables individuals to develop their capabilities, promotes a willingness to participate in organisational decision-making, and enhances their positive beliefs. Empirical evidence highlights that practices such as training, performance appraisal and participation, as embedded within HPWS, can improve performance (Messersmith et al., 2011).

Additionally, the implementation of HPWS may afford new opportunities for individuals to be trained in and work with AI as the new technology. They may experience new insights and be aware of new trends or new capabilities that AI can facilitate. In organisations that implement HPWS, employees are more likely to be motivated to develop themselves and be creative (Jeong & Shin, 2019). Therefore, HPWS with practices such as extensive training, clear job descriptions and results-oriented appraisal (Sun et al., 2007) may foster positive beliefs about AI and consequently facilitate change readiness for AI adoption.

In contrast, in organisations that do not implement HPWS, employees may not have positive beliefs about AI. For instance, if individuals have not been provided with opportunities for training in the application of AI, are not rewarded for their willingness to use AI, or are not given autonomy to determine the best way to do their job with the help of AI, they may feel that they are not ready for this significant change. In this way, their attitudes may not be as positive, and consequently, they may not be ready to adopt AI.

Adopting SCT in considering the environmental factor of HPWS, we argue that HPWS is interlinked with personal factors and behavioural outcomes. The way individuals perceive the existence and effectiveness of HPWS determines how they think (their beliefs about AI) and how they respond to the change (their change readiness for AI adoption). For example, Jones et al. (2005) found that employees' beliefs of their organisational support and values lead to higher levels of change readiness. Similarly, Gigliotti et al. (2019) suggested that employees' beliefs and perceptions of organisational support (in our case, the implementation of HPWS) enhance their change readiness. Based on the concepts of SCT of the inter-linkages between personal, environmental, and behavioural factors as earlier highlighted, we hypothesise that:

Hypothesis 3a: HPWS moderate the positive relationship between individuals' beliefs about AI and change readiness for AI adoption, such that the relationship is stronger for organisations that implement HPWS.

We earlier hypothesised that individuals' AI anxiety will have a negative effect on their change readiness for AI adoption. Employees may feel terrified about what AI may do to their job. Instead of feeling hopeful and being ready to adopt AI to reduce their time in undertaking tasks or improve their decision-making process, individuals may experience anxiety, partly because of a lack of communication from the top leaders on how AI will transform their workplace and partly due to their perceptions that their skills may not be adequate to handle the complexity of AI (Forbes Insights, 2019). Arguably, this effect could be lessened through the implementation of HPWS. Drawing on SCT, we argue that the implementation of HPWS in the organisation enables employees to perceive that their organisation provides opportunities for training, autonomy, rewards and participation. In this situation, employees are more likely to feel less anxious about the change as they are kept informed through participation, learning, and information sharing (Fu et al., 2017). On the other hand, if HPWS are not implemented, these employees may not receive the opportunity, training and information sharing that they expect from top managers in relation to how AI may affect their job. This consequently leads to their higher anxiety (Forbes Insights, 2019).

Based on the concepts of SCT of the inter-linkages between personal, environmental and behavioural factors, we argue that an organisation's HPWS as an environmental condition plays a role in potentially lessening the negative effect of AI anxiety through the use of practices such as training, employment security, clear job descriptions and results-oriented appraisal (Sun et al., 2007). When individuals feel they are involved in these various practices, they are less likely to feel anxious about how AI affects their employment future and organisational sustainability. In line with this theorising, HPWS and employees' anxiety are interlinked (Kehoe & Wright, 2013). As further highlighted by Jensen et al. (2013), employees who positively perceive HPWS utilisation are more likely to demonstrate lower levels of anxiety. We thus posit that employees who experience lower AI anxiety are more likely to display a positive behavioural outcome – in our case, they are ready to adopt AI, particularly when HPWS practices are implemented in the organisation. Thus:

Hypothesis 3b: HPWS moderate the negative relationship between individuals' AI anxiety and change readiness for AI adoption, such that the relationship is weaker for organisations that implement HPWS.

Method

Sample and procedure

We collected our data through an online panel, WJX, the largest online panels service in China. We specifically focused on HR managers as our sample for two reasons. First, HR as an organisational function is most likely to capitalise and adopt AI (Greeven, 2017; van Esch et al., 2019). For instance, Guenole and Feinzig (2018) noted that the HR function was one area disrupted by the new technology; the HR function in IBM was in fact one of the first business functions to adopt AI technology in terms of supporting the hiring process, ensuring motivation and engagement, facilitating retention, providing personalised learning and career development, and also enabling 24/7 employee interaction. Second, given that there are not many studies examining the perceptions of change agents (Bouckenooghe, 2010), HR managers' perceptions and involvement in the adoption of AI can play a crucial role in piloting the implementation of AI and then institutionalising it throughout the organisation to achieve the intended outcomes.

We did not make any distinctions in terms of the companies where these respondents worked (whether foreign firms, state-owned enterprises, publicly-traded firms, or privately-owned firms), as we wanted to explore the general perceptions of HR managers across the country. Additionally, distinguishing the types of companies operating in China is challenging given that the legal registration information of companies operating in China may not reflect the actual ownership status. Hsieh and Song (2015) highlighted some issues with this situation—for instance, many firms that are registered as foreign firms can be state-owned because the regulation permits firms with more than one-third of foreign-held ownership to be registered as foreign firms in China. Due to the potential complexity, we did not include information related to the legal status of our respondents' firms.

A total of 512 responses were received, of which 417 (81.4%) were useable after the deletion of incomplete entries and removal of those that did not fit our sampling criteria. The participants received compensation directly from WJX. Of the 417 respondents, 65.3% were female and 34.7% were male, with an average age of 32.68 years ($SD = 5.60$, ranging from 19 to 56). In terms of the company size, 52.5% of the respondents were from companies with fewer than 500 employees, and 24.7% and 22.6% of the sample were from companies with 501 to 1,000 employees and more than 1,000 employees, respectively. In terms of the educational background, 74.1% of the respondents held a bachelor's degree, and 22.9% listed a master's or doctoral degree as their highest academic qualification.

Measures

The surveys were presented in Mandarin Chinese, which was then back-translated into English, following the procedure proposed by Brislin (1970). The variables were measured using a seven-point Likert scale (1 = strongly disagree/never; 7 = strongly agree/always).

Change readiness for AI adoption ($\alpha = 0.76$). Change readiness for AI adoption was assessed with the five-item scale developed by Rafferty and Minbashian (2019). We wanted to be specific when using the term 'change'; thus, we used the term 'AI adoption' to illustrate 'change' as reflected in the original items to better fit with the context of our study. A sample item is: 'I am ready for the organisational change to adopt AI'.

Beliefs about AI ($\alpha = 0.83$). We used the 10-item scale developed by Durndell and Haag (2002) to measure individuals' beliefs about AI. The scale was originally developed to measure students' internet cognitive attitudes. Once again, to fit the current study context, we changed the word 'internet' to 'AI.' A sample item is: 'People are becoming slaves to AI' (reverse item). A high score for this measure reflected more positive beliefs about AI.

AI anxiety ($\alpha = 0.88$). AI anxiety was assessed with the 19-item scale developed by Durndell and Haag (2002), which originally measured students' computer anxiety. We also replaced the term 'computer' with 'AI' to fit the current study context. A sample item is: 'I do not think I would be able to learn AI programming language'. A high score for this measure suggested that individuals have a high level of AI anxiety.

HPWS ($\alpha = 0.91$). We measured HPWS using the 27-item scale developed by Sun et al. (2007). Sample items include: 'Great effort is taken to select the right person' and 'Employees have few opportunities for upward mobility'.

Control variables. Following previous research on organisational change (Avey et al., 2008), we included age, gender, company size (1 = fewer than 50; 2 = between 50 and 500; 3 = between 501 and 1,000; 4 = between 1,001 and 5,000; 5 = between 5,001 and 10,000; and 6 = more than 10,000) and education as the control variables.

Analysis and results

Our measures demonstrated internal consistency (reliability) with Cronbach's α values above 0.70 (Hair et al., 2006; Nunnally, 1978). Given that the data we collected were cross-sectional from a single source, we first tested whether common-method bias was an issue in this study (Podsakoff et al., 2003). We used Harman's one-factor test (Harman, 1976) to examine whether a single factor could explain more than half of the variance from the unrotated factor solution. The result showed that the largest single component accounted for only 22.04% of the variance, indicating that no single factor dominates. Therefore, common-method bias was not an issue in our study.

We used linear regression to examine the hypothesised model and test the main effects of beliefs and AI anxiety on change readiness. We first conducted CFA to examine our measurement model by first testing a four-factor model included in the study: beliefs about AI, AI anxiety, HPWS and change readiness for AI adoption. We used the robust weighted least squares estimator The model fit was: χ^2 (1,704) =

3,996.266; RMSEA = .056; CFI = .855; TLI = .849. This four-factor model was a better fit compared to the single-factor model (χ^2 (1,710) = 5,623.366; RMSEA = .074; CFI = .749; TLI = .741). The RMSEA for both models was less than 0.08 indicating a good fit (Loehlin, 2004), but the four-factor model indicated a better fit. Moreover, the CFI for the four-factor model is .855, which is within the range of 0.80 to 0.89 (Byrne, 1998) This also indicated a better fit than the single-factor model.

To test the moderation effects, we used hierarchical multiple regression analysis to examine the interactions. All predictors in the model were grand-mean centred to avoid issues of multicollinearity (Aiken & West, 1991). In all our models, the variance inflation factors (VIFs) for all variables were below 5, indicating that multicollinearity was not a problem (Neter et al., 1990). Table 1 presents the means, standard deviations and correlations for the variables used in the study.

As Table 2 shows, in Models 1 and 2, we predicted individuals' change readiness for AI adoption using the control variables and individuals' beliefs about AI. The results showed that beliefs about AI had a positive effect on change readiness towards AI adoption ($b = 0.40$, $p < .001$, VIF = 1.04), supporting Hypothesis 1. In Models 3 and 4, we included the HPWS and the interaction term with individuals' beliefs about AI. Our results as shown in Model 4 indicated that individuals' beliefs about AI ($b = 0.23$, $p < .001$, VIF = 1.20) and the HPWS ($b = 0.57$, $p < .001$, VIF = 1.21) were significantly related to change readiness for AI adoption, but the effect of the interaction term was not significant ($b = -0.1$, $p > .05$, VIF = 1.06). Given that the interaction in Model 4 was not significant, and the R^2 did not increase from Model 3 to Model 4, Model 3 was a better model for the relationship between beliefs about AI and the change readiness for AI adoption. Thus, Hypothesis 3a was not supported. Based on Model 1 to Model 4, we derived the regression equation as below (ϵ denotes the residual in the equation):

$$\text{Change readiness} = 0.83 + 0.23 \text{ Beliefs} + 0.57 \text{ HPWS} - 0.10(\text{Beliefs} * \text{HPWS}) + \epsilon$$

Table 1. Descriptive statistics and correlations ($N = 417$).

Variables	Mean.	SD.	1	2	3	4	5	6	7	8
1 Age	32.74	5.59	—							
2 Gender	1.66	.48	-.02	—						
3 Organization size	2.70	1.01	.28***	-.06	—					
4 Education	5.22	.48	.08	-.11*	.13**	—				
5 Beliefs about AI	5.29	.89	.18***	-.01	-.03	.02	—			
6 AI Anxiety	2.73	.77	.15**	.03	-.02	-.01	-.80***	—		
7 HPWS	5.35	.71	.15**	-.11*	.16**	.08	.37***	-.45***	—	
8 Change readiness for AI adoption	5.44	.92	.11*	-.02	.08	.05	.39***	-.52***	.53***	—

*$p \leq .05$.
**$p \leq .01$.
***$p \leq .001$.

Table 2. Multiple regression of change readiness for AI adoption on the individuals' beliefs about AI and high-performance work systems ($N=417$).

Independent variables	Model 1		Model 2		Model 3		Model 4	
	B	SE	B	SE	B	SE	B	SE
Intercept	4.49***	.58	2.76***	.57	.85***	.55	.83	.55
Age	.02	.01	.00	.01	.00	.01	.00	.01
Gender	-.03	.10	-.02	.09	.06	.08	.06	.08
Organization size	.05	.05	.08	.04	.02	.04	.02	.04
Education	.07	.09	.06	.09	.02	.08	.03	.08
Beliefs about AI	—	—	.40***	.05	.23***	.05	.23***	.05
HPWS					.58***	.06	.57***	.06
Beliefs about AI×HPWS					—	—	-.10	.05
F test	1.780		15.781***		32.961***		28.934***	
Adjusted R^2	.01		.15		.32		.32	
ΔR^2	—		.14		.17		.00	

Dependent variable: Change readiness for AI adoption.
*$p \leq .05$.
**$p \leq .01$.
***$p \leq .001$.
ΔR^2 is the change of R^2 between two models. ΔR^2 of Model X is calculated by the R^2 of Model X minus the R^2 of Model (X-1).

Table 3. Multiple regression of change readiness for AI adoption on the individuals' AI anxiety and high-performance work systems ($N=417$).

Independent variables	Model 5		Model 6		Model 7		Model 8	
	B	SE	B	SE	B	SE	B	SE
Intercept	4.49***	.58	6.49***	.52	3.67***	.59	3.64***	.59
Age	.02	.01	.00	.01	.00	.01	.00	.01
Gender	-.03	.10	.00	.08	.06	.08	.06	.08
Organization size	.05	.05	.06	.04	.02	.04	.02	.04
Education	.07	.09	.07	.08	.04	.08	.04	.07
AI Anxiety	—	—	-.61***	.05	-.42***	.05	-.41***	.05
HPWS					.48***	.06	.47***	.06
AI anxiety×HPWS					—	—	.11*	.06
F test	1.780		31.050***		41.753***		36.599***	
Adjusted R^2	.01		.27		.37		.38	
ΔR^2	—		.26		.10		.01	

Dependent variable: Change readiness for AI adoption.
*$p \leq .05$.
**$p \leq .01$.
***$p \leq .001$.
ΔR^2 is the change of R^2 between two models. ΔR^2 of Model X is calculated by the R^2 of Model X minus the R^2 of Model (X-1).

As Table 3 shows, in Models 5 and 6, we predicted individuals' change readiness for AI adoption using the control variables and individuals' AI anxiety. The results indicated that AI anxiety had a negative effect on change readiness for AI adoption ($b = -0.61$, $p < .001$, VIF $= 1.03$), supporting Hypothesis 2. In Models 7 and 8, we included the HPWS and the interaction term with individuals' beliefs about AI. As shown in Model 8, employees' AI anxiety ($b = -0.41$, $p < .001$, VIF $= 1.28$), HPWS ($b=0.47$, $p < .001$, VIF $= 1.31$) and the interaction term ($b=0.11$, $p < .05$, VIF $= 1.05$) were all significantly related to individuals' change readiness for AI adoption. Figure 2 shows the significant result of the interaction between AI anxiety and HPWS for AI adoption change

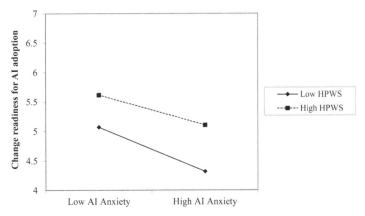

Figure 2. Moderation effect of HPWS on the relationship between AI anxiety and change readiness for AI Adoption

readiness. Given that the interaction in Model 8 was significant, and there was an increase in R^2 by 1 per cent from Model 7 to Model 8, Model 8 was deemed as a better model for the relationship between AI anxiety and the change readiness for AI adoption. Thus, Hypothesis 3b was supported. Based on Model 5 to Model 8, we derived the regression equation as below (ϵ denotes the residual in the equation):

Change readiness = 3.64 − 0.41 Anxiety + 0.47 HPWS + 0.11(AI Anxiety * HPWS) + ϵ

Discussion and conclusion

The study highlights that organisations must ensure that their employees are ready for change (Rafferty et al., 2013), particularly if the organisation is implementing a significant change as in the case of the adoption of AI. The results of the study indicated that HR managers' beliefs about AI and AI anxiety had a significant influence on their change readiness for AI adoption. Specifically, individuals with positive beliefs were more likely to accept the change to adopt AI, while individuals who experienced higher anxiety over AI were less ready to adopt AI. The findings contribute to empirical evidence of TMA in explaining that attitudes are a combination of cognitive/beliefs, feelings/affect, and behaviours (Ajzen, 2001, 2005; Eagly & Chaiken, 1993; Rosenberg & Hovland, 1960). Through the application of this theory, our findings provide insights that individual beliefs about AI (the cognitive element) are likely to influence the individual's change readiness for AI adoption (the behavioural element). Additionally, an employee's AI anxiety (the affective element) is also likely to influence his or her change readiness towards AI adoption (the behavioural element). Exploring the three elements of attitudes is important, as failure to address the different elements of attitudes may result in inertia or even organisational crisis, with individuals being reluctant to implement the change or, if they do implement such change, they may only apply these new technologies in a limited manner (Rafferty & Jimmieson, 2017).

As for the moderating effect of HPWS, our results illustrated that HPWS, as perceived by individuals, moderate the negative relationship between individuals' AI anxiety and change readiness to adopt AI. While previous theoretical explanations of HPWS highlight that HPWS influence organisational-level outcomes (e.g. Fu et al., 2017), the results from our study indicated that the way individuals perceive HPWS also influences their change readiness to adopt AI. Our findings supported the premise of SCT (Bandura, 1986, 2006) in that there are inter-relationships between personal, environmental, and behavioural factors, with the findings confirming that HPWS as an environmental condition needs to be implemented to attenuate individuals' AI anxiety (a personal factor). This implies that, when HPWS are implemented, individuals are less likely to feel anxious and frustrated because they may perceive the usefulness of AI (Venkatesh, 2000) through, for example, being provided opportunities to participate in decision-making involving AI and being trained in AI (Wei et al., 2010). They may also be rewarded for their results, be given opportunities for career mobility, and be assured that their jobs will be secure if they can use AI to improve their decision-making processes (Sun et al., 2007). As such, consistent with SCT (Otaye-Ebede et al., 2020), this study confirmed the need to consider the environmental factor through the implementation of HPWS in understanding employees' behaviours for change.

This study offers several theoretical implications. First, the consideration to integrate both the cognitive (beliefs) and affective (AI anxiety) elements to explain individuals' change readiness for AI adoption in the organisation contributes to the much-needed understanding of the individual-level predictors of change readiness (Eby et al., 2000; Rafferty & Minbashian, 2019; Shah et al., 2017). This is an important contribution to the literature on HRM in providing empirical evidence that successful change management considers the 'people side' of management more effectively. The adoption of AI potentially involves a radical shift in business and workforce transformation; thus, handling the 'people side' such as managing their beliefs, anxiety and change readiness are critical. Examining HR managers' perspectives and addressing concerns such as anxiety will also help facilitate the successful implementation of change (Jensen et al., 2013). More generally, our integration of cognitive, affective, and behavioural attitudes enriches the literature on TMA by highlighting the effects of cognitive and affective attitudes on a behavioural outcome in the context of technology adoption.

Second, the current study tests the role of HPWS as an environmental factor in influencing employees' beliefs, feelings and readiness for change as in the case of the adoption of AI. To the best of our knowledge, no previous work on organisational change that is related to AI draws on this perspective. This contributes to the literature on HRM, given that our study is focused on the individual-level perceptions of HPWS which remain under-explored in the literature (Kehoe & Wright, 2013). Our results are in line with SCT in exploring the inter-linkages between personal and environmental factors in influencing individual behavioural outcomes (Otaye-Ebede et al., 2020). Nonetheless, we contribute to the literature on SCT by demonstrating that the role of the environmental factor differs in their influence on the relationship between affective factor and behavioural outcome on the one hand (a significant relationship in our case), and cognitive factor and behavioural outcome on the other (a non-significant relationship in our study).

Finally, our data were drawn from HR managers in China and thus attempt to address the calls from previous research to understand whether HPWS may have different effects due to the variations in practices in different countries (Boxall & Macky, 2009), such as training, selective staffing, employment security and incentive reward. However, while China appears to be progressive in the adoption of AI (PwC, 2018; Sherman, 2019), it is still unclear as to whether individual organisations operating in China and their employees are ready for this change, which this study has sought to highlight.

This study also offers several practical implications. First, organisations intending to adopt AI in the workplace need to ensure that individual employees (i.e. HR managers in our case) not only have the skills to work with AI but also have positive beliefs about AI and are not anxious about the changes that AI may bring. With AI being perceived as a significant change, adopting AI throughout the workplace requires leaders of the organisation and HR managers to convince individuals of the benefits of AI, build their trust in AI applications (Hengstler et al., 2016), and address their concerns regarding how AI may affect their tasks and/or employment. Thus, it is not only important to ensure that individuals have positive beliefs about AI, but it is also fundamental that leaders understand the anxiety that some individuals may experience. Those with higher AI anxiety may be fearful about whether AI will remove their autonomy (Jensen et al., 2013; Johnson & Verdicchio, 2017), and such feelings of anxiety need to be acknowledged and managed, rather than ignored or treated as insignificant. This consequently may have implications in terms of the organisational culture (Jones et al., 2005) and even the organisation's selection criteria when choosing candidates—perhaps organisations should consider selecting employees who are adaptable to change.

Second, given that individuals may not have the necessary skills in AI-associated tasks, such as machine learning and big data analytics (Dubey et al., 2019), managers must ensure that employees have positive perceptions that their organisations are supporting them (Gigliotti et al., 2019). In this way, HPWS need to be implemented effectively to provide opportunities for individuals to develop their knowledge, skills and ability to deal with AI. For example, clear job descriptions that involve AI need to be provided. Training could also be provided to individuals already employed by the organisation to increase their participation and reduce their level of AI anxiety. The rewards structure may also be altered to reward those who can utilise AI (Wilson & Daugherty, 2018) to improve the efficiency, productivity and decision-making process (McKinsey, 2017). Organisations thus need to make the conscious decision to embed and implement HPWS, as doing so can increase individuals' level of affective commitment (Chang & Chen, 2011; Conway & Monks, 2008) and reduce their level of AI anxiety.

Given the relatively recent literature on AI, there are limitations to the study, prompting suggestions for future research. First, in our study, we did not explain the detailed mechanisms of the processes by which individuals' beliefs and anxiety are linked to their change readiness. Past studies, however, have noted that there are some possible mechanisms in facilitating positive beliefs and minimising anxiety towards change, which could be examined in future studies. Second, given our cross-sectional data, we were unable to reach general conclusions about the causality of the relationships (Podsakoff et al., 2003). Thus, future studies adopting a longitudinal research design can be conducted to test the hypothesised relationships in this study.

Third, the study suffers from the limitation of our sample consisting of only HR managers. Even though this study is one of the first to examine individual-level predictors of change readiness for AI adoption, we suggest that future research can examine the perceptions of general employees in terms of their beliefs, AI anxiety and change readiness, as they may experience the effects of AI differently in comparison to the HR managers. Further, we did not specifically distinguish the types of firms for which our respondents worked, for reasons outlined previously. While we were unable to make comparisons between how AI and HPWS are implemented in different types of organisations, our exploratory discussions with several HR managers in China indicated that the topic is still relatively new in China. Thus, future research may investigate and compare employees' change readiness for AI adoption in different types of firms.

Fourth, when considering change readiness, our study did not examine individuals' personal valence, perceived capabilities or resistance to change (Piderit, 2000; Rafferty & Jimmieson, 2017). Future studies can, therefore, incorporate the influence of specific individuals' attitudes towards AI, such as their resistance to change or their self-efficacy, to examine how ready they are to adopt AI. Our study was also limited to the study of attitudes and did not address actual behaviours. Future research can further explore the effect of other contextual factors in explaining individuals' behaviours in the adoption of AI as new technology. There is therefore a need for future research to examine change readiness for AI adoption by utilising different perspectives and theories. Finally, as this study was conducted in China, the generalisability of our findings requires further research in other contexts.

In conclusion, this study aimed to provide a more comprehensive approach to understanding individuals' readiness for radical change—in our case, their change readiness for AI adoption. In particular, the study provided insights into HR managers' change readiness for AI adoption by integrating their beliefs, their AI anxiety, and their perception of the implementation of HPWS in the organisation. Our findings shed light on the importance of acknowledging and addressing individuals' beliefs and anxiety. It also indicates that business leaders should devote attention to the implementation of HPWS, given that the effective implementation of HPWS, as perceived by their employees, plays a role in reducing individuals' AI anxiety and enhancing their change readiness for AI adoption. Despite the progress, a lot of work remains to be done to understand both the effects of AI on HR practices and how to ensure individuals in organisations are ready for this significant change.

Disclosure statement

No potential conflict of interest was reported by the authors.

Funding

The authors gratefully acknowledge the National Science Foundation of China (Grant #71750410693) for this project on innovation adoption in China.

ORCID

Yuliani Suseno http://orcid.org/0000-0002-7865-5213
Marek Hudik http://orcid.org/0000-0002-1670-2555

Data availability statement

The data that support the findings of this study are available from the corresponding author at [yuli.suseno@newcastle.edu.au], upon reasonable request.

References

Aiken, L. S., & West, S. G. (1991). *Multiple regression: Testing and interpreting interactions.* Sage.

Ajzen, I. (2001). Nature and operation of attitudes. *Annual Review of Psychology, 52*(1), 27–58. https://doi.org/10.1146/annurev.psych.52.1.27

Ajzen, I. (2005). *Attitudes, personality, and behavior* (2nd ed.). Open University Press.

Albarracín, D., Zanna, M., Johnson, B., & Tarcan Kumkale, G. (2005). Attitudes: Introduction and scope. In D. Albarracín, B. Johnson, & M. Zanna (Eds.), *Handbook of attitudes* (pp. 1–20). Psychology Press.

Albert, E. T. (2019). AI in talent acquisition: A review of AI-applications used in recruitment and selection. *Strategic HR Review, 18*(5), 215–221. https://doi.org/10.1108/SHR-04-2019-0024

Appelbaum, E., Bailey, T., Berg, P., & Kalleberg, A. L. (2000). *Manufacturing advantage: Why high-performance work systems pay off.* Cornell University Press.

Armenakis, A., Harris, S. G., & Mossholder, K. W. (1993). Creating readiness for organizational change. *Human Relations, 46*(6), 681–703. https://doi.org/10.1177/001872679304600601

Au, A. K. M., & Enderwick, P. (2000). A cognitive model on attitude towards technology adoption. *Journal of Managerial Psychology, 15*(4), 266–282.

Avey, J. B., Wernsing, T. S., & Luthans, F. (2008). Can positive employees help positive organizational change? Impact of psychological capital and emotions on relevant attitudes and behaviors. The Journal of Applied Behavioral Science, *44*(1), 48–70. https://doi.org/10.1177/0021886307311470

Bandura, A. (1986). *Social foundations of thought and action: A social cognitive theory.* Prentice Hall.

Bandura, A. (2005). The evolution of social cognitive theory. In K. G. Smith, & M. A. Hitt (Eds.), *Great minds in management* (pp. 9–35).Oxford University Press.

Bandura, A. (2006). Toward a psychology of human agency. *Perspectives on Psychological Science : A Journal of the Association for Psychological Science, 1*(2), 164–180. https://doi.org/10.1111/j.1745-6916.2006.00011.x

Bellini, C. G. P., Filho, M. M. I., de Moura Junior, P. J., & de Faria Pereira, R. D. C. (2016). Self-efficacy and anxiety of digital natives in face of compulsory computer-mediated tasks: A study about digital capabilities and limitations. *Computers in Human Behavior, 59*(1), 49–57. https://doi.org/10.1016/j.chb.2016.01.015

Bondarouk, T., & Brewster, C. (2016). Conceptualising the future of HRM and technology research. *The International Journal of Human Resource Management, 27*(21), 2652–2671. https://doi.org/10.1080/09585192.2016.1232296

Bouckenooghe, D. (2010). Positioning change recipients' attitudes toward change in the organizational change literature. The Journal of Applied Behavioral Science, *46*(4), 500–531. https://doi.org/10.1177/0021886310367944

Boxall, P., & Macky, K. (2009). Research and theory on high-performance work systems: Progressing the high-involvement stream. *Human Resource Management Journal, 19*(1), 3–23. https://doi.org/10.1111/j.1748-8583.2008.00082.x

Brislin, R. W. (1970). Back-translation for cross-cultural research. *Journal of Cross-Cultural Psychology, 1*(3), 185–216. https://doi.org/10.1177/135910457000100301

Byrne, B. M. (1998). *Structural equation modeling with LISREL, PRELIS, and SIMPLIS: Basic concepts, applications, and programming.* Sage.

Caldwell, R. (2001). Champions, adapters, consultants and synergists: The new change agents in HRM. *Human Resource Management Journal, 11*(3), 39–52. https://doi.org/10.1111/j.1748-8583.2001.tb00044.x

Chang, P.-C., & Chen, S. J. (2011). Crossing the level of employee's performance: HPWS, affective commitment, human capital, and employee job performance in professional service organizations. *The International Journal of Human Resource Management*, *22*(4), 883–901. https://doi.org/10.1080/09585192.2011.555130

Chen, B., Marvin, S., & While, A. (2020). Containing COVID-19 in China: AI and the robotic restructuring of future cities. *Dialogues in Human Geography*, *10*(2), 238–241. https://journals.sagepub.com/doi/full/10.1177/2043820620934267https://doi.org/10.1177/2043820620934267

China Institute for Science and Technology. (2018). *China: AI development report*. http://www.sppm.tsinghua.edu.cn/eWebEditor/UploadFile/China_AI_development_report_2018.pdf

Choi, M. (2011). Employees' attitudes toward organizational change: A literature review. *Human Resource Management*, *50*(4), 479–500. https://doi.org/10.1002/hrm.20434

Chowdhry, A. (2018, September 18). Artificial Intelligence to create 58 million new jobs by 2022, says report. *Forbes*. https://www.forbes.com/sites/amitchowdhry/2018/09/18/artificial-intelligence-to-create-58-million-new-jobs-by-2022-says-report/#32c3a9e44d4b

Conrad, A. M., & Munro, D. (2008). Relationships between computer self-efficacy, technology, attitudes and anxiety: Development of the computer technology use scale (CTUS). *Journal of Educational Computing Research*, *39*(1), 51–73. https://doi.org/10.2190/EC.39.1.d

Conway, E., & Monks, K. (2007). HR practices and commitment to change: An employee level analysis. *Human Resource Management Journal*, *18*(1), 72–89. https://doi.org/10.1111/j.1748-8583.2007.00059.x

Della Torre, E., & Solari, L. (2013). High-performance work systems and the change management process in medium-sized firms. The International Journal of Human Resource Management, *24*(13), 2583–2607. https://doi.org/10.1080/09585192.2012.744337

Deloitte. (2017). *The 2017 Deloitte State of Cognitive Survey*. https://www2.deloitte.com/content/dam/Deloitte/us/Documents/deloitte-analytics/us-da-2017-deloitte-state-of-cognitive-survey.pdf

Deng, I., Zhang, J., & Soo, Z. (2019, December 18). China dreams of becoming an AI utopia, pushing beyond surveillance and into education and health care. *South China Morning Post*. https://www.scmp.com/tech/big-tech/article/3042451/china-dreams-becoming-ai-utopia-pushing-beyond-surveillance-and

Dubey, R., Gunasekaran, A., Childe, S. J., Blome, C., & Papadopoulos, T. (2019). Big data and predictive analytics and manufacturing performance: Integrating institutional theory, resource-based view and big data culture. *British Journal of Management*, *30*(2), 341–361. https://doi.org/10.1111/1467-8551.12355

Durndell, A., & Haag, Z. (2002). Computer self-efficacy, computer anxiety, attitudes towards the Internet and reported experience with the Internet, by gender, in an East European sample. *Computers in Human Behavior*, *18*(5), 521–535. https://doi.org/10.1016/S0747-5632(02)00006-7

Eagly, A. H., & Chaiken, S. (1993). *The psychology of attitudes*. Harcourt, Brace, Jovanovich.

Eby, L. T., Adams, D. M., Russell, J. E., & Gaby, S. H. (2000). Perceptions of organizational readiness for change: Factors related to employees' reactions to the implementation of team-based selling. *Human Relations*, *53*(3), 419–442. https://doi.org/10.1177/0018726700533006

Ferguson, M. J., & Fukukura, J. (2012). Likes and dislikes: A social cognitive perspective on attitudes. In Susan T. Fiske and C. Neil Macrae (Ed.), *The SAGE handbook of social cognition*, (pp. 165–186). SAGE Publications Ltd.

Forbes Insights. (2019, March 27). AI anxiety: An ethical challenge for business. *Forbes.* https://www.forbes.com/sites/insights-intelai/2019/03/27/ai-anxiety-an-ethical-challenge-for-business/#a9b642578807

Frey, C. B., & Osborne, M. A. (2017). The future of employment: How susceptible are jobs to computerisation?*Technological Forecasting and Social Change, 114*, 254–280. https://doi.org/10.1016/j.techfore.2016.08.019

Fu, N., Flood, P. C., Bosak, J., Rousseau, D. M., Morris, T., & O'Regan, P. (2017). High-performance work systems in professional service firms: Examining the practices-resources-uses-performance linkage. *Human Resource Management, 56*(2), 329–352. https://doi.org/10.1002/hrm.21767

Gawronski, B., & Bodenhausen, G. V. (2006). Associative and propositional processes in evaluation: An integrative review of implicit and explicit attitude change. *Psychological Bulletin, 132*(5), 692–731. https://doi.org/10.1037/0033-2909.132.5.692

Gigliotti, R., Vardaman, J., Marshall, D. R., & Gonzalez, K. (2019). The role of perceived organizational support in individual change readiness. *Journal of Change Management, 19*(2), 86–100. https://doi.org/10.1080/14697017.2018.1459784

Greeven, M. (2017, November 3). Chinese Internet leaders are also HR pioneers. *Nikkei Asian Review.* https://asia.nikkei.com/Business/Chinese-internet-leaders-are-also-HR-pioneers2

Guenole, N., & Feinzig, S. (2018). *The business case for AI in HR.* IBM Corporation.

Hair, J., J. F., Black, W. C., Babin, B. J., Anderson, R. E., L., & Tatham, R. (2006). *Multivariant data analysis.* Pearson International Edition.

Han, J. H., Liao, H., Taylor, M. S., & Kim, S. (2018). Effects of high-performance work systems on transformational leadership and team performance: Investigating the moderating roles of organizational orientations. *Human Resource Management, 57*(5), 1065–1082. https://doi.org/10.1002/hrm.21886

Harman, H. H. (1976). *Modern factor analysis* (3rd ed.).The University of Chicago Press.

Harnish, R. J., & Roster, C. A. (2019). The tripartite model of aberrant purchasing: A theory to explain the maladaptive pursuit of consumption. *Psychology & Marketing, 36*(5), 417–430. https://doi.org/10.1002/mar.21159

Hengstler, M., Enkel, E., & Duelli, S. (2016). Applied artificial intelligence and trust: The case of autonomous vehicles and medical assistance devices. *Technological Forecasting and Social Change, 105*, 105–120. https://doi.org/10.1016/j.techfore.2015.12.014

Hoffman, C. P., Lutz, C., & Meckel, M. (2015). Content creation on the Internet: A social cognitive perspective on the participation divide. *Information, Communication & Society, 18*(6), 696–716. https://doi.org/10.1080/1369118X.2014.991343

Hsieh, C.-T., & Song, Z. (2015). *Grasp the large, let go of the small: The transformation of the state sector in China.* National Bureau of Economic Research, NBER Working Paper Series. https://www.nber.org/papers/w21006.pdf

Jarrahi, M. H. (2018). Artificial Intelligence and the future of work: Human-AI symbiosis in organizational decision making. *Business Horizons, 61*(4), 577–586. https://doi.org/10.1016/j.bushor.2018.03.007

Jensen, J. M., Patel, P. C., & Messersmith, J. G. (2013). High-performance work systems and job control: Consequences for anxiety, role overload, and turnover intentions. *Journal of Management, 39*(6), 1699–1724. https://doi.org/10.1177/0149206311419663

Jeong, I., & Shin, S. J. (2019). High-performance work practices and organizational creativity during organizational change: A collective learning perspective. *Journal of Management*, *45*(3), 909–925. https://doi.org/10.1177/0149206316685156

Jiang, K., Lepak, D. P., Hu, J., & Baer, J. C. (2012). How does human resource management influence organizational outcomes? A meta-analytic investigation of mediating mechanisms. *Academy of Management Journal*, *55*(6), 1264–1294. https://doi.org/10.5465/amj.2011.0088

Johnson, D. G., & Verdicchio, M. (2017). AI anxiety. *Journal of the Association for Information Science and Technology*, *68*(9), 2267–2270. https://doi.org/10.1002/asi.23867

Jones, R., Jimmieson, N., & Griffiths, A. (2005). The impact of organizational culture and reshaping capabilities on change implementation success: The mediating role of readiness for change. *Journal of Management Studies*, *42*(2), 361–386. https://doi.org/10.1111/j.1467-6486.2005.00500.x

Kehoe, R. R., & Wright, P. M. (2013). The impact of high-performance human resource practices on employees' attitudes and behaviors. *Journal of Management*, *39*(2), 366–391. https://doi.org/10.1177/0149206310365901

Kummer, T.-F., Recker, J., & Bick, M. (2017). Technology-induced anxiety: Manifestations, cultural influences, and its effect on the adoption of sensor-based technology in German and Australian hospitals. *Information & Management*, *54*(1), 73–89. https://doi.org/10.1016/j.im.2016.04.002

Loehlin, J. C. (2004). *Latent variables models: An introduction to factor, path, and structural analysis* (4th ed.). Erlbaum.

Madsen, S. R., Miller, D., & John, C. R. (2005). Readiness for organizational change: Do organizational commitment and social relationships in the workplace make a difference?*Human Resource Development Quarterly*, *16*(2), 213–233. https://doi.org/10.1002/hrdq.1134

McKinsey. (2017). A future that works: Automation, employment, and productivity. McKinsey Global Institute. https://www.mckinsey.com/~/media/mckinsey/featured%20insights/digital%20disruption/harnessing%20automation%20for%20a%20future%20that%20works/a-future-that-works-executive-summary-mgi-january-2017.ashx

Messersmith, J. G., Patel, P. C., Lepak, D. P., & Gould-Williams, J. S. (2011). Unlocking the black box: Exploring the link between high-performance work systems and performance. *The Journal of Applied Psychology*, *96*(6), 1105–1118. https://doi.org/10.1037/a0024710

Neter, J., Wasserman, W., & Kutner, M. H. (1990). *Applied linear statistical models*. Irwin.

Nunnally, J. C. (1978). *Psychometric theory* (2nd ed.). McGraw-Hill.

Olson, M. A., & Kendrick, R. V. (2008). Origins of attitudes. In W. Crano, & R. Prislin (Eds.), *Attitudes and attitude change* (pp. 111–131). Psychology Press.

Otaye-Ebede, L., Shaffakat, S., & Scott, F. (2020). A multi-level model examining the relationships between workplace spirituality, ethical climate, and outcomes: A social cognitive theory perspective. *Journal of Business Ethics*, *166*(3), 611–626. https://doi.org/10.1007/s10551-019-04133-8

Peccei, R., & Van De Voorde, K. (2019). Human Resource Management–well-being–performance research revisited: Past, present, and future. *Human Resource Management Journal*, *29*(4), 539–563. https://doi.org/10.1111/1748-8583.12254

Phipps, M., Ozanne, L. K., Luchs, M. G., Subrahmanyan, S., Kapitan, S., Catlin, J. R., Gau, R., Naylor, R. W., Rose, R. L., Simpson, B., & Weaver, T. (2013). Understanding the inherent complexity of sustainable consumption: A social cognitive framework.

Journal of Business Research, 66(8), 1227–1234. https://doi.org/10.1016/j.jbusres.2012.08.016

Piderit, S. K. (2000). Rethinking resistance and recognizing ambivalence: A multidimensional view of attitudes toward an organizational change. *Academy of Management Review*, 25(4), 783–794. https://doi.org/10.5465/amr.2000.3707722

Podsakoff, P. M., MacKenzie, S. B., Lee, J. Y., & Podsakoff, N. P. (2003). Common method biases in behavioral research: A critical review of the literature and recommended remedies. *The Journal of Applied Psychology*, 88(5), 879–903. https://doi.org/10.1037/0021-9010.88.5.879

PwC. (2018). What will be the net impact of AI and related technologies on jobs in China?https://www.pwc.com/gx/en/issues/artificial-intelligence/impact-of-ai-on-jobs-in-china.pdf

Rafferty, A. E., & Jimmieson, N. L. (2017). Subjective perceptions of organizational change and employee resistance to change: Direct and mediated relationships with employee well-being. *British Journal of Management*, 28(2), 248–264. https://doi.org/10.1111/1467-8551.12200

Rafferty, A. E., & Minbashian, A. (2019). Cognitive beliefs and positive emotions about change: Relationships with employee change readiness and change-supportive behaviors. *Human Relations*, 72(10), 1623–1650. https://doi.org/10.1177/0018726718809154

Rafferty, A. E., Jimmieson, N. L., & Armenakis, A. (2013). Change readiness: A multilevel review. *Journal of Management*, 39(1), 110–135. https://doi.org/10.1177/0149206312457417

Rosenberg, M. J., & Hovland, C. I. (1960). Cognitive, affective, and behavioral components of attitude. In M. Rosenberg, C. Hovland, W. McGuire, R. Abelson, & J. Brehm (Eds.), *Attitude organization and change: An analysis of consistency among attitude components* (1–14). Yale University Press.

Shah, N., Irani, Z., & Sharif, A. M. (2017). Big data in an HR context: Exploring organizational change readiness, employee attitudes and behaviors. *Journal of Business Research*, 70, 366–378. https://doi.org/10.1016/j.jbusres.2016.08.010

Sherman, N. (2019, November 12). Is China gaining an edge in Artificial Intelligence? BBC. https://www.bbc.com/news/business-50255191

Sun, L.-Y., Aryee, S., & Law, K. S. (2007). High-performance human resource practices, citizenship behavior, and organizational performance: A relational perspective. *Academy of Management Journal*, 50(3), 558–577. https://doi.org/10.5465/amj.2007.25525821

Thatcher, J. B., Loughry, M. L., Lim, J., & McKnight, D. H. (2007). Internet anxiety: An empirical study of the effects of personality, beliefs, and social support. *Information & Management*, 44(4), 353–363. https://doi.org/10.1016/j.im.2006.11.007

Van der Heijden, H. (2004). User acceptance of hedonic information systems. *MIS Quarterly*, 28(4), 695–704. https://doi.org/10.2307/25148660

van Esch, P., Black, J. S., & Ferolie, J. (2019). Marketing AI recruitment: The next phase in job application and selection. *Computers in Human Behavior*, 90, 215–222. https://doi.org/10.1016/j.chb.2018.09.009

Venkatesh, V. (2000). Determinants and perceived ease of use: Integrating control, intrinsic motivation, and emotion into the Technology Acceptance Model. *Information Systems Research*, 11(4), 342–365. https://doi.org/10.1287/isre.11.4.342.11872

Wei, Y.-C., Han, T.-S., & Hsu, I.-C. (2010). High-performance HR practices and OCB: A cross-level investigation of a causal path. The International Journal of Human Resource Management, 21(10), 1631–1648. https://doi.org/10.1080/09585192.2010.500487

Wilson, H. J., & Daugherty, P. R. (2018). Collaborative intelligence: Humans and AI are joining forces. *Harvard Business Review, 96*(4), 114–123.

Wood, S., Van Veldhoven, M., Croon, M., & de Menezes, L. M. (2012). Enriched job design, high involvement management and organizational performance: The mediating roles of job satisfaction and well-being. *Human Relations, 65*(4), 419–445. https://doi.org/10.1177/0018726711432476

Zhou, Y., Fan, X., & Son, J. (2019). How and when matter: Exploring the interaction effects of high-performance work systems, employee participation, and human capital on organizational innovation. *Human Resource Management, 58*(3), 253–268. https://doi.org/10.1002/hrm.21950

Artificial intelligence, robotics, advanced technologies and human resource management: a systematic review

Demetris Vrontis, Michael Christofi, Vijay Pereira (iD), Shlomo Tarba (iD), Anna Makrides and Eleni Trichina

ABSTRACT
Although academic production in intelligent automation (e.g. artificial intelligence, robotics) has grown rapidly, we still lack a comprehensive understanding of the impacts of the utilization of these technologies in human resource management (HRM) at an organizational (firms) and individual (employees) level. This study therefore aims to systematize the academic inputs on intelligent automation so far and to clarify what are its main contributions to and challenges for HRM. In a systematic search of 13,136 potentially relevant studies published in the top HRM, international business (IB), general management (GM) and information management (IM) journals, we found 45 articles studying artificial intelligence, robotics and other advanced technologies within HRM settings. Results show that intelligent automation technologies constitute a new approach to managing employees and enhancing firm performance, thus offering several opportunities for HRM but also considerable challenges at a technological and ethical level. The impact of these technologies has been identified to concentrate on HRM strategies, namely, job replacement, human-robot/AI collaboration, decision-making and learning opportunities, and HRM activities, namely, recruiting, training and job performance. This study discusses these shifts in detail, along with the main contributions to theory and practice and directions for future research.

Introduction

Today, innovative technologies are dynamically reinventing the human resource management (HRM) landscape on a global scale (Ancarani et al., 2019). Indeed, with the accelerating development and wide application of Artificial Intelligence (AI) and other breakthrough technologies, the interplay between firms, employees and customers is fundamentally changing and the automation of the administrative components of HRM activities and tasks is intensifying (Larivière et al., 2017; Marler & Parry, 2016).

Although the technological evolution in HRM can be traced back to the industrial revolution, technological advancements had simply altered either physical or mental services. Contemporary developments, however, are increasingly providing alternatives to human resources in functions traditionally requiring human interaction and communication (Malik et al., 2019; Luo et al., 2019), thereby changing both the organizational structures and the nature of work (Colbert et al., 2016). Humanoid service robots and artificial intelligence bots, for example, are increasingly attracting industry attention (Araujo, 2018; Go & Sundar, 2019; Larivière et al., 2017; Thomaz et al., 2020). These intelligent "beings" have revolutionized traditional human resource functions, providing growing strengths and potentialities for HRM but also formidable challenges including job-specific obsolescence (Malik et al., 2019; Larivière et al., 2017). At the same time, deep learning algorithms, smart objects and the Internet of Things (IoT) are particularly useful for businesses operating across borders as they can foster more productive coordination and cooperation (Cooke et al., 2019). Similarly, the introduction of electronic human resource information systems and other novel technologies offer several opportunities to improve upon and reduce the cost of HRM functions including, among others, the evaluation of job applicants (Bondarouk et al., 2017; Cooke et al., 2019) and employee performance appraisals (Abraham et al., 2019; Parry & Tyson, 2011).

HRM embodied by technological advancements is increasingly the focus of internationally oriented HRM studies (e.g. Bondarouk et al., 2017; Cooke et al., 2019; Dulebohn & Hoch, 2017; Schaubroeck & Yu, 2017). Remarkably, scholars emphasize how information technologies are changing HRM-related practices by introducing e-recruitment, e-training or e-competence management, contributing positively to HRM service quality in both local and international organizations (Bondarouk & Brewster, 2016; Bondarouk et al., 2017). As these technologies are introducing new actors like social robots to HRM practices, they unlock numerous possibilities and support various HRM services (Bondarouk & Brewster, 2016; Bondarouk et al., 2017). Consistent with this view, several studies highlight the ways in which computer-aided design, manufacturing and process planning are automating many tasks and enhancing effectiveness and speed (Buckley et al., 2004; Park, 2018). Most notably, an increasing body of knowledge pertains to HRM as an enabler of technological change and innovation at a global level through work reorganization, such as working conditions and employee training (Seeck & Diehl, 2017; Zanko et al., 2008).

Academic production in technology-enabled HRM has grown rapidly. Despite the fact that the topic is rooted in HRM literature, it is placed at the crossroads of HRM research and information management (IM) research as well as has apparently attracted considerable attention in the international business (IB) literature. Thus, this topic is inherently multidisciplinary, melding concepts from different disciplines. In fact, the study of the utilization of intelligent automation in HRM has been undertaken within four research fields: HRM, general management (GM), IM and IB. In the main, although related, these literatures have been developed in parallel and their analytical connections remain unconnected so that scholarly work remains partial and fragmented (Loebbecke & Picot, 2015; Newell & Marabelli, 2015). Moreover, several reviews of the latest HRM developments due to diverse technological advancements are available (Bondarouk & Brewster, 2016; Bondarouk et al., 2017; Fleming, 2019; Garcia-Arroyo & Osca, 2019; Stone et al., 2015), but have partially analyzed technology-enabled HRM and focused on some aspects of technology and HRM. A systematic review is therefore warranted in order to gain a holistic view of the topic, by building knowledge conduits among the literatures. While studies continue to be published from the point of view of HRM, IB and other disciplines, scholars should find a multidisciplinary synthesis invaluable. In fact, our study responds to several calls to synthesise the current state of knowledge beyond the boundaries of individual academic disciplines in reference to intelligent automation (e.g. AI, machine learning, digitization) and work (Loebbecke & Picot, 2015; Markus, 2015).

The aim of this paper therefore is to conduct a review of the literature to systematize the academic inputs so far, clarifying what it means for HRM the utilization of intelligent automation. Note that we would seek to exclude work that focuses on Big Data, as it is already the subject of excellent review studies. For example, Wenzel and Van Quaquebeke (2018) review potential opportunities and risks in organizational research based on the central characteristics of Big Data and Giacumo and Breman (2016) analyze the utilization of Big Data in workplace learning. In particular, our analysis is guided by three specific questions:

1. What themes around intelligent automation in HRM have been identified and examined to date by researchers?
2. How does the utilization of intelligent automation in HRM affect firm performance and employment conditions?
3. Which issues need to be addressed in future research?

Overcoming the approaches of previous reviews, partially emphasizing some aspects of technology and HRM, the contributions of our study are fivefold. First, our study clarifies the complex nature of intelligent automation technologies and HRM at both firm and employee level, focusing on the short-and long-term positive outcomes and challenges of these technologies at the different levels of HRM strategies and activities. Second, presenting the main research themes, namely advanced technologies, AI and robotics, and their sub-themes allows us to understand how HRM is progressively shifting from eHRM towards an HRM defined by intelligent automation. Third, we provide an organizing framework for previous research that draws linkages between AI, robotics and advanced technologies with firm performance and future of employment. In doing so, we hope to encourage theory development and guide further empirical research on this area. Fourth, our study highlights the role of intelligent automation in supporting HRM and suggests how HRM managers can overcome the obstacles arise both at local and international level through employees' involvement in technological implementation processes and collaboration between human and machines. Finally, we shed light on a number of streams of multidisciplinary research, involving HRM, GM, IM and IB fields. In essence, we consider that the incorporation of intelligent automation in the HRM field is multidisciplinary in nature, and, thus, HRM, GM, IM and IB knowledge domains should be assimilated.

The remainder of this paper is organized as follows. We begin by offering a description of the methodology employed to search and select articles relevant to our research topic. The results are categorized in three research themes, namely advanced technologies, AI and robotics, and thematically presented highlighting the emerging perspectives of the studies and describing their impact on HRM. We then present a framework to draw linkages between AI, robotics, advanced technologies and firm performance, and AI, robotics, advanced technologies and the future of employment. Subsequently, we point to the critical implications of this review. Finally, we provide a set of recommendations for future research that arise from the synthesis of the findings by taking specifically an international business approach.

Methodology

To delineate research patterns and discern avenues for future studies related to intelligent automation in HRM, we conducted a systematic literature review following the suggestions made by Tranfield et al. (2003) as well as Crossan and Apaydin (2010). A systematic approach was deemed appropriate because it enhances the overall quality of the review by using a transparent and easily reproduced procedure (Crossan & Apaydin, 2010; Tranfield et al., 2003). In this regard, a systematic literature review methodology enabled us to critically analyze, synthesize and map the extant research by identifying the broad themes involved.

Selection of articles

For the purpose of this review paper, we used two methods to search for the relevant articles (Cooke et al., 2017). First, we have focused on academic articles published in 38 premier journals in the HRM, GM and IB fields. For this part of our study, we have used the same lists adopted by Pisani (2009), Pisani et al. (2017), Hewett et al. (2018) and Gaur and Kumar (2018). It was deemed appropriate to also include IM journals. The reason is that these journals provide the foundations of research pertaining to technological advancements and information systems (Van Geffen et al., 2013). Considering that the lists we adopted from the afore-mentioned reviews (Gaur & Kumar, 2018; Hewett et al., 2018; Pisani, 2009; Pisani et al., 2017) focused on HRM, GM and IB journals ranked 3, 4 and 4* based on the Association of Business Schools (ABS) Journal Guide 2018, IM journals that have earned rankings of 3 or above were only included ($n = 21$). Table 1 reports the entire list of 59 journals used in our study. As the focus is mainly on HRM in this section, we included only those studies that overlap with HRM, excluding studies that did not cover HRM issues.

Second, following the systematic review conducted by Hewett et al. (2018) we have used two major databases: *Business Source Ultimate (EBSCO)* and *Science Direct*. The decision to use these databases is anchored in the observation that research related to technological advancements and HRM is mostly published in journals covered by EBSCO and Science Direct. Having selected our publication outlets and following other state-of-the-art systematic reviews, we limited our research to full-length, academic peer-reviewed publications written in the English language (Marler & Boudreau, 2017; Sheehan et al., 2010). We also decided to review both review, empirical and conceptual papers (Leonidou et al., 2020). In order to gain a deep and comprehensive picture of the topic, we chose not to set any timeframe restriction to the data collection (Andresen & Bergdolt, 2017) and thus included work published before the writing of this paper (January 2020).

To find relevant articles, we sought to establish the appropriate keyword formula. In order to do so, we performed an initial scoping search of relevant articles to identify trends in keyword usage. This process led to the identification of several keywords related to intelligent automation.

Table 1. List of academic journals searched in alphabetical order.

Academic Journals	
Specialized IB Journals	GM Journals
Asia Pacific Journal of Management	Academy of Management Annals
Global Strategy Journal	Academy of Management Journal
International Business Review	Academy of Management Review
International Marketing Review	Administrative Science Quarterly
Journal of International Business Studies	Decision Sciences
Journal of International Management	Human Relations
Journal of International Marketing	Industrial Relations
Journal of World Business	Journal of Applied Behavioral Science
Management and Organizational Research	Journal of Applied Psychology
Management International Review	Journal of Management
	Journal of Management Studies
IM Journals	Journal of Occupational and
	Organizational Psychology
Information Systems Research	Journal of Occupational Psychology
MIS Quarterly	Journal of Organizational Behavior
Journal of Management Information Systems	Strategic Management Journal
Journal of the Association of Information Systems	Journal of Service Research
Computers in Human Behavior	Journal of Vocational Behavior
Decision Support Systems	Management Science
European Journal of Information Systems	Organization Science
Expert Systems with Applications	Organization Studies
Government Information Quarterly	Organizational Behavior and Human
	Decision Processes
Information and Management	Personnel Psychology
Information and Organization	Psychological Bulletin
Information Society	
Information Systems Frontiers	
Information Systems Journal	
Information Technology and People	**Specialized HR Journals**
International Journal of Electronic Commerce	Human Resource Management
International Journal of Human-Computer Studies	Human Resource Management Journal
Journal of Computer Mediated Communication	Human Resource Management Review
Journal of Information Technology	Industrial & Labor Relations Review
Journal of Strategic Information Systems	International Journal of Human
	Resource Management
Journal of the American Society for Information	
Science and Technology	

The use of standard Boolean operators enabled the creation of a single search algorithm (Pisani et al., 2017). Thus, these keywords were combined with the Boolean operator 'OR' to search for relevant papers in the top-tier HRM, GM and IB journals. The keyword search algorithm performed was: technolog* OR autom* OR "intelligent automation" OR "smart device" OR "Internet of Things" OR "human involvement" OR "artificial intelligence" OR "conversational agent" OR "chatbot*" OR "service agent" OR machine* OR robot* OR virtual OR intelligen* OR "automated service interaction" OR computer*. For the IM journals, however, we took a different search approach. Given the vast and varied research on advanced technologies within the IM research field, HRM-related search terms were added to the keyword search algorithm so that the search results will exclude studies that do not cover HRM issues. The HRM-related keywords were drawn from previous systematic reviews within the area of HRM (e.g. Cooke et al., 2017; De Kock et al., 2020; Voegtlin & Greenwood, 2016). Consequently, we combined the selected search terms of each theme, namely intelligent automation and HRM, with the Boolean operator 'AND'. The search used for IM journals was as follows: (technolog* OR autom* OR "intelligent automation" OR "smart device" OR "Internet of Things" OR "human involvement" OR "artificial intelligence" OR "conversational agent" OR "chatbot*" OR "service agent" OR machine* OR robot* OR virtual OR intelligen* OR "automated service interaction" OR computer*) AND ("HR" OR "HRM" OR "human resource management" OR "human resource" OR "IHR" OR "IHRM" OR "international HRM" OR "employ* relation*" OR "human resource development" OR "human resource performance system" OR "HRPS" OR employ* OR human).

As frequently done by systematic literature reviews, we used this combination of keywords to search titles, keywords and/or abstracts (Crossan & Apaydin, 2010; Pisani et al., 2017). The first step thus included the title and abstract screening while for the studies for which the research focus was not clear from this initial step, we left it for full-text screening at the second step. We also employed a further step, by examining the selected articles' references lists to identify other relevant articles. Following that, we repeated the process of reviewing reference lists for any additional articles included.

Our initial sample of potentially relevant studies was 13,136 articles in the target databases. After reviewing titles and abstracts we omitted those studies that were not related to our research questions, leaving us with a total of 187 journal articles. Then, once we screened the full text of the remaining articles for their eligibility in regard to the inclusion criteria set, 42 passed the screening criteria. Cross-referencing led to the inclusion of 3 articles. Thus, a total of 45 articles were included for data analysis, 24 of which were empirical studies, 7 conceptual papers and 14 review articles. The oldest study included in our systematic literature review was published in 1986, while the most relevant study stems from the year 2020. These articles were published in 23 HRM, GM, IB and IM journals (see Table 2). Figure 1 shows the selection process of the articles included in the review.

It is important to acknowledge that the search might not have identified all articles relevant to the topic due to issues related to database unavailability or human error (oversight) (Cooke et al., 2017). Nevertheless, we feel confident that the pool of selected articles includes the majority of the articles in top-tier HRM, GM, IM and IB journals. Thus, it enables us to map out what has been researched and identify gaps and theory development opportunities.

Table 2. List of journals and number of articles found related to our study ($N = 45$).

No.	Journal titles in descending order of number of articles	No. of articles found
1.	International Journal of Human Resource Management	6
2.	Computers in Human Behavior	5
3.	Journal of Service Research	4
4.	Journal of Applied Psychology	3
5.	Journal of Management	3
6.	Organization Science	2
7.	Human Resource Management	2
8.	Human Resource Management Review	2
9.	Journal of Information Technology	2
10.	Information Systems Frontiers	2
11.	Human Resource Management Journal	2
12.	Academy of Management Review	1
13.	Human Relations	1
14.	Academy of Management Annals	1
15.	International Marketing Review	1
16.	Journal of International Management	1
17.	Journal of International Marketing	1
18.	Management Science	1
19.	Organization Studies	1
20.	Personnel Psychology	1
21.	Decision Support Systems	1
22.	Information and Organization	1
23.	Expert Systems with Applications	1

Coding

All articles deemed relevant for the purpose of this study were down-loaded. We screened each article with the aim of extracting relevant information (Andresen & Bergdolt, 2017) and adding them to a data extraction form. Following Tranfield et al. (2003), this is done to eliminate human error and document the procedure for replicability and transparency reasons. Based on the objectives of our systematic review, the coded data were entered into an Excel spreadsheet and were classified in a number of categories, including publication details, type of the paper (empirical, conceptual, review), definition(s) provided relevant to our research questions, unit of analysis, effects of intelligent automation on HRM, key findings, future research directions provided by the author(s) of each study.

Thematic analysis

Scholarly work on technology-enabled HRM has investigated diverse topics in different contexts, and thus the issues explored in the reviewed articles are many and heterogeneous. The aim of this section was to identify the key findings in the literature. We sought to find common features between articles in order to categorize them into research themes based on the unit of analysis, which would enable us to address our research questions (Bailey et al., 2017). Three main research themes were identified: (1) advanced technologies; (2) AI; and (3) robotics. We

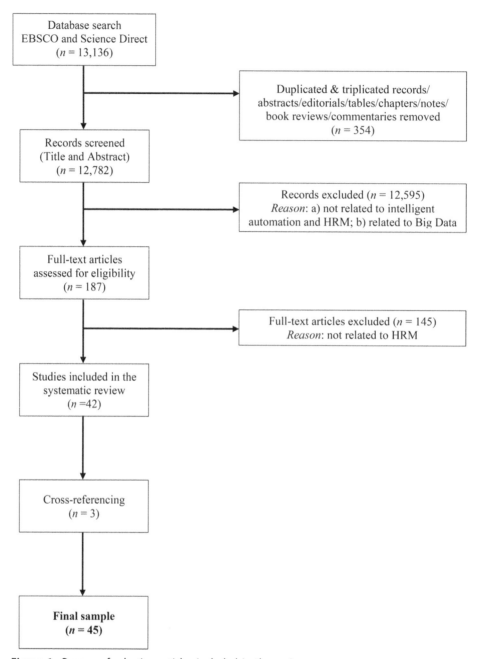

Figure 1. Process of selecting articles included in the review.

thus grouped the articles in these three research themes. The first theme (advanced technologies) included 16 articles that address the ways in which information technology and relevant technological innovations have started altering HRM in a more general perspective. The majority of articles ($n = 22$) belong to the second theme regarding AI and its influence on job replacement, human-AI collaboration, training, decision making, and recruiting. The third theme (robotics) included 7 articles aimed at understanding the impact of robots on employment in terms of job replacement and how collaboration between humans and robots can be achieved in support of HRM, as well as their role in the creation of learning opportunities. In line with other state-of-the-art systematic reviews (Christofi et al., 2017; Christofi et al., 2019; Leonidou et al., 2020; Vrontis & Christofi, 2019), we focus on key findings, rather than providing an exhaustive analysis of each article. Appendix A provides a summary of the final sample of articles included in the review according to the three broad research themes.

Advanced technologies

Information technologies have allowed significant transformations in the way people work and hence in organizational forms, routines and functions (Bondarouk et al., 2017). Consequently, the intersection between information technology and HRM, also referred to as eHRM, has gained increasing attention as scholars have sought to understand the external influences rather than internal influences on organizational operations and HRM practices in particular (e.g. Alcaraz et al., 2012; Parry & Tyson, 2011; Strohmeier, 2007; Strohmeier, 2009). These technologies not only have brought a new vocabulary to the HRM discourse but are altering the HRM profession. New ways of doing business are arising, thus leading to radical changes in workforce management practices and the creation of new products and services (Bondarouk & Brewster, 2016). Zammuto et al. (2007) describe five affordances – visualizing entire work processes, real-time/flexible product and service innovation, virtual collaboration, mass collaboration, and simulation/synthetic reality – that can result from this interplay.

The execution of the recruitment process online, resulting in what is commonly referred to as e-recruitment, has been widely addressed in the literature. Research thus far reveals that companies establish an e-recruiting system to reduce costs, to access more people, get quicker response and increase applicants' positive perceptions about the company (e.g. Parry & Tyson, 2008). Martinez-Gil et al. (2019) argue that automatic matching between job offers and suitable candidate profiles provides several advantages including reduced effort (in terms of cost and time) and elimination of the need for HR professionals to have knowledge pertaining to a specific professional field or skill. However, although the trend towards the use of information technology for e-recruitment has transformed the way firms recruit, select and retain employees (Stone et al., 2015), several issues impede its effectiveness. Feldman and Klaas (2002) and Stone et al. (2015) discuss these issues in depth.

Prior research also discusses other advanced technologies, for which information technology is the backbone, and their impact on HRM. The application of IoT in HRM involves changes and modifications in HR technologies (hardware, software and data), HR activities (flexibilization of employee working times, improvement of employee performance, personalization of employee working environments) and HR actors (tasks and qualifications) (Strohmeier, 2020). Employee self-service (ESS) technology allows employees to manage their own data rather than rely on HR professionals and register for training with the objective of efficiency-related gains (Marler et al., 2009). Electronic performance monitoring (EPM) has the potentiality to change various HR practices including evaluation, selection and training (Ravid et al., 2020). Many EPM forms are already widely used (e.g. call and internet usage monitoring, electronic medication administration records) and it is increasingly argued that technologies such as microchip wrist implants and body heat sensor desk hardware may be the future of work monitoring (e.g. Ravid et al., 2020). Algorithmic technologies can also help employers direct, evaluate and discipline workers (Kellogg et al., 2020). Of particular contemporary interest are virtualization technologies, that is to say, virtual representation of individuals who interact with each other in 3D digital environments. Although they have emerged from the computer games industry, they are increasingly being used to enhance interpersonal and organizational interaction and facilitate organizational learning (Dodgson et al., 2013).

Overall, research yielded contradictory results with regard to the strategic benefits of technology-enabled HRM. While information technology and other advanced technological innovations have offered several benefits (cost savings, harmonization and integration of HR activities, efficiency, support of international strategy), they have also created extra barriers (more HR administration, work stress, disappointments with technological properties) (e.g. Bondarouk et al., 2017; Stone et al., 2015; Strohmeier, 2007). Researchers also argue that the consequences of technology largely depend on context (Bondarouk et al., 2017). For some companies depending on the size, the industry and the country, technology-enabled HRM will have a negligible effect. For others, it can be seen as a key factor for success and survival in a highly competitive market.

As for employees, the implications still remain unclear. According to Levy and Murnane (2014) the number of jobs will increase, but the nature of these jobs will change. New skills will be required including problem-solving and communication that are particularly hard for computers to match. Bondarouk and Brewster (2016) argue that a decline in standard full-time employment and a growth in contingent forms of work are inevitable. HRM transformations undoubtedly eliminate distance constraints, but the risk for an increasing lack of direct contact between the various stakeholders is lurking. Stone et al. (2015) highlight that, although there are a number of advantages, there is a danger lurking behind technology-focused HRM and suggest that technology should be viewed as a decision support tool that enhances and does not replace the HR professionals in organizations.

Artificial intelligence

AI could be viewed as computing technologies that simulate or imitate intelligent behaviors relevant to the ones of humans despite that they act different from them (Bhave et al., 2020). Research areas around AI applications in workplace are related among others to machine learning and deep learning and they can be applied in industries across the globe (Bhave et al., 2020). Importantly, in reference to HRM, the domain of AI research encompasses AI in the context of job replacement, human-AI collaboration, training, decision making, and recruiting.

One way to comprehend AI and its applications in HRM is to think of the services that AI will replace and how this will affect the world of work in general. One theory related to this asserts that job replacement by AI will happen first at a task level instead of a job level and for "lower" intelligence tasks as these are easier and less complex to be performed by AI than human employees (Huang & Rust, 2018). Progressively, however, AI, having the ability to perform human tasks and being able to think and feel like humans, will replace human labor entirely and, thus, human interactions will fade from sight (Huang & Rust, 2018). Consider, for example, the potential impact of virtual assistants like Siri. Dealing with queries and customer support internationally, they may enable organizations to operate 24 h a day, without engaging human employees as representatives at physical locations (Glavas et al., 2019). Cano-Kollmann et al. (2018) argue that due to the dramatic advances in AI, automation and digitalization, unskilled workers in advanced economies may not only become unemployed but also "unemployable", as human tasks and jobs are either offshored, cease to exist altogether or decline.

Taking into consideration the above, we find that the progress of AI may change the fundamental nature of work and pose a serious threat to human employment. However, it can also create significant opportunities for human-machine collaboration and integration. Within this context, several authors support the view that AI can be of great value in facilitating service or sales and creating more favorable, customized and valued service interactions (Marinova et al., 2017; Singh et al., 2017). Notably, machine learning can assist in processing interaction-based knowledge, analyze variability across interactions and clarify ambiguous patterns using data from frontline employee (FLE) – customer interactions. In this way, it gives FLEs the possibility to use this data for the provision of efficient, effective and customized solutions to customers (Marinova et al., 2017). Similarly, artificially smart technologies, being capable of natural language processing and real time learning, play an important role in complementing human interactions and increasing problem-solving effectiveness (Singh et al., 2017). AI algorithms in the realm of journalism beyond the initial programming can also assist journalists in basic works, allowing them to focus on more investigative reporting, generating at the same time news faster, at a larger scale and with less errors (Jung et al., 2017). In addition, people can use AI, often in the form of personal digital assistants, to facilitate work activities regardless of temporal and spatial location (Golden & Geisler, 2007). Overall, these observations are consistent with the view that the effect of automation technology on staffing decisions greatly depends on a facility's vertical position in the local marketplace, thereby supporting the argument that automate intelligent technologies do not lead necessarily to reduced job opportunities.

AI concerns, inter alia, information processing, logical reasoning and mathematical skills (Huang & Rust, 2018). For employees, those challenging skills could be obtained through expertise and training. Researchers argue that AI applications could be of pivotal utility in HRM for training purposes. Simulations, defined as AI environments, can provide high degree of interactivity with other users and enhance learning opportunities (Bell et al., 2008). Despite the increased cost of using such technologies, simulation-based applications allow employees to interact and comprehend how to adapt their decisions to the interactive effects of the environment and multiple competitors (Bell et al., 2008). Research also highlights the use of intelligent animated characters for training purposes, giving feedback and providing support like a human trainer (Behrend & Thompson, 2011). These intelligent agents have the ability to learn in real time and amend their training to employees' preferences and external information, addressing issues related to low engagement and isolation in web-based training (Behrend & Thompson, 2011). Within the same context, AI computer agents have been examined as important tools in enhancing employees' skills when interacting in strategic and negotiation settings, saving considerable effort and offering better performance (Lin et al., 2014).

Recent research also discusses the ways in which contemporary advances in AI increasingly offer alternatives to the actual decision making of

HRM, offering several potentialities, risks as well as vulnerabilities to organizations. Early studies in considering AI as a decision-making tool in HRM suggest that expert systems – AI applications that embody the knowledge and decision-making abilities of a human expert – can increase the accuracy of HRM decisions made by non-experts and eliminate the time required by them to make HRM decisions (Lawler & Elliot, 1996; Hooper et al., 1998). Importantly, explanations produced by AI expert systems are useful to managers who are firstly assisted by this decision-making process and are able secondly to learn why a particular decision was made (Hooper et al., 1998). Other studies pertaining to AI applications in HRM decision-making highlight the ability to process large amounts of data at high speeds (Lindebaum et al., 2020), the possibility to help salespeople to acquire new customers more efficiently (Watson et al., 2018) and the potentiality to effectively evaluate and manage employee turnover risk (Wang et al., 2017). However, even when AI improves task performance and poses no immediate threat, its extensive use in HRM decision-making is likely to be perceived as a threat to human employees' autonomy, status and job security because it can provide more options to them and confuse them, increasing perceived complexity (Lawler & Elliot, 1996). Ötting and Maier (2018) emphasize the importance of procedural justice in decision situations because it enhances beneficial employee attitudes and behavior regardless of whether these decisions are taken by human leaders or AI systems.

Moreover, the adoption of AI technologies provides several opportunities for recruiting and can simulate real work conditions towards evaluation and recruitment. Specifically, the introduction of AI applications in HRM allows HR employees to conduct background checks of job applications and develop compensation packages for certain positions (Cooke et al., 2019). AI-enabled recruitment platforms can also extrapolate possible behaviors in terms of job fit and performance while being less biased and more objective than humans (Van Esch et al., 2019). Consistent with this view, Sajjadiani et al. (2019) suggest that machine learning can greatly assist HR practitioners and firms by transforming the selection process into a more systematic process by eliminating the occurrence of recruiters' biases or even applicants' influence methods to deviate the selection process. Certainly, the numerous advantages that AI provides to HRM recruiting constitute a positive development for HRM. However, these positive effects have been questioned in a number of ways in reference to ethicality of acquiring and progressing of data as well as in terms of favorability among applicants (Suen et al., 2019; Bhave et al., 2020). Indeed, AI machine learning and deep learning applications in HRM raise questions of privacy and offer a fruitful discussion of ethical challenges. Notably, direct applications in the employment and HR context through AI machine learning, including the analysis and collection of digital records to support traditional psychometric tests in evaluating talent and predicting work-related issues, entail several questions concerning human privacy (Bhave et al., 2020). Similar privacy issues arise when employing image and video recognition in digital interviews through AI deep learning in order to capture verbal and other interpersonal behaviors and amend them to create a psychological profile and predict possible fit (Bhave et al., 2020).

Overall, given the discussion above and recalling our analysis around advanced technologies, we can argue that with the increasing involvement of AI in the HRM field, we are witnessing a shift from eHRM to a new phase. In this phase, AI intelligent automation constitutes the tool that drives the transformation of HRM by utilizing AI applications in recruiting, training and decision-making. And although there are more paths yet to be uncovered and a number of challenges to be addressed, we need to acknowledge that AI has a say in the future of HRM.

Robotics

Robotics involves the creation of machines that can perform human movement and mimic human behavior. In a nutshell, the field of robotics is a set of sciences related to artificial intelligence, machine learning, electronics, nanotechnology and many others. The discourse focusing on the developments in the field of robotic technologies highlights the implications that robots will have on work and employment; whereas at the other end, there is considerable optimism about the learning and training opportunities that can create for business and people in organizations. Research efforts on robotic technologies can be therefore categorized in job replacement, human-robot collaboration, and learning opportunities.

Research on robotic technologies has predicted that many jobs will soon disappear and be replaced by automation and robotics. Chao and Kozlowski (1986) highlight that the jobs that are more possible to suffer the greatest effects of job displacement are those of welding, painting, and assembling jobs as well as those employees that are less educated, experienced and skilled. It is also plausible that humanoid robots like robot waiters in restaurants and virtual assistants that provide guidance to customers through a company's website will fully substitute human frontline employees (Van Doorn et al., 2017). Other studies suggest that the impact of robotics might be of great importance for HRM and more specifically for unemployment; however, this might occur in the future. Specifically, given the way that AI, digitalization and robotic technologies are being shaped by socioeconomic and organizational forces, predictions about mass joblessness and replacement by robotics are not likely to be realized (Fleming, 2019). Van Doorn et al. (2017) argue that situations defined by strong needs for empathy, in which developing original and creative solutions is required or that necessitate high levels of social intelligence are not at high risk for automation and replacement. Shifting away from job replacement, several researchers emphasize the need to combine human capabilities with robotic technologies in HRM to bring more insightful HR solutions. In this regard, more skilled and educated employees are needed in the era of human and robots symbiosis and collaboration to be benefited from possible opportunities and reverse potential threats (Aleksander, 2017). Robotics can support human employees by offering them opportunities for more technical positions that are either created or enhanced by robotic technologies (Chao & Kozlowski, 1986). Robotic surgery is a notable example. Although robotics can enhance precision and reduce errors if applied correctly, the human knowledge remains a vital component (Jonsson et al., 2018). Importantly, the features of technology as well as the manipulations and knowledge of the doctor are required (Jonsson et al., 2018).

Robotic technologies have also brought several learning opportunities to HRM. Work on robotics emphasizes the ways in which robotic technologies can eliminate repetitive and routine activities handled by human employees, offering to them the possibility to engage in opportunities to use their skills more effectively (Lindsay et al., 2014). At the same time, this creates new learning opportunities combined with extensive training in order for the employees to meet their altered responsibilities and acquire the skills required to work with a robot. However, employees may exhibit differential perceptions towards robots based on their occupations. Chao and Kozlowski (1986) find that high-skilled employees have more positive attitudes towards robots and their implementation as they offer them opportunities to expand further their skills and knowledge. Inevitably, jobs designed based on AI and robotic technologies are about to bring uncertainty. Yet, these technologies offer the opportunity for the design of problem-solving strategies that will be of great value (Wall et al., 1992).

Framework development

Based on the thematic analysis, an organizing framework that captures the impact of intelligent automation on HRM is proposed and shown in Figure 2. This model indicates that intelligent automation in HRM includes AI, robotics and other advanced technologies. These

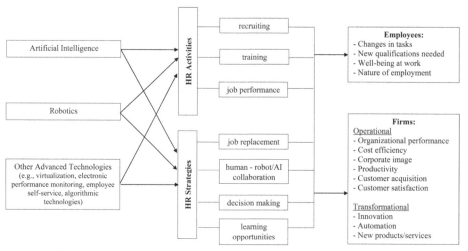

Figure 2. Framework summarizing the reviewed literature.

technologies are increasingly used in HRM transforming the practices of recruiting, training and job performance, altering organizations' decision-making processes, introducing job replacement issues, enabling collaboration between robots, AI technologies and employees and offering learning opportunities for employees. The model also highlights the consequences of intelligent automation in HRM for organizations and employees.

At first, AI, robotics and advanced technologies are obviously of relevance for HRM. As a model able to map the impact of these technologies on different levels, HR activities and HR strategies are considered. HR activities encompass HR functions like recruiting, training and job performance. HR strategies refer to the formulation of objectives and the implementation of HRM within the scope of job replacement, human – robot/AI collaboration, decision-making and learning opportunities. Taken together, an analysis of these components allows a depiction of intelligent automation's contribution to the future of work and overall organizational performance.

Having mapped intelligent automation within HRM settings in extant research, its actual consequences, whether beneficial or adverse, delineate a crucial aspect. Consequences occur at an individual or organizational level. Consequences at an individual level refer to impacts of technology on the nature of work like changes in tasks and qualifications and employee well-being. Leaning on extant work, consequences at an organizational level can be structured into operational and transformational. The operational consequences emphasize efficiency and overall performance outcomes. The transformational consequences refer to transformations in terms of doing business and business models.

The integrative framework proposed in this systematic review provides a road map for extant research on the topic and helps researchers in classifying and formulating the content. Hopefully, it will serve as a basis for advancement by future research incorporating other technologies, their impact on HRM and the subsequent employee-level and firm-level effects into the framework. Last, this framework relates academic research to the real-life situations that managers must deal with and thus offers important insights for practitioners.

Theoretical implications

The main objective of this study was to conduct a review of extant research on intelligent automation within HRM settings to clarify what are the major implications and challenges for HR strategies and activities. This review resulted in the identification of 45 journal articles that provided us with an overview of the state of the art on this subject. Issues of those studies were addressed as opportunities or challenges for HRM, however, studies specified on AI and intelligent automation are scarce and focus mainly on other technologies or more recently on big data. Even though this is a new and emerging topic and there is lack of a solid conceptualization about the role of AI in organizational life, there are some important theoretical implications that should be pointed out.

First, building on the theory of decision-making (Edwards, 1954) as well as on recent research that has analyzed how data allow HR managers to better informed about employees (Garcia-Arroyo & Osca, 2019), we found that AI algorithms and expert systems facilitate HR processes and allow better decision-making about human employees and HR practices. In doing so, they enhance the accuracy of HRM decisions made by non-experts and eliminate the time needed by them to make HRM decisions (Lindebaum et al., 2020; Lawler & Elliot, 1996). Hence, AI plays a crucial role in strengthening the quality of HR decisions.

Second, as our study has indicated, advanced technologies and AI technologies in HRM constitutes a multifaceted theme, which is associated with a variety of academic disciplines. Therefore, we suggest that it is studied adopting a multidisciplinary approach. For instance, HR researchers could be benefited from collaborating with IM researchers or computer scientists to analyze the ethical challenges of AI technologies in decision-making processes as well as the factors that affect the way that human employees can accept these technologies.

Third, the findings of this systematic review identify the effects of AI, robotics and advanced technologies on HRM strategies and activities at both firm and employee level, questioning the role of intelligent automation on job replacement. Notably, despite the expectations that these advancements will have a dramatic impact on employment (Frey & Osborne, 2017), our findings suggest that we are still years away from wide-ranging consequences on HRM and levels of employment.

Fourth, the development of AI, robotics and advanced technologies, involve complex processes that should consider possible challenges and risks. Important methodological and ethical challenges are associated with the novelty of the subject and are likely to be addressed progressively as the use of AI and related technologies goes on; in this sense several authors have offered helpful recommendations. For example, considering the conflicts and ethical challenges that could arise from privacy interests of employees and employers operating at a regional and international level, this could be diminished with the development of a conflict resolution model drawing on efficiency, equity, and voice that would assist stakeholders in reaching an agreement (Bhave et al., 2020).

Fifth, there are some methodological strengths of our study worth mentioning. Although other reviews of the literature related to eHRM or big data have been conducted (e.g. Garcia-Arroyo & Osca, 2019; Giacumo & Breman, 2016), the present review, applying a systematic review methodology, scopes the whole field of HRM, making it more robust. Notably, the inclusion of journal articles from a variety of disciplines adds value to this study as we map the different research sub-areas about this subject that occur in different disciplines, uncovering their key findings as well as their main concepts.

Last, by developing a framework that draws linkages between AI, robotics and advanced technologies with firm performance and future of employment, this study enables future scholars to examine the various possible roles that technology may play in HRM and enhance our understanding of underlying mechanisms and conditions under which technological advancements will result in certain outcomes.

Managerial implications

Considering that intelligent automation constitutes an emerging research stream in the HRM field, the findings of this systematic literature review are also of considerable practical worth. This research joins the scholarly voices calling upon managers to shift their attention to the benefits of these technologies on firm and employee performance. Artificially smart technologies complement human employees' interactions, enhance problem-solving for effectiveness, provide training, give feedback and support human employees (Behrend & Thompson, 2011; Singh et al., 2017). As a result, firms should establish an organizational environment in which human employees and technology could coexist. Moreover, as our findings suggest, firms should focus on training and ongoing development of employees in order for them to meet the criteria and skills needed for working with AI agents (Lindsay et al., 2014). Managers could encourage employees to get actively involved in trainings that will enhance their learning routines and existing knowledge base. It is the managers' responsibility to assist employees in being more engaged in such activities that will offer them the technological knowledge required in the competitive international market. Ferraris, Erhardt, and Bresciani (2019) suggest that the technological knowledge required could be acquired through numerous flexible alliances with various government and public actors, research centers and universities.Notably, although there are a number of advantages, there is a danger lurking behind technology-focused HRM, suggesting that technology should be viewed as a supporting tool that enhances and does not replace the HRM professionals in organizations. In essence, a human mind is needed for the knowledge and manipulations required. Given our findings, we would suggest that intelligence automation can boost the positive effects for HRM, if managers refrain from letting technology dominate and substitute the core meaning and role of HRM. On the contrary, practitioners should focus on the mutual development of HRM strengths and intelligent technologies.

Technological developments in HRM, including the introduction of AI, machine learning and deep learning applications for the analysis and collection of digital records in predicting work-related issues, have raised a number of concerns pertaining to human privacy (Bhave et al., 2020). Considering the privacy and ethical challenges that these positions hold, there is an emerging necessity for the development of regulations that guarantee the rights of employees or potential employees for the protection of their data. Although considerable progress has been made with the General Data Protection Regulation (EU, 2016/679), the rapid technological developments imply ongoing updates that will raise the awareness of society and employees.

Finally, in the context of global HRM, thinking of how AI technologies eliminate distance constraints but at the same time how they minimize the direct contact between the various stakeholders involving digital mediations, managers need to consider ways to use these technologies for the benefit of firms and employees. This entails assisting diverse actors to use different technologies to coherently perform shared work arrangements (Jonsson et al., 2018).

Limitations and future research directions

There are some limitations of this review that need to be acknowledged. First, the review is restricted to work published merely in peer-reviewed journals, which means that we do not have the complete picture. Valuable work published in non-peer-reviewed papers, books and book chapters may be available; thus, future work should be complemented by other forms of existing research, which may result in other ways of classifying extant body of work. Second, our search might not have identified all academic peer-reviewed articles related to our topic as stated earlier. Third, the keyword formula used might not have allowed relevant articles to surface. Given the increasing complexity of the HRM architecture due to the emergence of technology, and the strong interdependence between HRM, GM, IB and IM issues, there could be more articles with a focus on intelligent automation that the search keywords did not capture. As a result, despite the fact that our final sample includes articles that examine various issues related to intelligent automation from the perspective of HRM, this may not be exhaustive. In addition, there has been a plethora of technological innovations, which were examined from heterogeneous approaches, and thus it is difficult to draw a precise line of studies for inclusion and exclusion. Nevertheless, we feel confident that the pool of selected articles includes the majority of the articles in top-tier HRM, GM, IB and IM journals, thereby enabling us to identify a broad pattern.

Strohmeier (2007) suggests that the body of knowledge relevant to HRM is patchy and the question of whether eHRM is able to transform into a valued strategic partner have yet to be sufficiently addressed. Ten years later, Bondarouk et al. (2017) address the same issue and state that we still lack theory-driven and evidence-based eHRM studies in this still immature research field. Indeed, much remains to be examined and the possibilities are enormous.

We envision that in the years to come the HRM landscape will change dramatically, as the technological advancements are pushing the boundaries of business and management. Although there are many promising areas for further research, we chose to develop future research directions focused specifically on the international context for the following reasons. First, we acknowledge the call for studying technology-enabled HRM with the focus on the international context and for exploring the effects of the international context on the implementation processes (e.g. Bondarouk & Brewster, 2016). Second, the take up and use of technological innovations seem to be heavily dependent on context (Van Geffen et al., 2013). Third, the technological revolution and the more rapid pace of internationalization leads to a more strategic role for HRM, representing a major determinant of success or failure in international business (Cooke et al., 2019).

Research argues that, as far as organizational processes are concerned, the transfer of HR activities and strategies across borders can be challenging and problematic (e.g. Chang & Smale, 2013; Ferraris et al., 2019). Thus, it would be worth investigating more closely how technology-enabled HRM is delivered in different country contexts in order to identify whether country-specific factors change the dynamics pertaining to the role of intelligent automation in HR activities and strategies or whether a global HRM model can be achieved. Developing an understanding of the contexts under which technology-enabled HR practices converge or diverge would be of great importance to firms that operate in various countries (Kivimaa et al., 2019). Furthermore, research is needed to identify those macro-contextual barriers to the implementation of intelligent automation in HRM across borders and examine how they can be overcome.

Another rather unexplored area that is ripe for future research is employees' reactions and responses to the technologically induced shift in the organizational role of HRM. Adopting a cross-cultural perspective is particularly suited for gaining insight in possible cross-national differences and similarities pertaining to employee behavior that can support or hinder the implementation of intelligent automation in HRM. Moreover, it is increasingly clear that robots will replace certain human jobs. Yet, the use of robots is likely to significantly affect not only those displaced but also managers and supervisors. Thus, it would be an interesting avenue for future work to address not only what intelligent automation has in store for various actors across the organization hierarchy but also internationalization's added layers of complexity that managing people must deal with.

From the customer's perspective, Watson et al. (2018) argue that evidence of customers' acceptance of AI is unambiguous. It would thus be an interesting avenue for future work to examine whether customers are receptive of these technologies and in which contexts AI is more effective for building customer relationships. More importantly, there is a need to identify customers' acceptance levels with an eye to specific contexts internationally, rather than accepting a universalized perspective. Undertaking cross-national comparative research in future will inform practice on how to make international strategic decisions of whether and when to replace workers with AI. While exploring the trade-offs that customers are willing to make is crucial for implementing new technologies, we argue that the impact of smart technologies on customer engagement is nonlinear and can increase and decrease over time. Thus, the time-level effect of AI and robotics in HR practices is another issue worthy of future study.

On a final note, the role of technological advancements in HRM is much more complex than just supporting or altering HR processes.

When we take into account internationalization aspects, a question is inevitably raised as to how universal the processes and effects may be. Multidisciplinary research to address this complex and hybrid topic and illustrate how traditional and new ways of managing the workforce can be balanced for the benefit of all stakeholders across the world is sorely needed. We hope that this paper will inspire future research to explore and expand on our proposed pathways, which ultimately will be of paramount importance for practice.

Conclusion

The objective of this paper was to conduct a review of research related to intelligent automation in HRM. We searched for potentially relevant studies in 59 top-tier HRM, GM, IB and IM journals in order to clarify what is the novelty of intelligent automation for HRM. The selection process led to the identification of 45 articles that offered an overview of the state of the art on this topic. Although not exhaustive, this article shed light on the impact of AI, robotics and other advanced technologies on HRM. Recommendations for future research were also provided, which target opportunities for theoretical and empirical advancement of the field by taking specifically an international business approach. Collectively, we hope that the contributions of our study will advance the next generation of research, which will be meaningfully extended and validated in practice.

Disclosure statement

No potential conflict of interest was reported by the authors.

ORCID

Vijay Pereira (iD) http://orcid.org/0000-0001-6755-0793
Shlomo Tarba (iD) http://orcid.org/0000-0002-1919-084X

References

Abraham, M., Niessen, C., Schnabel, C., Lorek, K., Grimm, V., Möslein, K., & Wrede, M. (2019). Electronic monitoring at work: The role of attitudes, functions, and perceived control for the acceptance of tracking technologies. *Human Resource Management Journal*, *29*(4), 657–675. https://doi.org/10.1111/1748-8583.12250

Alcaraz, J. M., Domènech, M., & Tirado, F. (2012). eHR software, multinational corporations and emerging China: Exploring the role of information through a postcolonial lens. *Information and Organization*, *22*(2), 106–124. https://doi.org/10.1016/j.infoandorg.2012.01.004

Aleksander, I. (2017). Partners of humans: A realistic assessment of the role of robots in the foreseeable future. *Journal of Information Technology*, *32*(1), 1–9. https://doi.org/10.1057/s41265-016-0032-4

Ancarani, A., Di Mauro, C., & Mascali, F. (2019). Backshoring strategy and the adoption of Industry 4.0: Evidence from Europe. *Journal of World Business*, *54*(4), 360–371. https://doi.org/10.1016/j.jwb.2019.04.003

Andresen, M., & Bergdolt, F. (2017). A systematic literature review on the definitions of global mindset and cultural intelligence–merging two different research streams. *The International Journal of Human Resource Management*, *28*(1), 170–195. https://doi.org/10.1080/09585192.2016.1243568

Araujo, T. (2018). Living up to the chatbot hype: The influence of anthropomorphic design cues and communicative agency framing on conversational agent and company perceptions. *Computers in Human Behavior*, *85*, 183–189. https://doi.org/10.1016/j.chb.2018.03.051

Bailey, C., Madden, A., Alfes, K., & Fletcher, L. (2017). The meaning, antecedents and outcomes of employee engagement: A narrative synthesis. *International Journal of Management Reviews*, *19*(1), 31–53. https://doi.org/10.1111/ijmr.12077

Behrend, T. S., & Thompson, L. F. (2011). Similarity effects in online training: Effects with computerized trainer agents. *Computers in Human Behavior*, *27*(3), 1201–1206. https://doi.org/10.1016/j.chb.2010.12.016

Bell, B. S., Kanar, A. M., & Kozlowski, S. W. (2008). Current issues and future directions in simulation-based training in North America. *The International Journal of Human Resource Management*, *19*(8), 1416–1434. https://doi.org/10.1080/09585190802200173

Bhave, D. P., Teo, L. H., & Dalal, R. S. (2020). Privacy at work: A review and a research agenda for a contested terrain. *Journal of Management*, *46*(1), 127–164. https://doi.org/10.1177/0149206319878254

Bondarouk, T., & Brewster, C. (2016). Conceptualising the future of HRM and technology research. *The International Journal of Human Resource Management*, *27*(21), 2652–2671. https://doi.org/10.1080/09585192.2016.1232296

Bondarouk, T., Harms, R., & Lepak, D. (2017). Does e-HRM lead to better HRM service? *The International Journal of Human Resource Management*, *28*(9), 1332–1362. https://doi.org/10.1080/09585192.2015.1118139

Bondarouk, T., Parry, E., & Furtmueller, E. (2017). Electronic HRM: Four decades of research on adoption and consequences. *The International Journal of Human Resource Management*, *28*(1), 98–131. https://doi.org/10.1080/09585192.2016.1245672

Buckley, P., Minette, K., Joy, D., & Michaels, J. (2004). The use of an automated employment recruiting and screening system for temporary professional employees: A case study. *Human Resource Management*, *43*(2-3), 233–241. https://doi.org/10.1002/hrm.20017

Cano-Kollmann, M., Hannigan, T. J., & Mudambi, R. (2018). Global innovation networks–organizations and people. *Journal of International Management*, *24*(2), 87–92. https://doi.org/10.1016/j.intman.2017.09.008

Chang, Y. Y., & Smale, A. (2013). Expatriate characteristics and the stickiness of HRM knowledge transfers. *The International Journal of Human Resource Management*, *24*(12), 2394–2410. https://doi.org/10.1080/09585192.2013.781436

Chao, G. T., & Kozlowski, S. W. (1986). Employee perceptions on the implementation of robotic manufacturing technology. *Journal of Applied Psychology*, *71*(1), 70–76. https://doi.org/10.1037/0021-9010.71.1.70

Christofi, M., Vrontis, D., Thrassou, A., & Shams, S. R. (2019). Triggering technological innovation through cross-border mergers and acquisitions: A micro-foundational perspective. *Technological Forecasting and Social Change*, *146*, 148–166. https://doi.org/10.1016/j.techfore.2019.05.026

Christofi, M., Leonidou, E., & Vrontis, D. (2017). Marketing research on mergers and acquisitions: A systematic review and future directions. *International Marketing Review*, *34*(5), 629–651. https://doi.org/10.1108/IMR-03-2015-0100

Colbert, A., Yee, N., & George, G. (2016). The digital workforce and the workplace of the future. *Academy of Management Journal*, *59*(3), 731–739. https://doi.org/10.5465/amj.2016.4003

Cooke, F. L., Liu, M., Liu, L. A., & Chen, C. C. (2019). Human resource management and industrial relations in multinational corporations in and from China: Challenges and new insights. *Human Resource Management*, *58*(5), 455–471. https://doi.org/10.1002/hrm.21986

Cooke, F. L., Veen, A., & Wood, G. (2017). What do we know about cross-country comparative studies in HRM? A critical review of literature in the period of 2000-2014. *The International Journal of Human Resource Management*, *28*(1), 196–233. https://doi.org/10.1080/09585192.2016.1245671

Cooke, F. L., Wood, G., Wang, M., & Veen, A. (2019). How far has international HRM travelled? A systematic review of literature on multinational corporations (2000–2014). *Human Resource Management Review*, *29*(1), 59–75. https://doi.org/10.1016/j.hrmr.2018.05.001

Crossan, M. M., & Apaydin, M. (2010). A multi-dimensional framework of organizational innovation: A systematic review of the literature. *Journal of Management Studies*, *47*(6), 1154–1191. https://doi.org/10.1111/j.1467-6486.2009.00880.x

De Kock, F. S., Lievens, F., & Born, M. P. (2020). The profile of the 'Good Judge'in HRM: A systematic review and agenda for future research. *Human Resource Management Review*, *30*(2), 100667. https://doi.org/10.1016/j.hrmr.2018.09.003

Dodgson, M., Gann, D. M., & Phillips, N. (2013). Organizational learning and the technology of foolishness: The case of virtual worlds at IBM. *Organization Science*, *24*(5), 1358–1376. https://doi.org/10.1287/orsc.1120.0807

Dulebohn, J. H., & Hoch, J. E. (2017). Virtual teams in organizations. *Human Resource Management Review*, *27*(4), 569–574. https://doi.org/10.1016/j.hrmr.2016.12.004

Edwards, W. (1954). The theory of decision making. *Psychological Bulletin*, *51*(4), 380–417. https://doi.org/10.1037/h0053870

Feldman, D. C., & Klaas, B. S. (2002). Internet job hunting: A field study of applicant experiences with on-line recruiting. *Human Resource Management*, *41*(2), 175–192. https://doi.org/10.1002/hrm.10030

Ferraris, A., Erhardt, N., & Bresciani, S. (2019). Ambidextrous work in smart city project alliances: Unpacking the role of human resource management systems. *The International Journal of Human Resource Management*, *30*(4), 680–701. https://doi.org/10.1080/09585192.2017.1291530

Fleming, P. (2019). Robots and organization studies: Why robots might not want to steal your job. *Organization Studies*, *40*(1), 23–38. https://doi.org/10.1177/0170840618765568

Frey, C. B., & Osborne, M. A. (2017). The future of employment: How susceptible are jobs to computerisation? *Technological Forecasting and Social Change*, *114*, 254–280. https://doi.org/10.1016/j.techfore.2016.08.019

Garcia-Arroyo, J., & Osca, A. (2019). Big data contributions to human resource management: A systematic review. *The International Journal of Human Resource Management*, 1–26. https://doi.org/10.1080/09585192.2019.1674357

Gaur, A., & Kumar, M. (2018). A systematic approach to conducting review studies: An assessment of content analysis in 25 years of IB research. *Journal of World Business*, *53*(2), 280–289. https://doi.org/10.1016/j.jwb.2017.11.003

Giacumo, L. A., & Breman, J. (2016). Emerging evidence on the use of big data and analytics in workplace learning: A systematic literature review. *Quarterly Review of Distance Education*, *17*(4), 21.

Glavas, C., Mathews, S., & Russell-Bennett, R. (2019). Knowledge acquisition via internet-enabled platforms: Examining incrementally and non-incrementally internationalizing SMEs. *International Marketing Review*, *36*(1), 74–107. https://doi.org/10.1108/IMR-02-2017-0041

Go, E., & Sundar, S. S. (2019). Humanizing chatbots: The effects of visual, identity and conversational cues on humanness perceptions. *Computers in Human Behavior*, *97*, 304–316. https://doi.org/10.1016/j.chb.2019.01.020

Golden, A. G., & Geisler, C. (2007). Work–life boundary management and the personal digital assistant. *Human Relations*, *60*(3), 519–551. https://doi.org/10.1177/0018726707076698

Hewett, R., Shantz, A., Mundy, J., & Alfes, K. (2018). Attribution theories in human resource management research: A review and research agenda. *The International Journal of Human Resource Management*, *29*(1), 87–126. https://doi.org/10.1080/09585192.2017.1380062

Hooper, R. S., Galvin, T. P., Kilmer, R. A., & Liebowitz, J. (1998). Use of an expert system in a personnel selection process. *Expert Systems with Applications*, *14*(4), 425–432.

Huang, M. H., & Rust, R. T. (2018). Artificial intelligence in service. *Journal of Service Research*, *21*(2), 155–172. https://doi.org/10.1177/1094670517752459

Jonsson, K., Mathiassen, L., & Holmström, J. (2018). Representation and mediation in digitalized work: Evidence from maintenance of mining machinery. *Journal of Information Technology*, *33*(3), 216–232. https://doi.org/10.1057/s41265-017-0050-x

Jung, J., Song, H., Kim, Y., Im, H., & Oh, S. (2017). Intrusion of software robots into journalism: The public's and journalists' perceptions of news written by algorithms and human journalists. *Computers in Human Behavior*, *71*, 291–298. https://doi.org/10.1016/j.chb.2017.02.022

Kellogg, K., Valentine, M., & Christin, A. (2020). Algorithms at work: The new contested terrain of control. *Academy of Management Annals*, *14*(1), 366–410. https://doi.org/10.5465/annals.2018.0174

King, K. G. (2016). Data analytics in human resources: A case study and critical review. *Human Resource Development Review*, *15*(4), 487–495. https://doi.org/10.1177/1534484316675818

Kivimaa, P., Boon, W., Hyysalo, S., & Klerkx, L. (2019). Towards a typology of intermediaries in sustainability transitions: A systematic review and a research agenda. *Research Policy*, *48*(4), 1062–1075. https://doi.org/10.1016/j.respol.2018.10.006

Larivière, B., Bowen, D., Andreassen, T. W., Kunz, W., Sirianni, N. J., Voss, C., Wünderlich, N. V., & De Keyser, A. (2017). Service Encounter 2.0": An investigation into the roles of technology, employees and customers. *Journal of Business Research*, *79*, 238–246. https://doi.org/10.1016/j.jbusres.2017.03.008

Lawler, J. J., & Elliot, R. (1996). Artificial intelligence in HRM: An experimental study of an expert system. *Journal of Management*, *22*(1), 85–111. https://doi.org/10.1177/014920639602200104

Leonidou, E., Christofi, M., Vrontis, D., & Thrassou, A. (2020). An integrative framework of stakeholder engagement for innovation management and entrepreneurship development. *Journal of Business Research, 119*, 245-258.

Levy, F., Murnane, R. (2014). Dancing with robots. Human skills for computerized work. NEXT report. http://content.thridwayorg/publications/715/Dancing-with-Robots.pdf

Lin, R., Gal, Y., Kraus, S., & Mazliah, Y. (2014). Training with automated agents improves people's behavior in negotiation and coordination tasks. *Decision Support Systems, 60*, 1–9. https://doi.org/10.1016/j.dss.2013.05.015

Lindebaum, D., Vesa, M., & den Hond, F. (2020). Insights from The Machine Stops to better understand rational assumptions in algorithmic decision-making and its implications for organizations. *Academy of Management Review, 45*(1), 247–263. https://doi.org/10.5465/amr.2018.0181

Lindsay, C., Commander, J., Findlay, P., Bennie, M., Dunlop Corcoran, E., & Van Der Meer, R. (2014). Lean', new technologies and employment in public health services: Employees' experiences in the National Health Service. *The International Journal of Human Resource Management, 25*(21), 2941–2956. https://doi.org/10.1080/09585192.2014.948900

Loebbecke, C., & Picot, A. (2015). Reflections on societal and business model transformation arising from digitization and big data analytics: A research agenda. *The Journal of Strategic Information Systems, 24*(3), 149–157. https://doi.org/10.1016/j.jsis.2015.08.002

Luo, X., Tong, S., Fang, Z., & Qu, Z. (2019). Frontiers: Machines vs. humans: The impact of artificial intelligence chatbot disclosure on customer purchases. *Marketing Science, 38*(6), 937–947.

Malik, A., Budhwar, P., Srikanth, N. R., Varma, A. (2019). May the Bots Be with You! Opportunities and Challenges of Artificial Intelligence for Rethinking Human Resource Management Practices. Paper Accepted for presentation BAM 2019. https://www.bam.ac.uk/sites/bam.ac.uk/files/contribution294_0.pdf

Marinova, D., de Ruyter, K., Huang, M. H., Meuter, M. L., & Challagalla, G. (2017). Getting smart: Learning from technology-empowered frontline interactions. *Journal of Service Research, 20*(1), 29–42. https://doi.org/10.1177/1094670516679273

Markus, M. L. (2015). New games, new rules, new scoreboards: The potential consequences of big data. *Journal of Information Technology, 30*(1), 58–59. https://doi.org/10.1057/jit.2014.28

Marler, J. H., & Boudreau, J. W. (2017). An evidence-based review of HR Analytics. *The International Journal of Human Resource Management, 28*(1), 3–26. https://doi.org/10.1080/09585192.2016.1244699

Marler, J. H., & Parry, E. (2016). Human resource management, strategic involvement and e-HRM technology. *The International Journal of Human Resource Management, 27*(19), 2233–2253. https://doi.org/10.1080/09585192.2015.1091980

Marler, J. H., Fisher, S. L., & Ke, W. (2009). Employee self-service technology acceptance: A comparison of pre-implementation and post-implementation relationships. *Personnel Psychology, 62*(2), 327–358. https://doi.org/10.1111/j.1744-6570.2009.01140.x

Martinez-Gil, J., Paoletti, A. L., & Pichler, M. (2019). A novel approach for learning how to automatically match job offers and candidate profiles. *Information Systems Frontiers, 22*, 1–10.

Newell, S., & Marabelli, M. (2015). Strategic opportunities (and challenges) of algorithmic decision-making: A call for action on the long-term societal effects of 'datification. *The Journal of Strategic Information Systems, 24*(1), 3–14. https://doi.org/10.1016/j.jsis.2015.02.001

Ötting, S. K., & Maier, G. W. (2018). The importance of procedural justice in human--machine interactions: Intelligent systems as new decision agents in organizations. *Computers in Human Behavior, 89*, 27–39. https://doi.org/10.1016/j.chb.2018.07.022

Park, R. (2018). The roles of OCB and automation in the relationship between job autonomy and organizational performance: A moderated mediation model. *The International Journal of Human Resource Management, 29*(6), 1139–1156. https://doi.org/10.1080/09585192.2016.1180315

Parry, E., & Tyson, S. (2008). An analysis of the use and success of online recruitment methods in the UK. *Human Resource Management Journal, 18*(3), 257–274. https://doi.org/10.1111/j.1748-8583.2008.00070.x

Parry, E., & Tyson, S. (2011). Desired goals and actual outcomes of e-HRM. *Human Resource Management Journal, 21*(3), 335–354. https://doi.org/10.1111/j.1748-8583.2010.00149.x

Pisani, N. (2009). International management research: Investigating its recent diffusion in top management journals. *Journal of Management, 35*(2), 199–218. https://doi.org/10.1177/0149206308321552

Pisani, N., Kourula, A., Kolk, A., & Meijer, R. (2017). How global is international CSR research? Insights and recommendations from a systematic review. *Journal of World Business, 52*(5), 591–614. https://doi.org/10.1016/j.jwb.2017.05.003

Ravid, D. M., Tomczak, D. L., White, J. C., & Behrend, T. S. (2020). EPM 20/20: A review, framework, and research agenda for electronic performance monitoring. *Journal of Management, 46*(1), 100–126. https://doi.org/10.1177/0149206319869435

Sajjadiani, S., Sojourner, A. J., Kammeyer-Mueller, J. D., & Mykerezi, E. (2019). Using machine learning to translate applicant work history into predictors of performance and turnover. *Journal of Applied Psychology, 104*(10), 1207–1225. https://doi.org/10.1037/apl0000405

Schaubroeck, J. M., & Yu, A. (2017). When does virtuality help or hinder teams? Core team characteristics as contingency factors. *Human Resource Management Review, 27*(4), 635–647. https://doi.org/10.1016/j.hrmr.2016.12.009

Seeck, H., & Diehl, M. R. (2017). A literature review on HRM and innovation–taking stock and future directions. *The International Journal of Human Resource Management, 28*(6), 913–944. https://doi.org/10.1080/09585192.2016.1143862

Sheehan, C., Fenwick, M., & Dowling, P. J. (2010). An investigation of paradigm choice in Australian international human resource management research. *The International Journal of Human Resource Management, 21*(11), 1816–1836. https://doi.org/10.1080/09585192.2010.505081

Singh, J., Brady, M., Arnold, T., & Brown, T. (2017). The emergent field of organizational frontlines. *Journal of Service Research, 20*(1), 3–11. https://doi.org/10.1177/1094670516681513

Stone, D. L., Deadrick, D. L., Lukaszewski, K. M., & Johnson, R. (2015). The influence of technology on the future of human resource management. *Human Resource Management Review, 25*(2), 216–231. https://doi.org/10.1016/j.hrmr.2015.01.002

Strohmeier, S. (2007). Research in e-HRM: Review and implications. *Human Resource Management Review, 17*(1), 19–37. https://doi.org/10.1016/j.hrmr.2006.11.002

Strohmeier, S. (2009). Concepts of e-HRM consequences: A categorisation, review and suggestion. *The International Journal of Human Resource Management, 20*(3), 528–543. https://doi.org/10.1080/09585190802707292

Strohmeier, S. (2020). Smart HRM–A Delphi Study on the application and consequences of the internet of things in human resource management. *The International Journal of*

Human Resource Management, 31(18), 2289–2230. https://doi.org/10.1080/09585192.2018.1443963

Suen, H. Y., Chen, M. Y. C., & Lu, S. H. (2019). Does the use of synchrony and artificial intelligence in video interviews affect interview ratings and applicant attitudes? *Computers in Human Behavior, 98*, 93–101. https://doi.org/10.1016/j.chb.2019.04.012

Thomaz, F., Salge, C., Karahanna, E., & Hulland, J. (2020). Learning from the Dark Web: Leveraging conversational agents in the era of hyper-privacy to enhance marketing. *Journal of the Academy of Marketing Science, 48*(1), 43–63. https://doi.org/10.1007/s11747-019-00704-3

Tranfield, D., Denyer, D., & Smart, P. (2003). Towards a methodology for developing evidence-informed management knowledge by means of systematic review. *British Journal of Management, 14*(3), 207–222. https://doi.org/10.1111/1467-8551.00375

Van Doorn, J., Mende, M., Noble, S. M., Hulland, J., Ostrom, A. L., Grewal, D., & Petersen, J. A. (2017). Domo arigato Mr. Roboto: Emergence of automated social presence in organizational frontlines and customers' service experiences. *Journal of Service Research, 20*(1), 43–58. https://doi.org/10.1177/1094670516679272

Van Esch, P., Black, J. S., & Ferolie, J. (2019). Marketing AI recruitment: The next phase in job application and selection. *Computers in Human Behavior, 90*, 215–222. https://doi.org/10.1016/j.chb.2018.09.009

Van Geffen, C., Ruël, H., & Bondarouk, T. (2013). E-HRM in MNCs: What can be learned from a review of the IS literature? *European Journal of International Management, 7*(4), 373–392.

Voegtlin, C., & Greenwood, M. (2016). Corporate social responsibility and human resource management: A systematic review and conceptual analysis. *Human Resource Management Review, 26*(3), 181–197. https://doi.org/10.1016/j.hrmr.2015.12.003

Vrontis, D., & Christofi, M. (2019). R&D internationalization and innovation: A systematic review, integrative framework and future research directions. *Journal of Business Research*, https://doi.org/10.1016/j.jbusres.2019.03.031

Zammuto, R. F., Griffith, T. L., Majchrzak, A., Dougherty, D. J., & Faraj, S. (2007). Information technology and the changing fabric of organization. *Organization Science, 18*(5), 749–762. https://doi.org/10.1287/orsc.1070.0307

Zanko, M., Badham, R., Couchman, P., & Schubert, M. (2008). Innovation and HRM: Absences and politics. *The International Journal of Human Resource Management, 19*(4), 562–581. https://doi.org/10.1080/09585190801953616

Wall, T. D., Jackson, P. R., & Davids, K. (1992). Operator work design and robotics system performance: A serendipitous field study. *Journal of Applied Psychology, 77*(3), 353–362. https://doi.org/10.1037/0021-9010.77.3.353

Wang, X., Wang, L., Zhang, L., Xu, X., Zhang, W., & Xu, Y. (2017). Developing an employee turnover risk evaluation model using case-based reasoning. *Information Systems Frontiers, 19*(3), 569–576. https://doi.org/10.1007/s10796-015-9615-9

Watson, G. F., IV, Weaven, S., Perkins, H., Sardana, D., & Palmatier, R. W. (2018). International market entry strategies: Relational, digital, and hybrid approaches. *Journal of International Marketing, 26*(1), 30–60. https://doi.org/10.1509/jim.17.0034

Wenzel, R., & Van Quaquebeke, N. (2018). The double-edged sword of big data in organizational and management research: A review of opportunities and risks. *Organizational Research Methods, 21*(3), 548–591. https://doi.org/10.1177/1094428117718627

Appendix A. Categorization of articles based on research theme.

Research Theme	Topics Included	Relevant Articles
Advanced Technologies (16 articles)	The application of IoT and visualization technologies in HRM involves changes and modifications in HR technologies, HR activities and HR actors. Electronic performance monitoring (EPM) and employee-self-service technology can change various HR practices including evaluation, selection and training. Algorithmic technologies can help employers direct, evaluate and discipline workers. Some HR activities have benefited by using eHRM (cost savings, harmonization and integration of HR activities, efficiency, support of international strategy), whereas others created extra barriers (more HR administration, work stress, disappointments with technological properties).	Alcaraz, Domènech, and Tirado (2012); Bondarouk and Brewster (2016); Bondarouk, Parry, and Furtmueller (2017); Dodgson, Gann, and Phillips (2013); Feldman and Klaas (2002); Kellogg, Valentine, and Christin (2020); Marler, Fisher, and Ke (2009); Martinez-Gil, Paoletti, and Pichler (2019); Parry and Tyson (2008); Parry and Tyson (2011); Ravid et al. (2020); Stone et al. (2015); Strohmeier (2007); Strohmeier (2009); Strohmeier (2020); Zammuto et al. (2007)
Artificial Intelligence (22 articles)	AI techniques, manifested by machines defined by human intelligence have been applied in various HR aspects. AI, including machine learning or intelligent agents could be used in HRM to improve recruiting of staff and training purposes. Potential uses include also collecting and analyzing digital records or large amount of data to supplement decision-making and evaluation of employees' processes or predict work-related outcomes such as employees' turnover. Using video recognition of candidates profile based on AI assists to capture candidates, analyze candidates' behaviors, translate them into a psychological profile, and predict potential job placement. The wide use however of employees' data entails also important implications for privacy issues and data protection laws. Additional research on AI and HR, debates on whether AI and technologies will replace humans and result in jobs loss or they can be employed to complement and support human employees.	Behrend and Thompson (2011); Bell, Kanar, and Kozlowski (2008); Bhave, Teo, and Dalal (2020); Cano-Kollmann, Hannigan, and Mudambi (2018); Cooke, Liu, Liu, and Chen (2019); Glavas, Mathews, and Russell-Bennett (2019); Golden and Geisler (2007); Hooper, Galvin, Kilmer, and Liebowitz (1998); Huang and Rust (2018); Jung et al. (2017); Lawler and Elliot (1996); Lin, Gal, Kraus, and Mazliah (2014); Lindebaum, Vesa, and den Hond (2020); Lu, Rui, and Seidmann (2017); Marinova et al. (2017); Sajjadiani, Sojourner, Kammeyer-Mueller, and Mykerezi (2019); Singh et al. (2017); Suen, Chen, and Lu (2019); Van Esch, Black, and Ferolie (2019); Wang et al. (2017); Watson et al. (2018); Ötting and Maier (2018)
Robotics (7 articles)	Robotics technologies are deployed in a growing variety of work activities in which they may act as coworkers and technological tools for human employees. Robots have the potential to alter several HR practices, including the elimination of routine HR activities and allowing for opportunities for employees to use their skills more effectively and receive new learning opportunities. Research on AI and HR has also emphasized on how robots can act as employees' partners or how automation and robotics can progressively replace jobs. For employees, the implications of robotics on job replacement still remain questionable.	Aleksander (2017); Chao and Kozlowski, (1986); Fleming, (2019); Jonsson, Mathiassen, and Holmström (2018); Lindsay et al. (2014); Van Doorn et al. (2017); Wall, Jackson, and Davids, (1992)

Conclusion: AI and HRM - Future Research Agendas

Ashish Malik and Pawan Budhwar

1. Introduction

The field of artificial intelligence (AI) and its impact on work, workers and the workplace has already gained significant attention to warrant several dedicated special issues on the topic in journals, such as HRMR, IJHRM, and HRM (see Budhwar et al., 2022; Malik et al., 2020a, b, 2021, 2022 a, b and c). A significant worry among scholars and practitioners is the disruption that AI is causing to HRM practices and underpinning theories of the nature of work and work design and the unavoidable displacement of tasks that will happen in a range of service occupations, including the feeling economy (Huang & Rust, 2018, 2019, 2020). Some have focussed on the macro-level influences such as ethical and legal issues (Agar, 2019, 2020), whereas others have tended to focus on meso-(organisational) and micro-(individual) level influences of AI adoption and implementation issues. In this chapter, we summarise the future research agendas for shaping further scholarship in AI and HRM. We broadly group this into three levels: macro-, meso- and micro-level influences and offer some comments on methodological choices concerning future research directions for this vital area of scholarship and practice. We begin by highlighting the macro-level gaps, followed by meso- and micro-level gaps, an interrelationship between some of these gaps and a brief commentary on methodological challenges and gaps.

2. Macro-level Gaps

Our review suggests three types of gaps at this level: institutional change and ethics, cross-cultural influences, and further technological changes and disruptions. A major macro-level issue is ensuring that the digital and disruptive technological changes align with the UN's sustainable development goals and ensure that there are no human rights breaches with the adoption of AI for business and work so that global sustainability issues are not compromised. Instead, the focus should be on asking whether AI can improve equality at work, and decent work, especially with the adoption of disruptive technologies and algorithmic management. How do we deal with ethical issues relating to the growth of AI in general (Agar, 2019, 2020) and HRM (Malik et al., 2022) in particular is a key question? First, limited research provides a way to resolve the tension about regulation and law governing the design and implementation of AI applications and algorithmic solutions or humanoids and intelligent digital agents as co-workers. This area of the ethics of AI in business, particularly in the work and employment domain, is scant. Malik et al. (2022a, b and c) highlight various ethical issues in AI-HRM implementation and design choices. Further research is needed to articulate the role of a diverse group of internal and external stakeholders, for example, a panel of experts, in co-designing AI applications and solutions.

Another major macro-level gap relates to the quality of the AI technology chosen and its features and functionality chosen that have an impact on the efficacy of the solutions and helps deal with some of the legal and ethical issues relating to AI transparency and opacity, which then helps under-stand the extent to which AI is explainable or unexplainable (Chowdhury et al., 2022; Langer & König, 2022; Prikshat, Malik & Budhwar, 2022). An understanding of AI as well as ease of its use is becoming an imperative, which then helps to facilitate greater adoption of such applications (Nguyen & Malik, 2021, 2022). Additional technological disruptions in blockchain and Metaverse have implications for work and employment and how they will shape the HRM practice (Dwivedi et al., 2021).

A third area increasingly gaining importance at a macro-level is gaps in our understanding of AI-HRM from a cross-cultural perspective. We know from the extant literature on International Business (IB) and International Human Resource Management (IHRM) that there are huge differences that persist across cultures, especially in global organisations in the adoption of AI-assisted HRM in the future is another fertile area of inquiry. Del Giudice et al. (2021) identify the need to promote macro-level learning initiatives that promote a culture of openness to learning and engaging with humanoids and other intelligent digital assistants at the workplace.

3. Meso-Level Gaps

The next most significant gaps lie at an organisational level. A primary focus is naturally on identifying the nature and extent of new skills and compe-tencies needed by employees as disruptive technologies displace tasks and roles. Jaiswal and colleagues (2021) found skills gaps in five critical core skill areas: data analysis, digital skills, complex cognitive decision-making, and continuous learning. The authors highlight that individuals need a broad portfolio of skills, such as social, emotional, technological, and physical skills and how employees must learn to embrace human–machine interactions and engage productively and fruitfully rather than in an adversarial manner.

Del Giudice et al. (2021) highlight the need for further research on the role of senior leadership teams (SLT) in managing the transition of automation and adopting service robots.

Further research is also needed on how they maintain the balance between exploratory and exploitative routines. At a meso-level, another implication of this research is that organisations must remain open-minded to acquire new skill gaps that may be filled quickly by contingent and gig economy workers but what is important is how we leverage their specialist knowledge and skills and integrate it into the organisation's productive routines (Malik et al., 2022). Further, Malik et al. (2022) also highlight the need to consider meso-level influences of a culture of innovation and the broader ecosystem of enablers that encourage employees to engage in creative solutions, including adopting new disruptive technologies, such as AI-assisted applications (Malik et al., 2021). Also, at a meso-level, Malik et al. (2021, 2022) highlight the need for cross-comparative studies of end-users and not creators of AI solutions and firms that are creators of such AI-assisted HR applications and platforms.

Vrontis et al. (2021) present evidence of increasing job replacement thesis, human–robot interactions, and decision-making, including evidence of HRM algorithms showing adaptive and self-learning. Further, the authors have found little integration of the findings with concepts of meso-level understanding of strategic choices in the field of strategic HRM though some scholars have made inroads by developing a strategic framework for AI-assisted HRM (Malik et al., 2023). The internationalisation of digital transformation is also expected to increase. Hence, it is timely for IB and IHRM scholars to engage cross-cultural differences in both technology adoption and employees' and managers' attitudes towards engaging and interacting with such technology applications.

Moreover, highlighting the challenge of managing the anxiety of the perceived and actual effects of AI adoption and resultant job displacement fears requires the managers and leaders to allay some of the unrealistic fears and invest in boosting the self-efficacy of their staff to manage the change process. Yet, limited research captures what specific skills are needed to boost change readiness. Therefore, this study directs to essential and micro-level skills of managers and leaders of organisations in building employee resilience and well-being in times of disruptive technological change.

4. Micro-level Gaps

Suseno et al. (2021) note that the data that needs further understanding is micro-level attitudinal data for adoption and implementation, as it will, in part, determine the success of these applications. Also, at a micro-level, the authors identify the drivers of anxiety and fear of alienation and adoption by employees and leaders as AI technologies are introduced. This micro-level area of research directs scholars to consider the framework of the values-attitudes and behaviours to delineate the individual and organisational factors that can develop appropriate values that drive employees' positive attitudes and behaviours towards AI adoption and implementation. Suseno et al. (2021) highlight the need for a deeper understanding of individuals' cognitive and affective domains and how it affects meso-level decisions such as adoption, change readiness and skills development.

There is then a need to gain a deeper understanding of the interactions of communications and sharing of information between AI applications and humans (Malik et al., 2022d), as there might be trust issues and a lack of reciprocity in an AI-mediated social exchange, especially if the AI applications and algorithmic management have resulted in adverse or unexplainable outcomes.

5. Methodological considerations

Methodologically, Pan et al. (2021) highlight the need for multilevel, longitudinal, and in-depth qualitative case designs as the adoption of AI at work is still a relatively new phenomenon. Given that the nature of interactions between humans and AI applications is still not well understood, there is also a need to develop contextualised measures for the nature of AI technologies employed and their service quality to gauge its impact on a range of meso- and micro-level outcomes. While there has been some evidence of adaptation of existing scales to AI adoption contexts on AI quality (Nguyen & Malik, 2021), anxiety (Suseno et al., 2021) and Pan et al. (2021) these need to be validated for further research inquiry. Another methodological choice that can offer rich data is the observation of interactions between humans and machines as they use and engage with machines. Additionally, getting humans to partake in completing directed essays with follow-up interviews can deliver rich narrations of their experiences in an unbiased, psychologically safe and free-flowing manner. We hope the above multilevel gaps identified through our reviews and scholarship contributes to sustained scholarship in this rapidly emerging area.

References

Agar, N. (2019). *How to be human in the digital economy*. MIT Press.

Agar, N. (2020). How to treat machines that might have minds. *Philosophy & Technology*, *33*(2), 269–282. https://doi.org/10.1007/s13347-019-00357-8

Budhwar, P., & Malik, A. (2020). Call for papers for the special issue on Leveraging artificial and human intelligence through Human Resource Management. *Human Resource Management Review*. Retrieved June 24, 2020, from www.journals.elsevier.com/human-resource-man agement-review/call-for-papers/leveraging-artificia l-and-human-intelligence

Chowdhury, S., Joel-Edgar, S., Dey, P. K., Bhattacharya, S., & Kharlamov, A. (2022). Embedding transparency in artificial intelligence machine learning models: managerial implications on predicting and explaining employee turnover. *The International Journal of Human Resource Management*, 1–32.

Del Giudice, M., Scuotto, V., Ballestra, L. V., & Pironti, M. (2021, this issue). Humanoid robot adoption and labour productivity: A perspective on ambidextrous product innovation routines. *International Journal of Human Resource Management*, ahead-of-print. 1–27. https://doi.org/10.1080/09585192.2021.1897643

Dwivedi, Y. K., Hughes, L., Ismagilova, E., Aarts, G., Coombs, C., Crick, T., Duan, Y., Dwivedi, R., Edwards, J., Eirug, A., Galanos, V., Ilavarasan, P. V., Janssen, M., Jones, P., Kar, A. K., Kizgin, H., Kronemann, B., Lal, B., Lucini, B., ... Williams, M. D. (2021). Artificial Intelligence (AI): Multidisciplinary perspectives on emerging challenges, opportunities, and agenda for research, practice and policy. *International Journal of Information Management*, *57*, 101994. https://doi.org/10.1016/j.ijinfo- mgt.2019.08.002

Huang, M. H., & Rust, R. T. (2018). Artificial intelligence in service. *Journal of Service Research*, *21*(2), 155–172. https://doi.org/10.1177/1094670517752459

Huang, M. H., & Rust, R. T. (2020). Engaged to a robot? The role of AI in service. *Journal of Service Research*, *24*(1), 30–41. https://doi.org/10.1177/1094670520902266

Huang, M. H., Rust, R., & Maksimovic, V. (2019). The feeling economy: Managing in the next generation of artificial intelligence (AI*). California Management Review*, *61*(4), 43–65. https://doi.org/10.1177/0008125619863436

Jaiswal, A., Arun, C. J., & Varma, A. (2021, this issue). Rebooting employees: Upskilling for artificial intelligence in multinational corporations. *International Journal of Human Resource Management*, 1–30. ahead-of-print. https://doi.org/10.1080/0958519 2.2021.1891114

Langer, M., & König, C. J. (2021). Introducing a multi-stakeholder perspective on opacity, transparency and strategies to reduce opacity in algorithm-based human resource management. *Human Resource Management Review*, 100881.

Malik, A., Budhwar, P., & Srikanth, N. R. (2020a). Gig economy, 4IR and artificial intelligence: Rethinking strategic HRM. In P. Kumar, A. Agrawal, & P. Budhwar (Eds.), *Human & technological resource management (HTRM): New insights into revolution 4.0* (pp. 75–88). Emerald Publishing Limited.

Malik, A., Srikanth, N. R., & Budhwar, P. (2020b). Digitisation, artificial intelligence (AI) and HRM. In J. Crawshaw, P. Budhwar, & A Davis (Eds.), *Human resource management: Strategic and international perspectives* (pp. 88–111). Sage.

Malik, A., Budhwar, P., Patel, C., & Srikanth, N. R. (2022a). May the bots be with you! Delivering HR cost-effectiveness and individualised employee experiences in an MNE. *International Journal of Human Resource Management*, 1–31. ahead-of-print. https://doi.org/10.1080/09585192.2020.1859582

Malik, A., De Silva, M. T. T., Budhwar, P., & Srikanth, N. R. (2021). Elevating talents' experience through innovative artificial intelligence-mediated knowledge sharing: Evidence from an IT-multinational enterprise. *Journal of International Management*, *27*(4), 100871. https://doi.org/10.1016/j.intman.2021.100871

Malik, A., Sreenivasan, P., & De Silva, T. (2022b). Artificial intelligence, employee engagement, experience and HRM. In A. Malik (Ed.), *Strategic human resource man- agement and employment relations: An international perspective* (2nd ed.). Springer.

Malik, A., Budhwar, P. Mohan, H., & Srikanth, NR (2022c) Employee experience –The missing link: Insights from an MNE's AI-based employee engagement ecosystem. *Human Resource Management.* doi:https://doi.org/10.1002/hrm.22133

Malik, A., Nguyen, M., & Budhwar, P. (2022d). Antecedents and consequences of an artificial intelligence mediated knowledge-sharing social exchange: Towards a conceptual model. *IEEE Transactions on Engineering Management*, 97–115. doi: 10.1109/TEM.2022.3163117

Malik, A., Budhwar, P. & Kazmi, B. (2023, forthcoming). Artificial intelligence (AI)-assisted HRM: Towards an extended strategic framework. *Human Resource Management Review*, *33*(1), 100940.

Nguyen, T. M., & Malik, A. (2021). A twowave crosslagged study on AI service quality: The moderating effects of the job level and job role. *British Journal of Management*. ahead-of-print. https://doi.org/10.1111/1467-8551.12540

Nguyen, T. M., & Malik, A. (2022). 'Impact of knowledge sharing on employees' service quality: The moderating role of artificial intelligence. *International Marketing Review*, ahead-of-print. https://doi.org/10.1108/IMR-02-2021-0078

Pan, Y., Froese, F., Liu, N., Hu, Y., & Ye, M. (2021). The adoption of artificial intelligence in employee recruitment: The influence of contextual factors. *International Journal of Human Resource Management*, 1–23. ahead-of-print. https:// doi.org/10.1080/ 09585192.2021.1879206

Prikshat, V., Malik, A., & Budhwar, P. (2022). AI-augmented HRM: Antecedents, assimilation and multilevel consequences. *Human Resource Management Review, 100860*.

Suseno, Y., Chang, C., Hudik, M., & Fang, E. S. (2021). Beliefs, anxiety and change readiness for artificial intelligence adoption among human resource managers: The moderating role of high-performance work systems. *International Journal of Human Resource Management*, ahead-of-print. 1–28. https://doi.org/10.1080/09585192.2021.1931408

Vrontis, D., Christofi, M., Pereira, V., Tarba, S., Makrides, A., & Trichina, E. (2021). Artificial intelligence, robotics, advanced technologies and human resource management: A systematic review. *International Journal of Human Resource Management*, 1–30. ahead-of-print. https://doi.org/10.1080/09585192.2020.1871398

Index

Note: Figures are indicated by *italics*. Tables are indicated by **bold**.

absorptive capacity 62, 65, 67
academic journals **177**
Acemoglu, D. 37–8
advanced technologies 1, 3–6, 9, 14, 175, 177, 179–82, 187–90, 194, 201
Agrawal, A. 19
AI adoption: change readiness 146–7, 152–4; in China 150–1; employee recruiting 75; and ethical issues 103; HR managers 26, 146; individuals' AI anxiety and high-performance work systems **160**, 160–1; individuals' beliefs about AI and high-performance work systems **160**; and TFPG 108; TOE 61; total factor productivity growth 108
AI anxiety 26, 146, 147, 149, 150, 152–6, 158–65, **160**
AI-enabled HRM applications 13–15, 86, 89, 104
AI-mediated social exchange 2, 17, 18, 20, 22, 25, 26, 84–6, 93–106; employee experience 89–90
AI usage 60, 67–9, 71, **72**, 74–8; domestic, government and global multinational enterprises 23–4; HRM 61; organizational context 73; regression results of **73**
Ajzen, I. 152
Albert, E. T. 145
Alos-Simo, L. 50
Amazon 13, 19, 90, 115–16
Apaydin, M. 175
Argyris, C. 89
Armenakis, A. 152
articles: categorization of 201; journals and the frequencies of **8**; selection *180*
Association of Business Schools (ABS) 176
asynchronous video interviews (AVIs) 10
attitudes 12–14, 40, 45, 53, 61, 65, 85–9, 105, 106, 108, 146–9, 151–5, 158, 161, 162, 165, 187, 204, 205
Australian Business Deans Council (ABDC) 6
Autry, C. W. 70
average variance extracted (AVE) 71

Barrett, M. 50
basic statistics skills **127**
Bayesian information criterion (BIC) 47
Beane, M. 50
beliefs about AI 26, 146, 147, 149–52, 155, 158–61, **159**, 163
Benner, M. J. 49
big data 1, 13, 174
biometrics 1, 13
Bondarouk, T. 182, 192
Boolean operator 177–8
Bots 93; coaching assessment and performance management 98–9; and humanoids 108; recruitment and selection 97–8; talent supply chain 99–100; training and development 99
Breman, J. 174
Brewster, C. 182
Brislin, R. W. 157
Brougham, D. 14
Brown, F. 38
Budhwar, P. 2, 20
Business Source Ultimate (EBSCO) 176

Canada 121
Cano-Kollmann, M. 183
Castellacci, F. 12
change readiness 26, 145–7, 152–62, **160**, 164, 165, 204, 205
Chao, G. T. 186–7
Chaudhuri, K. 115
China 18, 41, 60, 69, 115, 156, 157, 163, 164; AI adoption 150–1
cloud automation 133
cloud automation (Slack, Google Cloud Provider) 127
Cobb-Douglas production function 38
cognitive skill 132
common method bias (CMB) 71
communication skills **127**, 129
complex cognitive skills **126**, 127–8
computer anxiety 152, 158
confirmatory factor analysis (CFA) 71

INDEX

contextual ambidexterity 36–9, 51
continuous learning skills **126**, 128–9
control variables 43, 47, 71, 158–60
Convergys 90
conversational agent 177–8
cost-effective service excellence (CESE) 2, 13
Crépon, B. 38
Cronbach's a 69, 70, 158
Crossan, M. M. 175
cybersecurity 127, 133
Cyprus 42

data analysis skills 125, **126**
Daugherty, P. R. 17
Davenport, T. H. 37, 52
decision making skills **126**, 128
Del Giudice, M. 24, 203, 204
Denmark 42, 121
dependent variable 69, 71
De Stefano, V. 21
development-operations (DevOps) 130, 134
digital skills 125, **126**, 127
digitization 174
dummy variable 71
Durndell, A. 158
Dwivedi, Y. K. 14, 20
dynamic managerial capabilities (DMC) 136

electronic performance monitoring (EPM) 182
employability 34, 37, 136
employee experience (EX) 16–17, 25,
    84–9, 95–7, 103, 105, 106, 145; and HR
    costeffectiveness 95–7; individualisation
    and AI-mediated exchanges 89–90;
    individualised 100–1; social exchange and
    person-organisation 88–9
employee-level outcomes 5–6
employee self-service (ESS) 182
employee upskilling: skills for 131, *131*
environmental context 68
equity, diversity and inclusion (EDI) 19
Ererdi, C. **8**
EUROSTAT 43–5, 48
evergreen skills 129, 131
exploitative product innovation
    (ProdInnExploit) 44, 46–9
exploitative routines 25, 33–6, 39, 40, 42,
    49–52, 204
explorative product innovation
    (ProdInnExplor) 43–4, 46–9
explorative routines 35, 39–42, 49

feeling of doing a useful work
    (UsefulWork) 44
Feinzig, S. 156
Feldman, D. C. 181
Fourth Industrial Revolution (4IR) 1, 14
France 121
frontline employee (FLE) 184

Gaur, A. 176
General Data Protection Regulation
    (GDPR) 42
generalized linear model (GLM) 47, **48**
general management (GM) 174
geo-tagging 1, 13
Giacumo, L. A. 174
Gigliotti, R. 155
Gioia, D. A. 123
Glikson, E. 20
Global Data Protection Regulation (GDPR) 21
Greece 42
Green, T. 50
Guenole, N. 156
Guzmán, A. 38

Haag, Z. 158
Haar, J. 14
Haenlein, M. 42
Hancock, B. 115
Henkel, A. P. 18, 19
Hewett, R. 176
high commitment human resource
    (HCHR) 135
high-performance work systems
    (HPWS) 26, 87, 146–8, 150, 158–65,
    160, *161*; AI adoption 146, 159; conceptual
    model *147*; environmental factor of 155–6;
    measurement 157–8; moderation effect
    of *161*, 162; role of 154–6; sample and
    procedure 156–7; social cognitive theory 147,
    149–50; tripartite model of attitudes 148–9
Hitachi 90
HR cost-effectiveness 3, 25, 85, 86, 94–6,
    104, 105
HRM practices 24, 35–8, 40, 50, 60, 62, 68, 76,
    84–90, 93–6, 100, 103, 104, 173, 181,
    202, 203; MNE's 95; person-organisation
    fit 95
HR planning 9–10
HR practices 182, 189, 193, 201; personalised,
    hyper-personalised and individualised
    experience of 104–5; social exchange and
    idiosyncratic deals, personalisation and
    individualisation 105
Hsieh, C.-T. 157
Huang, M. H. 15, 132, 136
human-AI-enabled technologies 15–19
human-humanoid interactions 34, 35, 41
human involvement 177–8
human–machine integration 100, 101, 105,
    136, 183
humanoid robot adoption (HumRob) 34–8,
    41, 43, 46–8
humanoids 37–8, 40, 42, 93
human resource development 178
human resource management (HRM) 5, 178;
    AI and its impact 117–18; automation
    technologies in 3; cost efficiency 5–6

human resource management functions (HRM functions) 2–6, 21–4, 87, 89, 97, 104, 173; AI and intelligent technologies 9–12
human resource performance system 178
human–robot collaboration (HRC) 38, 43
hyper-personalisation 90, *94*, 96, 100, 104, 105

IBM 115–16
IFR 43
independent variable 70
India 26, 93, 101–2, 115, 121
Indian context 116–17
India's IT industry 91
individualisation 85, 94, 100, 104, 105; AI and HR cost-effectiveness 90; AI-mediated exchanges and employee experience 89–90; HRM practices 87–8
industrial robots (IndRob) 48
Industry 4.0 3, 34, 36, 52
information management (IM) 174
Infosys 90, 115–16
INSEAD's Global Innovation Index 91–2
intelligent automation (Blueprism, vision plotting) 26, **126**, 126–7, 133, 135, 174–9, 186–94
international business (IB) 174, 175, **177**, 192, 194, 203
International Federation of Robotics (IFR) 41
Internet of Things (IoT) 1, 13, 133, 173, 177–8
interpersonal skills **127**, 129, 131, 134
intrusion detection 127
Ireland 121, **122**

Jackson, S. E. 62
Jaiswal, A. 25, 203
Jasmand, C. 51
Jensen, S. H. 156
Jones, R. 155
journals and number of articles **179**

Kaplan, A. 42
Kazmi, B. 2
Klaas, B. S. 181
Kozlowski, S. W. 186, 187
Kraemer, K. L. 66
Kristof, A. L. 88
Kshetri, N. 23
Kumar, M. 176
Kurt, S. 38
Kurt, Ü. 38

labour productivity (LabProd) 35–47, **45**, 49–52; and CA product innovation 38–41
leadership skills **127**, 129, 132
Levinthal, B. 52
Levy, F. 182
Li, J. J. 18
Luxemburg 42

machine learning 1, 2, 13, 115, **126**, 133, 164, 174, 183–6, 191, **201**
macro-level gaps 202–3
Madsen, S. R. 145
Maier, G. W. 185
Malik, A. 2, 20
Malik, M. T. 17, 25, 203, 204
Malik, P. T. 50, 52
March, J. G. 52
Martinez-Gil, J. 181
meso-level gaps 203–4
micro-level gaps 204–5
Microsoft 90
Minbashian, A. 152
mobile technology 1, 13
moderating variables 70
Mueller, J. 37
multinational corporations (MNCs) 24–6, 91, 115–17, 119–21, 124, 133, 138; IT sector in India 124, **125**, 133
multinational enterprises (MNEs) 2, 3, 21, 84–7, 89–93, 95–7, 99–104, 106; organisational culture of innovative practices 101–3
Murnane, R. 182

National Association of Sofware and Services Companies (NASSCOM) 92
Nelson, R. R. 40
neo-human capital theory (NHCT) 117, 119–20, 135, 137
new technologies 13, 15, 34, 35, 37, 39, 62, 64–5, 67, 68, 83, 99, 108, 146, 148–9, 151–6, 162, 165, 193
Nguyen, M. 20
Nguyen, T. M. 20
Norlander, P. 137

organizational context 37, 64, 66–7, 73–5
Orlikowski, W. J. 50
Otting, S. K. 185

Pan, Y. 25, 205
personalised bot (PBOT) 95–7
person-organisation (P-O) 88–9, 93–4, 105
Pessach, D. 10
Piao, M. 50
Pisani, N. 176
Power BI 125
product innovation 34–6, 38, 40–4, **45**, 46, 47, 49, **49**, 50, 52
project management skills **127**
ProQuest 6
Python 125

qualitative assessment 6–7

Rafferty, A. E. 152
regulatory environment 68, 70, 75, 82
Restrepo, P. 37, 38

INDEX

Robert, L. P. 21
Robotic Process Automation (Kapow, Selenium) 115, **126**, 127, 133
robotics 5, 14, 21, 43, 48, 151, 175, 181, 186–7
Robot Report, The 41
robustness tests 47–9
Ronanki, R. 37, 52
R programming 125
runtime applications (Angular, JBOSS) 127
Rust, R. T. 15, 132, 136

Sajjadiani, S. 185
SAS 125
SCOPUS 6
Scuotto, V. 37
second job (SecondJob) 48, 49
senior leadership teams (SLT) 204
Service Robot Deployment (SRD) Model 35
smart device 177–8
Snyder, H. 5
social cognitive theory (SCT): concepts of 156
social skills 129, 134
Song, Z. 157
Son, J. Y. 70
speech recognition 1, 13
Stokes, P. 40, 51
Stone, D. L. 181, 183
Strohmeier, S. 62, 192
structural ambidexterity 37
Sun, L.-Y. 158
Suseno, Y. 26, 204, 205
Sutcliffe, K. M. 63
Switzerland 121
systematic review 4–6, 26, 174, 176, 177, 179, 181, 189, 190

Tableau 125
Tambe, P. 15, 20, 86, 87, 92
team working (TeamWork) 45
technological skill 132
technology, organization, and environment (TOE) 61–4, 66, 67, 76–8
total factor productivity growth (TFPG) 108

Tranfield, D. 5, 175, 179
transaction cost theory 25, 61–7, 73, 75–8
tripartite model of attitude (TMA) 151–2; elements of an attitude 153–4
Tushman, M. L. 49

UK 6, 24, 26
United States 42, 121, 151
upskilling 3, 18, 23–5, 115–17, 121, 124, 125, 133–8; AI 118–19, **126**; cognitive skills **126**, 127–9; evergreen skills **127**, 129; importance of skills 129–32; technological skills 125–7, **126**; theories of 119–20

Van Doorn, J. 34, 187
Van Quaquebeke, N. 174
variables of model 45–6
variance inflation factor (VIF) 45, 71, 159
Viñas-Bardolet, C. 12
virtual reality 1, 13
volatile, uncertain, complex and ambiguous business environment (VUCA) 128
Vrontis, D. 26, 204

Walmart 115–16
Wang, Y. M. 70
Watson, G. F. 193
Web of Science 6
Wenzel, R. 174
Wilson, H. J. 17
Winter Sidney, G. 40
Wipro 90
Wirtz, J. 34, 35
Woolley, A. W. 20
WorkHome 49
working from home (WorkHome) 48
working time (TimeWork) 45

Yin, R. 93

Zaheer, A. 63
Zajac, E. J. 50
Zammuto, R. F. 181

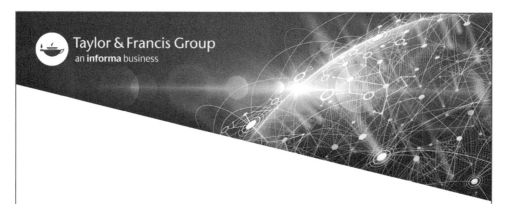